W9-BVI-382

101 Cost-Effective Ways to Increase the Value of Your Home

STEVE BERGES

Dearborn™
Trade Publishing
A **Kaplan Professional** Company

This publication is designed to provide accurate and authoritative information in regard to the subject matter covered. It is sold with the understanding that the publisher is not engaged in rendering legal, accounting, or other professional service. If legal advice or other expert assistance is required, the services of a competent professional should be sought.

Vice President and Publisher: Cynthia A. Zigmund
Acquisitions Editor: Mary B. Good
Senior Project Editor: Trey Thoelcke
Interior Design: Lucy Jenkins
Cover Design: Scott Rattray, Rattray Design
Typesetting: Elizabeth Pitts

© 2004 by Steve Berges

Published by Dearborn Trade Publishing
A Kaplan Professional Company

All rights reserved. The text of this publication, or any part thereof, may not be reproduced in any manner whatsoever without written permission from the publisher.

Printed in the United States of America

04 05 06 10 9 8 7 6 5 4 3 2 1

Library of Congress Cataloging-in-Publication Data

Berges, Steve, 1959–
    101 cost-effective ways to increase the value of your home / Steve Berges.
        p.   cm.
    Includes bibliographical references and index.
    ISBN 0-7931-8575-0
    1. House selling—United States. 2. Dwellings—United States—Maintenance and repair. 3. Housing—Prices—United States. I. Title: One hundred one cost-effective ways to increase the value of your home. II. Title: One hundred and one cost-effective ways to increase the value of your home. III. Title: Cost-effective ways to increase the value of your home. IV. Title.
    HD259.B468   2004
    643'.7—dc22

                                                                    2004003272

Dearborn Trade books are available at special quantity discounts to use for sales promotions, employee premiums, or educational purposes. Please call our Special Sales Department to order or for more information at 800-245-2665, e-mail trade@dearborn.com, or write to Dearborn Trade Publishing, 30 South Wacker Drive, Suite 2500, Chicago, IL 60606-7481.

DEDICATION

This book is dedicated to the millions of people throughout this great nation who are living the American dream of being homeowners. You have no doubt worked hard and sacrificed much over the years to have achieved this dream. I congratulate you for your patience, your persistence, and your prudence in the attainment of this wonderful dream!

C o n t e n t s

PART ONE
GETTING STARTED

1. YOUR HOME IS YOUR GREATEST ASSET 3

Introduction 3
Background and Personal Experience 6
Visibility Adds Value 7
Value Is Relative 9
Impact Value Rating System 11
Consumer Preferences 12

2. REQUIRED APPROVALS 19

1: Meeting with the Local Building Inspector 19
2: Required Permits and Related Fees 21
3: Required Inspections 23
4: Applying for a Building Permit 25
5: Revisions and Approvals 26
6: Deed Restrictions and Homeowner Associations 32

3. EVERYTHING YOU NEED TO KNOW ABOUT SUBCONTRACTORS 34

7: Do the Work Yourself or Hire a Subcontractor? 34
8: Pros and Cons of Using Subcontractors 37
9: How to Find Qualified Subcontractors 40
10: Licensing, Insurance, and Bonding Requirements 42
11: Protect Yourself Using the Right Contractor Agreements 43
12: Warranties 47
13: Comparing and Accepting Proposals 48
14: Payments to Subcontractors 50
15: Mechanics' Liens and How They Can Affect You 51

PART TWO
EXTERIOR IMPROVEMENTS

4. GENERAL PROPERTY AND GROUNDS 55

16: General Cleanup   55
17: Lawns   58
18: Landscaping   61
19: Irrigation Systems   63
20: Outdoor Lighting   67
21: Pets   69
22: Combining Grounds Improvements   72

5. EXTERIOR STRUCTURES 75

23: Decks   75
24: Patios   77
25: Gazebos   78
26: Pools   80
27: Hot Tubs and Spas   82
28: Storage Sheds   84
29: Garages   86
30: Playground Equipment   88

6. GENERAL EXTERIOR 91

31: Painting   91
32: Siding   94
33: Roofing Replacement   96
34: Roof Cleaning   98
35: Rain Gutters   100
36: Brick and Masonry   102
37: Exterior Doors   105
38: Windows   107
39: Fences   110
40: Improve an Existing Porch   113
41: Adding a Porch to Your Home   114
42: Sidewalk and Driveway Improvements   118
43: Sidewalk and Driveway Repairs   120
44: Junky Cars, Boats, and RVs   122
45: Combining Exterior Improvements   123

PART THREE
INTERIOR IMPROVEMENTS

7. GENERAL INTERIOR   129

46: Overall Cleanliness   129
47: Flooring   132
48: Drywall Repairs   135
49: Painting   137
50: Wallpaper   140
51: Cabinets   142
52: Countertops   144
53: Trim and Molding   148
54: Doors and Hardware   151
55: Furnishings and Decor   152
56: Ceilings   156
57: Mirrors   158
58: Fireplaces   160
59: Window Coverings   163
60: Odors   165
61: Attic and Wall Insulation   168

8. INTERIOR ROOMS AND COMPONENTS   171

62: Foyer and Entryway   171
63: Stairway   172
64: Living Room   174
65: Dining Room   176
66: Kitchen   177
67: Appliances   179
68: Pantry   181
69: Family Room   183
70: Study or Home Office   185
71: Powder Room   186
72: Utility Room   188
73: Bedrooms   190
74: Bathrooms   191
75: Closets   193
76: Basement   195
77: Room Additions   197

PART FOUR

STRUCTURAL AND MECHANICAL IMPROVEMENTS

9. STRUCTURAL 203

78: Slab Foundations 203
79: Basement Foundations 206

10. HEATING AND PLUMBING 208

80: Furnaces 208
81: Air-Conditioning Systems 211
82: Thermostats 213
83: Hot Water Heaters 214
84: Water and Sewer Lines 216
85: Kitchen and Bathroom Faucets 218
86: Whirlpool Tubs 219
87: Sinks 221

11. ELECTRICAL 223

88: Lighting 223
89: Wiring and Breakers 226
90: Switches and Outlets 227

PART FIVE

PUTTING IT ALL TOGETHER

12. CASE STUDY ANALYSIS 231

91: Primary Principles of Valuation 231
92: Secondary Principles of Valuation 234
93: Appraisal Methods 235
94: Appraisal Method #1 236
95: Appraisal Method #2 238
96: Appraisal Method #3 238
97: Case Study Analysis—Assumptions 239
98: Case Study Analysis—Estimates 242
99: Case Study Analysis—Comparable Sales 243
100: Case Study Analysis—Output Analysis 244
101: Summary and Conclusion 247

Appendix Sample Subcontractor Agreement 249
Glossary 253
Resources 285
Index 287

Part One

GETTING STARTED

1

YOUR HOME IS
YOUR GREATEST ASSET

INTRODUCTION

According to the U.S. Census Bureau, home prices have risen from an average sales price of $19,300 in 1963 to $228,300 in 2002 (see Figure 1.1). This represents a positive change of 1,082.9 percent over a 40-year period and an annualized increase of 6.37 percent in the average sales price of a home. While home prices may not have risen every year out of those 40 years, a home has been on average one of the most stable investments a person could make, especially when compared to other asset classes such as stocks and commodities that tend to be much more volatile.

Although there are certain macro economic factors over which you have little control, such as a weak economy or rising interest rates that may have an adverse effect on the value of your home, there are numerous micro economic factors over which you have direct control and that will enable you to minimize the negative effect of a soft housing market should one occur. Furthermore, factors under your control can greatly enhance the

FIGURE 1.1 *Average Home Sales Price*

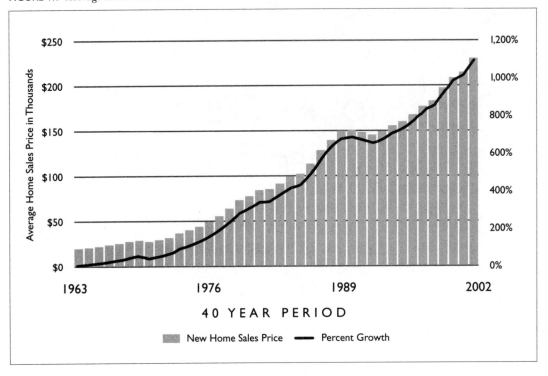

value of your home in a moderate to strong housing market and can give you an edge over other sellers in your area.

Even if you are not expecting to sell your home right away, you should still be aware of the impact that making certain improvements has on the value of your home. These factors include a wide range of repairs and modifications you can make, from minor home improvements, such as painting, to major renovations, such as adding a room addition. While some improvements, such as minor repairs, are made out of necessity and will add little to no value to your home, other improvements, such as new flooring and cabinets, can have a substantial positive impact on your home's value.

With more than 74 million homeowners continuing to find ways to improve their houses, the home improvement market likewise continues to remain strong year after year. The following excerpt, taken from the May 20, 2003, issue of *Home Improvement Retailing*, suggests that people are continuing to invest in their homes by making improvements to them at a record pace.

The residential renovation industry is overtaking home construction as a major economic driver, says the chief economist of the American Institute of Architects. Kermit Baker, speaking at the group's annual convention, said spending on home renovations has risen compared with spending on new home construction. Between 1994 and 2001, remodeling spending accounted for 51 percent of all residential construction dollars spent. Americans spent $214 billion on residential remodeling projects in 2001, according to the Joint Center for Housing Studies. The bulk of the spending, $131 billion, came from homeowner improvements, a category that generally includes projects involving an addition. Another $34 billion was spent on homeowner maintenance.

According to Mr. Baker, spending on home improvements is on the rise and accounts for over half of all money spent on residential construction. It appears that many homeowners already recognize the benefit of investing in their home.

101 Cost-Effective Ways to Increase the Value of Your Home is organized into four primary sections. Part One focuses on the process of getting started, or preparing to make your home improvements, and includes topics such as the benefits to doing it yourself versus hiring a subcontractor, meeting with local building inspectors, if necessary, understanding the building permit process, and learning how to protect yourself when dealing with subcontractors. Part Two focuses on the various structural and mechanical improvements that can be made, including topics such as shifting or settling foundations, heating and air-conditioning systems, electrical systems, and plumbing components such as hot water heaters and sump pumps. Part Three deals with making exterior improvements to your home and addresses topics such as lawns and landscaping, decks and swimming pools, and painting, siding, and roofing. Finally, Part Four addresses the various interior improvements that can be made to beautify and enhance the value of your home and includes topics such as flooring and painting, cabinets and countertops, and lighting, mirrors, and fireplaces. All in all, we describe here at least 101 tips, techniques, and strategies you can use to begin to immediately improve the value of what is likely your greatest asset, that being your home.

BACKGROUND AND PERSONAL EXPERIENCE

Although there are numerous books currently available that provide readers with the "how to" type of information needed to make improvements, only a handful of them discuss the concept of making home improvements specifically for the purpose of adding value to a property. My extensive experience over the past 25 years in buying real estate for the sole purpose of creating value in it and subsequently selling it to capture the gain created by the increase in value qualifies me to write about this topic. This experience includes buying and selling houses and apartment buildings, as well as adding value to land by building new houses on it and making them available for sale, again to capture the gain created by the increase in property values. Using a term I coined, "the value play," I describe this process in great detail for investors in the following books:

- *The Complete Guide to Buying and Selling Apartment Buildings* (New Jersey; John Wiley & Sons; 2002)
- *The Complete Guide to Flipping Properties* (New Jersey; John Wiley & Sons; 2003)
- *The Complete Guide to Investing in Rental Properties* (New York; McGraw Hill; 2004)

In addition, as a principal of Symphony Homes http://www .symphony-homes.com, a residential construction company, I am thoroughly familiar with the cost of each and every component of a house. This level of familiarity has allowed me to gain additional insight into the value of making home improvements. Another factor that must be taken into consideration is that the cost of each component or structural element can vary widely from neighborhood to neighborhood due to differing market demands. For example, when building new homes at the lower end of the price spectrum for budget conscious consumers, a less expensive three-tab shingle may be used on a roof with a low pitch. The pitch of a roof refers to its slope, or how steep the roof is. The lower the pitch, the less it costs to construct because there are fewer materials needed. On the other hand, in a higher end market where consumers are willing to pay for stronger curb appeal, dimensional shingles are used on roofs that have higher pitches and take on more angles with gables and possibly hip roof designs. These design elements are important to understand because as you consider making improvements to your home, you want to ensure that you will get the greatest return for your invested dollars on the improvements that you will make. If you go all out by spending money for wood shingles or dimensional shingles in a neighborhood where your house is the only one with superior shingles, chances are that you will not be able to fully recoup the money you spent.

VISIBILITY ADDS VALUE

It helps to know from a resale standpoint where you will be able to get the greatest "bang for the buck" on various types of home improvements that are made. For example, while spending $7,500 on a foundation repair may be required to get a house sold, the repair itself is not very visible and does nothing to improve the appearance of a house. On the other hand, spending the same $7,500 on sprucing up the landscaping, installing new flooring in the kitchen and baths, and perhaps painting the interior of the house have a potentially much greater return for the same amount of dollars invested. This is due to the fact that these improvements are all highly visible and can greatly enhance the beauty of the home.

People tend to buy what they "see." In general, repairs and modifications that have a greater propensity to improve the aesthetics of a home will realize a greater return for an equal amount of money spent than a repair that does nothing to improve a house's appearance. In *The Complete Guide to Investing in Rental Properties* (New York; McGraw Hill; 2004), I address the importance of visibility as it applies to the principle of perceived value as follows:

> While visibility refers to *what* can be seen, perception is the *way* something is seen. I often think of my one-year-old son, Benjamin, and the world he lives in. From his perspective, I must look like the giant, Goliath, from the story in the Bible. He lives in a world where everything within his reach is only one foot to two feet above the floor. Little Ben doesn't seem to mind, though, as he's perfectly content to play in the kitchen, bathroom, and living room cabinets. He pulls out pots and pans, shampoo and toilet paper, books and toys, and just about anything else he can get his hands on. By the time he's done, it looks like a cyclone has blown through. When I think about Ben in his tiny world, he really doesn't seem to mind being a little guy. In fact, it's a safe bet to say that he's just as content to play with pots and pans as he is anything else. Although Ben's perception of life is much different than yours or mine, his perception will change with corresponding changes in what becomes visible to him.

This "perceived value" concept applies equally to changes in what becomes visible to prospective buyers. Give them the opportunity to visibly see the benefit they are receiving and their over-all perception of your home is certain to improve. Ultimately, if we like what we see, it is of greater worth to us.

VALUE IS RELATIVE

Although the value or worth of a house or an improvement can be quantified in terms of dollars, it is difficult to do so for two reasons. First, the concept of value is relative. For example, a house that is worth $100,000 in one neighborhood may be worth $125,000 in another neighborhood only two miles away. These differences in value may be due to supply and demand, desirability of location, differences in tax rates, or any other number of reasons. Second, although property values can be quantified, there is a degree of subjectivity in doing so.

For instance, two different appraisers who appraise the exact same house will more than likely come up with two different values. This is due in part to the appraiser's selection process of comparable houses that have sold in the subject property's surrounding neighborhood. While one appraiser may select what he or she believes to be the three or four most appropriate comparable sales, the other appraiser may select three or four entirely different comparable sales. Because each appraiser has used different comparable sales to derive a value for the subject property, the two values for the same house are almost certain to be different. So although there is a high degree of objectivity in the appraisal process because appraisers follow the same standard appraisal guidelines, there is also a varying degree of appraiser subjectivity that is likely to result in differences in values.

By now, you may be asking, "So what? Why do I care about which practices appraisers use and how they might affect property values?" The answer is: It will help you gain a better understanding of how value is derived so that you can realize the greatest possible return on the various home improvements you choose to make. You must be able to think about property values in your own area and relate them to your specific needs. It would be impossible for me to recommend, for example, that you spend $2,000 on installing an air-conditioning unit in your house if it doesn't already have one so that you could realize an extra $2,500 in value for your house.

What I can recommend, however, is that if you live in a warmer climate and your house is the only one in the neighborhood that doesn't have an air conditioner, then yes, you should definitely consider investing the $2,000 in the needed equipment just to bring your house up to the same standard as those in your area. Conversely, if you live in a cooler climate and very few people have air-conditioning units, then it may not make sense to spend the money on that type of equipment. You would probably be better off investing that same $2,000 in another type of home improvement. For instance, you could add a small deck off the back of the house. Keep in mind the "visibility adds value" rule. A deck built onto the rear of the house is certainly more visible than an air-conditioning unit.

A report published by *Remodeling* magazine entitled "Cost Versus Value Report," (2003, Hanley-Wood, LLC) lends further evidence to the broad differences in value found throughout the country. One example in the study examines the cost of adding a 16 foot by 20 foot deck to a house, and the value of the deck when the house is sold. The study reports that the national average cost of adding the deck is $6,304, while its value at the time the house is sold is $6,661, which represents 104 percent of the initial cost of the project. When you break the data down by region, however, the costs and resale values vary widely. For example, in Boston the cost of adding a deck this size is $7,163 compared to its value at the time of sale of $18,333, representing 256 percent of the initial cost of the project. Now let's compare these results to those of Cleveland. In Cleveland, the cost of adding a deck this size is $6,454 compared to its value at the time of resale of $2,283, representing only 35 percent of the initial cost of the project. As the empirical data in this report clearly shows, the value of adding a deck as a home improvement varies widely by region.

IMPACT VALUE RATING SYSTEM

Because we have seen that the value of home improvements varies from area to area, it would be difficult, if not impossible, to devise a system to rate them that would apply equally in all markets. What we can do, however, is devise a system based upon generalizations. Before proceeding any further, let's take a minute to examine a simple rating system I have developed in an effort to somewhat quantify the value of each home improvement discussed in the remainder of this book.

As we've already established, calculating an exact dollar amount for the value of an improvement is difficult at best, if not impossible, to do because there are so many factors that influence value. An air conditioner, for example, would certainly be worth more to a prospective buyer in Texas than to a buyer in Alaska, and conversely, a high-efficiency furnace would be worth more to a prospective buyer in Alaska than to a buyer in Texas.

The rating system I have devised is based on a scale of five stars, with one star having the lowest impact on value, three stars having a neutral impact on value, and five stars having the strongest impact on value.

Impact value: ★ Weak. The impact value of a home improvement given a one-star rating is weak. For example, for every dollar spent on an improvement, the expected return on that improvement could potentially be negative and range from zero cents to 50 cents ($.00–$.50).

Impact value: ★★ Low. The impact value of a home improvement given a two-star rating is low. For example, for every dollar spent on an improvement, the expected return on that improvement could potentially be negative and range from 50 cents to 90 cents ($.50–$.90).

Impact value: ★★★ Moderate. The impact value of a home improvement given a three-star rating is moderate. For example, for every dollar spent on an improvement, the expected return on that improvement could potentially be range from 90 cents to one dollar and 10 cents ($.90–$1.10).

Impact value: ★★★★ High. The impact value of a home improvement given a four-star rating is high. For example, for every dollar spent on an improvement, the expected return on that improvement could potentially be positive and range from one dollar and 10 cents to one dollar and 50 cents ($1.10–$1.50).

Impact value: ★★★★★★ Strong. The impact value of a home improvement given a five-star rating is strong. For example, for every dollar spent on an improvement, the expected return on that improvement could potentially be positive and range from one dollar and 50 cents to two dollars or more ($1.50–$2.00+).

The five-star rating system should be used as a general guideline only when considering which home improvements to make. It is based on my experience in the real estate market over the past 25 years and may or may not hold true for your particular area. Keep in mind that there are many factors that affect value and that must be considered collectively as they apply to your region, to your city, and to your neighborhood.

CONSUMER PREFERENCES

Although I cannot quantify the actual impact of making certain home improvements in your area will have on the value of your home due to the diverse nature of communities, locations, climates, and other factors, I can provide some generalizations about consumer preferences. The more you can align the features and attributes of your home with those preferred by consumers, the greater the value you will be able to create.

According to data compiled in 2002 by the National Association of Home Builders and as illustrated in Figure 1.2, the three most important features in the next home purchased by consumers are that the houses should be spread out more, there be less traffic in the neighborhood, and property taxes should be lower. Following these three choices are a bigger home, a larger lot, better schools, and a good neighborhood.

Now take a moment to review Figure 1.3 that shows the results of a survey taken to gauge the relative importance of various community amenities among consumers. Respondents to this survey indicated that the three most important community amenities are access to a major highway; trails to accommodate walking, biking, or jogging; and sidewalks on both sides of the street. Ranking slightly below sidewalks, consumers also desire communities to have a park area, playgrounds, and to be within close walking distance to shops.

Now take a moment to review Figure 1.4 that shows the findings of a survey taken to determine consumer preferences regarding the most important features taken into account before purchasing a new home. The single most important factors in order of consumer preference were price, location, and home amenities. Note that while 41 percent of respondents were most concerned about price and 39 percent were most concerned about location, only 11 percent were concerned about home amenities. This data suggests that, by far, consumers are more concerned about the price and location of a home when making a purchase decision than any other factors. Notice also that price is only slightly more important than is location. You could reasonably infer from this result that although price is slightly more important to respondents than is location, there are almost just as many consumers who are willing to pay more for a more desirable location.

Now take a moment to review Figure 1.5 that outlines the findings of a survey taken to determine the desirability of specific

FIGURE 1.2 *Importance of Features in Next Home*

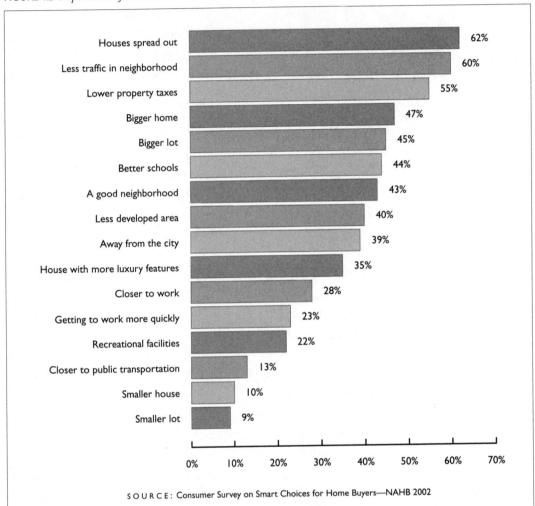

Feature	Percentage
Houses spread out	62%
Less traffic in neighborhood	60%
Lower property taxes	55%
Bigger home	47%
Bigger lot	45%
Better schools	44%
A good neighborhood	43%
Less developed area	40%
Away from the city	39%
House with more luxury features	35%
Closer to work	28%
Getting to work more quickly	23%
Recreational facilities	22%
Closer to public transportation	13%
Smaller house	10%
Smaller lot	9%

SOURCE: Consumer Survey on Smart Choices for Home Buyers—NAHB 2002

features within an average home, as well as an upscale home. The most preferred size for an average home was 2,300–2,400 square feet, while for an upscale home, it was 4,000+ square feet. "Must haves" for an average home include an island work area in the kitchen, a walk-in pantry, a laundry room, and a dining room. In addition to must haves for an average home, must haves for an upscale home include a work table or computer table in the kitchen, a whirlpool tub, a sunroom, media room, and a home office. Ad-

FIGURE 1.3 *Importance of Community Amenities*

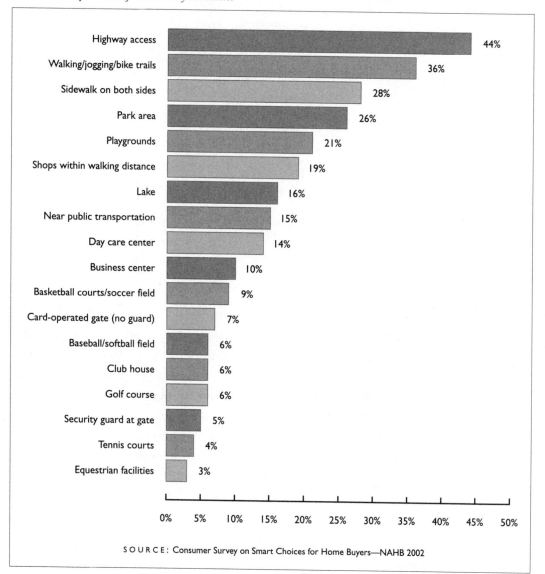

SOURCE: Consumer Survey on Smart Choices for Home Buyers—NAHB 2002

ditional must haves for upscale homes include a deck or patio, a monitored security system, and an audio system that distributes sound throughout the house. Now take a few minutes to review those preferences shown in Figure 1.5 that are not considered to be "must haves," but are nevertheless still "preferred."

FIGURE 1.4 *Most Important Considerations When Purchasing a Home*

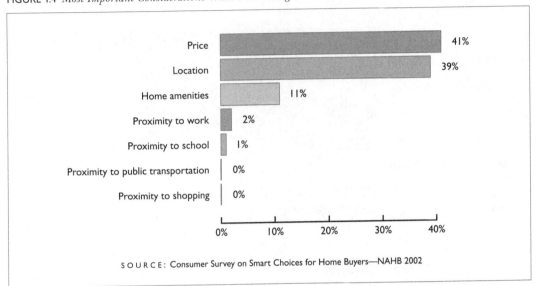

SOURCE: Consumer Survey on Smart Choices for Home Buyers—NAHB 2002

In summary, the three most important concepts for you to remember when considering making a home improvement are the visibility of the improvement, its relative value to other homes in the area, and its degree of desirability according to consumer preferences. In general, those improvements that are more visible and help to beautify a home will add more value than less visible improvements that do not beautify the home. In addition, improvements made to a home must be of relative value to the specific area it is in. Finally, consumer preferences should be kept in mind when making home improvement decisions.

FIGURE 1.5 *Consumer Preference for Homes of the Future*

	Average Home	Upscale Home
Single story vs. two story	Single or two story, depending on area	Two story
Location	Outlying or close-in suburb	Outlying or close-in suburb
Finished area	2,300 – 2,400 sq. ft.	4,000 + sq. ft.
Bedrooms	3 or 4	4 or 5
Bathrooms	2½ or 3	4 or 5
Parking	2-car garage	3- or 4-car garage
Siding	Vinyl or brick	Brick/stucco/wood
Fireplace	1	2
Ceiling height	1st floor 9'; upper floor 8'	1st floor 9½' or 10'; upper floor 9'
Skylight	Not necessary	Necessary
French door	Preferred, but not necessary	Necessary
Microwave	Built-in	Built-in
Kitchen cabinets	About 16; light wood	About 20; light wood
Island work area	Must have	Must have
Counter space	23 linear ft.	28 linear ft.
Walk-in pantry	Must have	Must have
Work/computer table in kitchen	Preferred, but not necessary	Must have
Kitchen sinks	2 stainless steel	2 stainless steel/vitreous china
Eat-in table space in kitchen	Necessary	Necessary
Breakfast counter	Not necessary	Necessary
Toilet, tub, shower	White	White
Separate shower	Preferred	Preferred
Multiple shower heads in master bedroom bath	—	Preferred
Whirlpool tub	—	Must have
Bidet	—	Preferred
Bathroom walls	Ceramic tiles	Ceramic tiles
Linen closet	Necessary	Necessary
Laundry room	Must have	Must have
Dining room	Must have	Must have
Sunroom	Preferred, but not necessary	Must have
Media room	—	Must have
Home office	—	Must have
Exercise room	—	Preferred
Front porch	Preferred	Preferred
Deck/patio	Preferred	Must have
Exterior light	Preferred	Must have
Central vacuum	Not necessary	Necessary
Entry foyer	Necessary	Necessary
Butler pantry	Not necessary	Necessary

FIGURE 1.5 *Consumer Preference for Homes of the Future (continued)*

	Average Home	Upscale Home
Technology		
Structured wiring	Necessary	Necessary
Monitored security	Preferred	Must have
Distributed Audio	Not necessary	Must have
Home theater	Not necessary	Preferred
Flooring		
Kitchen	Vinyl/ceramic tiles	Hardwood/ceramic tiles
Bathrooms	Vinyl/ceramic tiles	Ceramic tiles
Living room	Carpet	Hardwood
Family room	Carpet	Hardwood
Dining room	Carpet	Carpet/hardwood
Foyer/hallways	Carpet	
Community		
Park area	Preferred	Preferred
Playground	Preferred	Preferred
Walking/jogging trail	Preferred	Preferred
Open space	Preferred	Preferred

2

REQUIRED APPROVALS

I: MEETING WITH THE LOCAL BUILDING INSPECTOR

Depending on the magnitude and scope of your home improvement project, it may be a good idea to meet with your local building inspection department. If your project is relatively small, chances are you won't need to apply for a permit and therefore you won't need to meet with the inspection department. On the other hand, if you are considering a more complex project, such as a room addition, then it is a good idea to schedule a meeting with one of the local building inspectors. If the town or city you live in is small with very little new construction activity, then there is likely to be only one inspector who is responsible for ensuring that all work performed is in compliance with the requisite building codes. Moderate to large cities often have an inspection department with several inspectors who oversee work performed. Regardless of how many there may be, generally one or two inspectors are available for meeting with homeowners and contractors.

There are two primary reasons for meeting with your building inspector. The first reason is that it is important for you to learn as much as possible about what the legal requirements are for your project. You are on a fact-finding mission to educate yourself not only about what is mandated by the applicable building codes, but also about any items in particular that the building inspectors themselves may require. In my experience as a builder, most inspectors have their own specific things they look for that may not necessarily be covered by the building code. Usually these additional requirements are small and inexpensive to do, but the inspector will nevertheless want to see them completed.

For example, one inspector we work with always requires additional bracing underneath the stairwell. Although our framing crews may use just as much bracing underneath the stairwell in this community as they do in all of the other communities they work in, the inspector will "red tag" the work if it is not reinforced with additional bracing. In order to appease the inspector so as not to cause any unnecessary work delays, our crews know they must build the extra bracing into the stairwell. Because the additional work only takes a few minutes and is inexpensive to do, we just do it.

The second primary reason for meeting with your local building inspector is to establish rapport with him. You want to get to know the inspector and, at the same time, give him the opportunity to gain a level of trust and confidence in you. If you already have a set of preliminary drawings, I recommend taking them to the meeting to seek his or her advice and input. By offering suggestions to you regarding your project, the inspector is in a very real sense buying in to it. You want and need his or her approval to ensure as smooth a building-and-inspection process as possible.

Before going into any new community, a representative such as a site superintendent from our company, Symphony Homes, arranges to meet with the building officials. The site superintendent spends a few minutes providing the necessary introductions and company background, describes the nature of our project, and then inquires about anything in particular that the building inspector may be looking for that falls outside of the code. Finally, the site superintendent assures the inspector that we want to work together in a cooperative effort with the community to complete our project in a timely manner. We have found that this approach works well and is generally appreciated by the building officials.

2: REQUIRED PERMITS AND RELATED FEES

Depending on the type of home improvements you make, you may or may not need to get a permit from your local city or town building department. Minor home improvements, such as landscaping, painting, and replacing flooring, typically do not require a permit. On the other hand, most municipalities do require a permit for more complex improvements that require more than just general home improvement knowledge. Typical improvements that require permits include most any type of electrical work, roofing, room additions, and decks, to name a few. Minor plumbing problems such as a backed up sewer line often do not require a permit to be issued, but other more involved plumbing, such as digging up a sewer line to replace it, most likely would. The best thing to do is check with your local building department to determine exactly what type of work requires the issuance of a permit.

It may be necessary to check back with the local building department each time you get ready to take on a major home improvement because the ordinances or codes that govern construction can change at any time. For example, as a builder of new homes, a permit to pour a driveway was never required until just recently. The county, and not the local city, now requires a permit to be issued before pouring concrete for a driveway. Although the fee is only $20, it is one more form we have to fill out and one more fee we have to pay to ensure that we are in compliance with the local ordinances. If we pour the driveway without the proper permit, our company runs the risk of incurring a fine or penalty. In addition, a final certificate of occupancy will not be issued until the matter is resolved. In some cases, only licensed professionals, such as an electrician, can pull, that is, secure a permit for work to be performed. This does not mean that the individual holding the license has to do the actual work himself, but rather that the work performed must be done under his supervision and direction. The individual who is licensed is ultimately responsible for ensuring that the work performed meets all local, state, and national building code requirements.

Be careful not to fall into the trap of thinking you can get away with not pulling the requisite building permits. Believe it or not, our local government officials actually pay people to drive around neighborhoods and communities in search of any work being performed without the proper permits. I know of two neighbors just down the street who recently decided to build decks in their back yards at about the same time without getting the required permits. Their houses back up to woods, and there are no streets running behind their houses. Due to the location of the decks in the neighbors' respective back yards, they are barely visible from the front. About a week or so after starting their projects, in addition to being required to obtain the necessary permits by the city, both neighbors were fined for performing the work illegally. Although I don't condone the actions of my neighbors, I do think our government gets a little carried away at times.

Here is another case in point. I had a contractor build a deck on the back of my house a couple of years ago (the required permits were obtained). Within a few days of his completing the deck, my wife saw a strange woman wandering around up on our deck. My wife opened the door to ask her who she was and why she was on our deck. The woman replied that she was from the tax assessor's office and that she was assessing the value of our newly added deck. So my deck ended up costing me more than I had originally planned and to this day is still costing me more due to the immediate increase in property taxes. It's not so much that

I believe the tax increase wasn't justified. I suppose what bothered me the most was that it seems as if the tax assessor couldn't wait to come out and raise them. The bottom line is to be sure to check with the local building department before doing any major home improvements to determine if a permit will be required.

Permit fees vary widely by both the type of project and by locale. Some permit fees are very reasonable, such as the $20 driveway fee previously mentioned, while others can be quite high and can range from several hundred dollars to several thousand dollars. In addition, some permit fees are assessed at a flat rate, such as $20 for a driveway regardless of its length or width, while other permit fees are assessed by an estimate of the value of the project and are charged at a rate of so much per hundred dollars of value. Check with your local building inspector to obtain a list of the permit fees that may affect your next home improvement project.

3: REQUIRED INSPECTIONS

Although the types of inspections required vary widely from municipality to municipality, there are several that almost all cities or counties require. To be sure you are in compliance with the requirements in your area, the best approach is to check with your local building department to determine exactly what inspections are necessary. Following are some of the more common ones:

- *Footings.* Footings are used to support the walls of a foundation, such as a basement wall, and are typically eight-inches to ten-inches thick by about twelve-inches to twenty-inches wide. After the basement area has been excavated to the proper depth, the footing is framed in a continuous fashion around the perimeter of the area and wherever a basement wall will be erected. The footings area is then typically lined with steel for additional strength before being filled with concrete. After the concrete hardens, the forms for the basement walls can then be erected directly on the newly formed footings that will then provide the necessary support for them.

- *Slab foundation.* Prior to cement being poured for a slab foundation, the area must be inspected to ensure that the footings and supports for load bearing walls are dug properly and in accordance with the foundation engineer's design. Plumbing lines must also be inspected because they will be embedded in the concrete once it is poured. In addition, some areas may require a moisture barrier between the surface of the ground and the slab to help reduce any moisture penetration.

- *Rough inspection.* Once a house or room addition is framed, electrical wiring, plumbing lines, and air vents and ducts must be "roughed in." The rough-in portion of the work is everything behind the walls that homeowners don't see because it gets covered up with drywall. The workmanship must be inspected prior to the drywall being hung or insulation being installed to ensure that the work is in compliance with the requisite building codes. In addition, the framing of the house or room addition is also inspected at this time. Building inspectors examine the framing to ensure that it has been constructed in accordance with the required codes and engineered design.

- *Insulation inspection.* Many areas require the insulation to be inspected once the rough-in work has been completed and inspected. All new residential construction requires a minimum R-value of insulation in the exterior walls of a house or room addition. Because the insulation will be hidden once the drywall is hung, an inspection is often required.

- *Final inspection.* After all work has been completed, the building inspector will make one final inspection to ensure that the plumbing, electrical, air conditioning, and virtually every aspect of the newly completed work is in full compliance. Upon a satisfactory approval, the building inspector issues a final certificate of occupancy.

I recommend that you keep in mind several general guidelines when working with inspectors. First and foremost, be polite, professional, and courteous with them. If you assume an argumentative or adversarial role with them, they can make your life miserable. Remember that it is the inspector and no one else who holds the power to approve the completed work. Second, determine how much advance notice is required to schedule an inspection so that you can plan accordingly. If you live in a small town where there is not much construction activity, sometimes the inspector will come out the same day you call him or her. Other towns have more stringent notification requirements and may take as long as a one-day to three-day advance notice. Finally, try to be available when the inspector shows up so that any issues that may arise can be addressed directly with the inspector. Otherwise, you may get a red tag on an item that isn't in compliance and not understand what exactly the inspector wants done. I might point out that it is not always possible or convenient to be on the job site when the inspector arrives because he or she could show up first thing in the morning, at lunchtime, or even late in the afternoon. In my experience, more often than not the inspectors show up at random, so it is difficult at best to meet with them when they do arrive.

4: APPLYING FOR A BUILDING PERMIT

If your home improvement project requires a building permit, the size and scope of the project will determine what information needs to be submitted. If the project is relatively simple, such as adding a small deck, then the application process is fairly straightforward. If, however, you are adding a room addition, then quite a bit more information must be submitted. The building department will most likely require architectural drawings imprinted with an engineer's seal, along with detailed plans that identify electrical, plumbing, water, and sewer lines, to name a

FIGURE 2.1 *Permit Application Checklist*

- Completed application
- Legal description of property
- Scope of project defined
- Estimated construction costs (to determine permit fees)
- Site plan illustrating room additions, etc.
- Blueprints with all appropriate drawings
- Engineer's stamp or seal on drawings and calculations
- Plumbing and mechanical drawings as required
- Location of sewer, water, gas, and electrical utilities
- Soil erosion reports
- Other miscellaneous reports as required by the building department

few. Although local building departments can provide you with a checklist of the documents they require, outlined in Figure 2.1 are some of the more common items that may be required to be submitted to get your project approved.

Now take a moment to review Figure 2.2, containing a sample building permit application required by one of the local townships in Michigan. This particular application is fairly comprehensive and is a good example of what you might expect find in your area. Once again, be sure to check with your own building department because it is likely to have its own forms for permit applications.

5: REVISIONS AND APPROVALS

After submitting a building permit application, architectural drawings, and whatever other documentation your city or town requires, the building inspector will then review the information to ensure that it is in full compliance with the existing building code. If the application is incomplete, or if something is not in compliance, the application package may be rejected, in which case you will be notified so that the requisite corrections can be made. Often the corrections are very minor and can be made in a matter of minutes. Sometimes, plans may have to be redrawn for

FIGURE 2.2 *Sample Building Permit Application*

APPLICATION FOR BUILDING PERMIT AND PLAN EXAMINATION

CITY OF GRAND BLANC

NOTICE TO ALL APPLICANTS
THE APPROVAL OF THIS PERMIT DOES NOT CONSTITUTE APPROVAL TO CONTRADICT REQUIRED DEED RESTRICTIONS. THE CITY OF GRAND BLANC IS NOT RESPONSIBLE FOR THE ENFORCEMENT OF ANY RECORDED DEED RETRICTIONS. YOU ARE RESPONSIBLE FOR VERIFYING IF YOUR PROPOSED CONSTRUCTION VIOLATES ANY PROPERTY COVENANTS OR DEED RESTRICTIONS. IF YOU HAVE ANY QUESTIONS YOU MAY WISH TO CONTACT YOUR HOMEOWNERS ASSOCIATION.

AUTHORITY: P.A. 230 OF 1972, AS AMENDED COMPLETION: MANDATORY TO OBTAIN PERMIT PENALTY: PERMIT WILL NOT BE ISSUED	THE DEPARTMENT WILL NOT DISCRIMINATE AGAINST ANY INDIVIDUAL OR GROUP BECAUSE OF RACE, SEX, RELIGION, AGE, NATIONAL ORIGIN, COLOR, MARITAL STAUS, HANDICAP, OR POLITICAL BELIEFS.

APPLICANT TO COMPLETE ALL ITEMS IN SECTION I, II, III, IV, V AND VI
NOTE: SEPARATE APPLICATIONS MUST BE COMPLETED
FOR PLUMBING, MECHANICAL AND ELECTRICAL WORK PERMITS

I. PROJECT INFORMATION

PROJECT TYPE		ADDRESS		
CITY	VILLAGE	TOWNSHIP	COUNTY	ZIP CODE
BETWEEN		AND		

II. IDENTIFICATION

A. OWNER OR LESSEE

NAME		ADDRESS		
CITY		STATE	ZIP CODE	TELEPHONE NUMBER

B. ARCHITECT OR ENGINEER

NAME		ADDRESS		
CITY		STATE	ZIP CODE	TELEPHONE NUMBER
LICENSE NUMBER				EXPIRATION DATE

C. CONTRACTOR

NAME		ADDRESS		
CITY		STATE	ZIP CODE	TELEPHONE NUMBER
BUILDERS LICENSE NUMBER				EXPIRATION DATE

FEDERAL EMPLOYER ID NUMBER OR REASON FOR EXEMPTION

WORKERS COMP INSURANCE CARRIER OR REASON FOR EXEMPTION

MESC EMPLOYER NUMBER OR REASON FOR EXEMPTION

III. TYPE OF IMPROVEMENT AND PLAN REVIEW (COPY OF CONTRACT REQUIRED)

A. TYPE OF IMPROVEMENT   COST OF IMPROVEMENT $ _____

1. ☐ NEW BUILDING	3. ☐ ALTERATION	5. ☐ DEMOLITION	7. ☐ FOUNDATION ONLY	9. ☐ RELOCATION
2. ☐ ADDITION	4. ☐ REPAIR	6. ☐ MOBILE HOME SET-UP	8. ☐ PREMANUFACTURE	10. ☐ SPECIAL INSPECTION

B. REVIEW(S) TO BE PERFORMED

☐ BUILDING	☐ ELECTRICAL	☐ MECHANICAL	☐ PLUMBING	☐ FOUNDATION

PAGE 1

FIGURE 2.2 *Sample Building Permit Application (continued)*

IV. PROPOSED USE OF BUILDING

A. RESIDENTIAL

1. ☐ ONE FAMILY

2. ☐ TWO OR MORE FAMILY
   NO. OF UNITS _____

3. ☐ HOTEL, MOTEL
   NO. OF UNITS _____

4. ☐ ATTACHED GARAGE

5. ☐ DETACHED GARAGE

6. ☐ OTHER

B. NON-RESIDENTIAL

7. ☐ AMUSEMENT
8. ☐ CHURCH, RELIGION
9. ☐ INDUSTRIAL
10. ☐ PARKING GARAGE

11. ☐ SERVICE STATION
12. ☐ HOSPITAL, INSTITUTIONAL
13. ☐ OFFICE, BANK, PROFESSIONAL
14. ☐ PUBLIC UTILITY

15. ☐ SCHOOL, LIBRARY, EDUCATIONAL
16. ☐ STORE, MERCANTILE
17. ☐ TANKS, TOWERS
18. ☐ OTHER

NONRESIDENTIAL-DESCRIBE IN DETAIL PROPOSED USE OF BUILDING, E.G. FOOD PROCESSING PLANT, MACHINE SHOP, LAUNDRY BUILDING AT HOSPITAL, ELEMENTARY SCHOOL, SECONDARY SCHOOL, COLLEGE, PAROCHIAL SCHOOL, PARKING GARAGE FOR DEPARTMENT STORE, RENTAL OFFICE BUILDING, OFFICE BUILDING AT INDUSTRIAL PLANT. IF USE OF EXISTING BUILDING IS BEING CHANGED, ENTER PROPOSED USE.

_____

_____

_____

V. SELECTED CHARACTERISTICS OF BUILDING

A. PRINCIPAL TYPE OF FRAME

1. ☐ MASONRY, WALL BEARING   2. ☐ WOOD FRAME   3. ☐ STRUCTURAL STEEL   4. ☐ REINFORCED CONCRETE   5. ☐ OTHER

B. PRINCIPAL TYPE OF HEATING FUEL

6. ☐ GAS   7. ☐ OIL   8. ☐ ELECTRICITY   9. ☐ COAL   10. ☐ OTHER

C. TYPE OF SEWAGE DISPOSAL

11. ☐ PUBLIC OR PRIVATE COMPANY   12. ☐ SEPTIC SYSTEM

D. TYPE OF WATER SUPPLY

13. ☐ PUBLIC OR PRIVATE COMPANY   14. ☐ PRIVATE WELL OR CISTERN

E. TYPE OF MECHANICAL

15. WILL THERE BE AIR CONDITIONING? ☐ YES ☐ NO   16. WILL THERE BE FIRE SUPPRESSION? ☐ YES ☐ NO

F. DIMENSIONS/DATA

17. NUMBER OF STORIES _____

18. USE GROUP _____

19. CONSTUCTION TYPE _____

20. NO. OF OCCUPANTS _____

21. FLOOR AREA:	EXISTING	ALTERATIONS	NEW
BASEMENT	_____	_____	_____
1ST & 2ND FLOOR	_____	_____	_____
3RD - 10TH FLOOR	_____	_____	_____
11TH - ABOVE			
TOTAL AREA	_____	_____	_____

G. NUMBER OF OFF STREET PARKING SPACES

22. ENCLOSED _____   23. OUTDOORS _____

FIGURE 2.2 *Sample Building Permit Application (continued)*

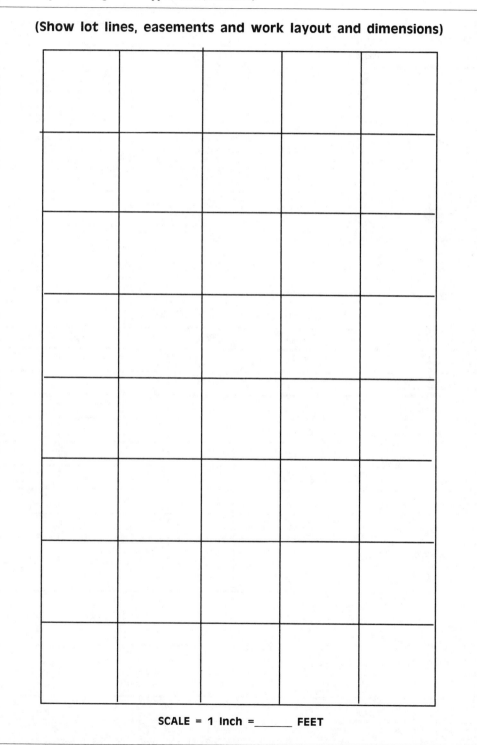

(Show lot lines, easements and work layout and dimensions)

SCALE = 1 Inch =_____ FEET

PAGE 3

FIGURE 2.2 *Sample Building Permit Application (continued)*

VI. APPLICANT INFORMATION

APPLICANT IS RESPONSIBLE FOR THE PAYMENT OF ALL FEES AND CHARGES APPLICABLE TO THIS APPLICATION AND MUST PROVIDE THE FOLLOWING INFORMATION.

NAME		TELEPHONE NO.	
ADDRESS	CITY	STATE	ZIP CODE

FEDERAL I.D. NUMBER/SOCIAL SECURITY NUMBER

I HEREBY CERTIFY THAT THE PROPOSED WORK IS AUTHORIZED BY THE OWNER OF RECORD AND THAT I HAVE BEEN AUTHORIZED BY THE OWNER TO MAKE THIS APPLICATION AS HIS/HER AUTHORIZED AGENT AND WE AGREE TO CONFORM TO ALL APPLICABLE LAWS OF THE STATE OF MICHIGAN. ALL INFORMATION SUBMITTED ON THIS APPLICATION IS ACCURATE TO THE BEST OF MY KNOWLEDGE.

> Section 23a of the state construction code act of 1972, 1972PA 230, MCL 125.1523A, prohibits a person from conspiring to circumvent the licensing requirements of this state relating to persons who are to perform work on a residential building or a residential structure. Violators of section 23a are subjected to civil fines.

SIGNATURE OF APPLICANT

PLAN REVIEW FEE ENCLOSED $ _____	BUILDING PERMIT FEE ENCLOSED $ _____

VII. LOCAL GOVERNMENT AGENCY TO COMPLETE THIS SECTION

ENVIRONMENTAL CONTROL APPROVALS

	REQUIRED?	APPROVED	DATE	NUMBER	BY
A - ZONING	☐ YES ☐ NO				
B - FIRE DISTRICT	☐ YES ☐ NO				
C - POLLUTION CONTROL	☐ YES ☐ NO				
D - NOISE CONTROL	☐ YES ☐ NO				
E - SOIL EROSION	☐ YES ☐ NO				
F - FLOOD ZONE	☐ YES ☐ NO				
G - WATER SUPPLY	☐ YES ☐ NO				
H - SEPTIC SYSTEM	☐ YES ☐ NO				
I - VARIANCE GRANTED	☐ YES ☐ NO				
J - OTHER	☐ YES ☐ NO				

VIII. VALIDATION - FOR DEPARTMENT USE ONLY

USE GROUP _____	BASE FEE _____
TYPE OF CONSTRUCTION _____	NUMBER OF INSPECTIONS _____
SQUARE FEET _____	

APPROVAL SIGNATURE

TITLE	DATE

PAGE 4

one reason or another, or perhaps some of the detail may be missing. For example, if the engineer's seal was inadvertently left off of the foundation plan, the package would be returned so that the necessary correction could be made. If a home improvement project is quite involved, such as enlarging a house by adding on to it, there is most likely quite a bit of documentation and detail required. Most experienced builders and contractors are familiar with the application process and generally know all that is required, but homeowners who seldom take on an improvement of this magnitude may be prone to overlook some of the required details.

Once satisfied with everything you have submitted, the building inspector will issue a permit. The length of time required for approval can vary anywhere from a few minutes to a few days to a few weeks. If a licensed electrician, for example, needs to pull an electrical permit, it will usually be issued on the spot. Building permits for new construction of an addition or a house, on the other hand, can take longer. If the town you live in is small with little building activity, the inspector can most likely review the application and issue a permit within a day or two. On the other hand, if you live in an area where there is strong growth, it may take several weeks to get an approval. One of our building superintendents recently submitted an application for the construction of a new house in a community in which the average time for approval is typically one week. On this occasion, however, a larger national builder had just submitted 23 applications for new residential construction the day before. Our usual one week approval turned into a little over three full weeks causing us a two-week delay. Fortunately the family for whom we were building the home was very understanding and not on a tight time schedule.

6: DEED RESTRICTIONS AND HOMEOWNER ASSOCIATIONS

Before considering making any improvements to your home, it's a good idea to review the deed restrictions that may govern your community, as well as the bylaws of your homeowners association (HOA). Restrictions and bylaws vary widely from area to area, so while a cedar fence may be the norm in one community, it may be expressly prohibited in another. For example, when I lived in Texas in a suburb of the Houston metropolitan area, cedar fences were quite common. In fact, in the neighborhood I lived in, all of the houses had yards that were completely fenced. Furthermore, most all of the newer communities had fenced yards and if for some reason one of them didn't, it made you wonder why not. When I moved to Michigan, I found just the opposite to be true. Very few of the new communities have fenced yards, and in most areas, they are prohibited unless, of course, the homeowner has a swimming pool, in which case state and federal laws require a fence for reasons of safety.

Many HOAs require certain home improvements to be approved before making them by a committee that oversees activity in the community. For instance, in one particular neighborhood I lived in, storage sheds were allowed, but they had to be constructed in accordance with specific guidelines using only approved materials and placed a certain distance from the property line. Although the local building department did not require a building permit because there was no digging or electrical work involved, the HOA committee nevertheless required drawings to be submitted for approval before construction began. Approval also had to given for minor improvements as well, such as painting your house. If a homeowner did not get the required approval from the governing HOA, they found themselves subject to a fine.

Deed restrictions and HOA bylaws are largely designed to help preserve the value of a community by ensuring that the residents who live there maintain their homes and property in a manner that is consistent with the governing restrictions. On the one hand, this can be of great value and can help protect property values. If, for example, I wanted to paint my house neon purple and the bylaws expressly stated that only earth tones can be used, the bylaws would help provide a more consistent appearance throughout the neighborhood. On the other hand, if I'm the type of individual who really values his privacy and prefers to have a fenced yard but the deed restrictions won't allow it, then it seems as if I don't have as much control over my property as I would like.

In summary, schedule a meeting with the local building inspector to learn all you can about what may be required before starting a project. Fill out all of the information requested on the building application and submit it with the required drawings and documentation. Be prepared to make revisions and, finally, be sure to verify that the home improvement you want to make is allowed in your neighborhood before starting any new projects.

3

EVERYTHING YOU NEED TO KNOW ABOUT SUBCONTRACTORS

7: DO THE WORK YOURSELF OR HIRE A SUBCONTRACTOR?

When getting ready to take on any new home improvement project, the question of whether or not to do the work yourself or to hire a subcontractor naturally arises. The answer to that question depends on several factors that must be taken into consideration. They include your own personal degree of skill and ability, the availability of time that you have to complete the project, and whether or not licensed contractors will be needed.

While many homeowners shun the idea of having anyone but themselves perform the work required to successfully complete a home improvement project, others prefer to do as little as possible. This is in large part due to the level of skill required for various types of projects. If you happened to grow up with parents who were "do-it-yourselfers," there's a good chance that you are quite comfortable operating tools such as power saws and sanders. On the other hand, many people with a different set of life experiences may not even know what a power saw is. If you're anything like my brother, Tim, it's quite possible that you have a natural gift for working with tools. Sometimes I think that Tim, who is the epitome of someone who is mechanically inclined, must have been born with a hammer in his hand. In *The Complete Guide to Flipping Properties* (New Jersey; John Wiley and Sons; 2003), I wrote the following:

> For those of you may be more mechanically inclined, it is natural for you to feel and believe that you should do as much of the work yourself in an effort to save money. Allow me to share a personal example with you of the differences between two individuals who have different skill sets. The first individual is my brother, Tim, who has very strong mechanical skills and can fix almost anything. In fact, one of my earliest memories of him "fixing something" occurred when I was about three years old. Tim would have been five at the time. I remember coming outside to play one day only to discover that he had taken all of the wheels off of my shiny, red tricycle. Another time, he completely disassembled our swing set. While Tim was exceptionally good at taking things apart, he had unfortunately not learned how to put them back together yet, thereby rendering my tricycle and the swing set useless. Tim has come a long way since that time. Not only has he become an expert at taking things apart, but he is now extremely proficient at putting them back together.
>
> The second individual in this example is none other than yours truly. While I lack the natural mechanical skills that Tim has, I do have very good organizational and management skills. I recall in my teenage years that I was always very particular about keeping my bedroom as neat and orderly as possible. I was probably the only child in the family who made his bed without having to be asked to do so. My personality demanded structure and order. Later, my service in the United States Air Force reinforced

these concepts, especially the training I received at boot camp (also known as basic training) at Lackland Air Force Base in San Antonio, TX. Our beds had to be made perfectly with blankets folded taut enough to literally bounce a quarter off of. Everything in our footlockers had to be placed in exact and precise order according to our training manuals. If it wasn't, believe me, you would hear about it from the drill sergeant.

So here you have two individuals who were raised by the same set of parents who happened to have two very different sets of skills. While Tim is more of the hands-on mechanical type, I am more of the hands-off organizational type, and while Tim loves to tackle almost any type of home improvement project himself, I prefer to take on only the smallest of projects.

Your availability of time will also play a large role in whether or not you decide to take on a home improvement project yourself or hire a subcontractor. The size and scope of the project will in part be a determining factor. The larger and more extensive the project, the more time will be required to complete it. Some people have more time than money while other people have more money than time. I have several neighbors who are the do-it-yourself types who have taken, for example, up to a year or more to finish a basement.

For those of you who live in an area where basements are uncommon, unfinished basements have concrete walls and a concrete floor and maybe a few steel posts for support. To finish a basement means converting the space into actual living area where interior walls are framed, electrical outlets are installed, plumbing lines are run, drywall is hung, and, finally, some type of flooring is laid. Although there are many companies that specialize in doing this type of work, there is probably an equal number of homeowners who prefer to finish their own basements. Because the work takes place inside, it can be done at the homeowner's leisure—during the day, on weekends, at night, in the rain, or in the snow. It really doesn't matter. So before taking on your next project, be sure to consider the element of time before committing yourself.

Another factor to consider in determining whether or not to do a home improvement yourself or hire a subcontractor is whether the work to be performed will require a licensed individual. If you're doing some minor or less extensive work, such as repainting or putting in new flooring, then a licensed contractor will most likely not be required. On the other hand, larger projects that require the installation of plumbing and electrical lines will almost surely require a licensed contractor.

In summary, whether you decide to do the work yourself or hire a subcontractor will depend the personal level of skill you have, your availability of time, and whether or not a licensed contractor is required. The primary advantage of doing the work yourself is, of course, the money you can save by not having to pay someone else for their labor. A secondary advantage or benefit, and perhaps one that is equally as important as the money you will save, is the personal satisfaction derived from successfully completing a project. Finally, how many times have you said to yourself something like, "That's not the way I wanted that done. Why did they do it like that?" If you are the type of person who is very particular and wants something done a certain way, then you will most likely want to do the project yourself. I'm sure you're familiar with the old adage, "If you want something done right, do it yourself." It seems that more often than not, the principle is quite true.

8: PROS AND CONS OF USING SUBCONTRACTORS

If you've decided that a subcontractor is needed for your home improvement project, then it is important for you to know and understand some of the advantages and disadvantages of employing them. Let's start with some of the advantages of employing a qualified subcontractor. First, believe it or not, using a subcontractor or a general contractor can actually save you money. "How can that be?" you ask, especially if you do a lot of the work yourself. The answer is really quite simple. Successful contractors who have been in business for several years have the necessary expertise to do the job right the first time. They are skilled and proficient and can do a job much quicker than the weekend do-it-yourselfer can. They already know where to find the materials needed at the best price and can probably purchase them cheaper than a typical homeowner can.

As a builder for Symphony Homes, I have seen this all too often. Individuals, such as a young couple, who want to take on the task of building their own house and think they will save money are often disappointed. For example, most of them have very little, if any, experience building a house. They spend time searching and shopping for the best prices for materials and labor and may think they are getting a good deal. In reality, the people they hire to help them may quote a low price, then add on a lot of extras for problems they didn't anticipate, or they may show up a week or two late and cause unnecessary delays that add to the carrying costs of the project. A young couple's dream of building a new home together can quickly turn into a nightmare, and the home that was supposed to be completed in four months has instead taken a full year.

As an experienced builder, on the other hand, our company has already negotiated competitive prices for materials based on volume discounts. Furthermore, we have weeded through the many trades and subcontractors who attempt to take advantage of the unsuspecting homeowner, as well as those who have proven to be unreliable. Our subcontractors work with us every day and are therefore familiar with the high standard of quality we expect. Moreover, our subcontractors know that if they fail to show up for a job as scheduled, they might as well not bother to show up at all. We strive to complete each job on time and do not tolerate delays caused by irresponsible and unreliable subcontractors. I certainly don't mean to imply that people cannot build a house or complete a major home improvement on their own, but rather point out that there are pitfalls to be aware of and that things aren't necessarily as easy as they look on the surface.

Some of the disadvantages of using subcontractors have just been pointed out in the preceding text. Subcontractors are, for example, notoriously late. Sometimes they don't bother to show up for a job at all. Furthermore, they don't even bother to call you to tell you they're not showing up. They just don't show up. Other subcontractors like to play games with their prices. For instance, if a cement contractor quotes a price of $2 per square foot for a driveway, you need to know what that price includes. If you operate under the premise that the quoted price is a "turnkey" price, you may be in for a big surprise. There may be additional charges for the steel rod that is laid to strengthen the concrete, or charges for cutting out the area to be poured with a small bulldozer, or adding chloride to the cement if the ambient air temperature is too low, or any number of other reasons the subcontractor can think of. Your $2 per square foot quote can quickly turn into $3 per square foot or more.

Not only is it important to get a firm quote from any company you may be considering doing business with, but you should also be sure you both agree upon what all is included in the quote. It's a good idea to ask the contractor directly if there are any other charges that may arise during the course of the work and to establish up front what all is included in the quote. Finally, be sure to outline not only the work to be done but also the materials that will be used. Many years ago, I hired a painter to paint the entire interior of my home. I was very clear with him about the brand of paint that I wanted used, a brand I believed to be of a quality superior to that of others. It was also, of course, more expensive than the inferior paints typically used by contractors. It wasn't until about halfway through the project that I noticed that the empty cans were some off-brand paint that I didn't recognize. As it turns out, the painter took it upon himself to match the color I had requested to the cheaper off-brand he used on all of his other jobs. The painter adamantly refused to use the higher quality paint I had initially wanted, so I allowed him to finish the job with the paint he started with, and then took it upon myself to reduce his fee by an amount equal to the difference in the cost of the two paints.

9: HOW TO FIND QUALIFIED SUBCONTRACTORS

Finding qualified and reliable subcontractors can prove to be challenging for the typical person who isn't in the business of working with them day in and day out. While the average home-owner may think to look in the Yellow Pages for a brick mason or carpenter, for example, chances are they wouldn't be listed there. Many of the smaller, independent contractors who are good at what they do don't need to advertise in the Yellow Pages because they often have all the work they can handle. These contractors are generally content to work by themselves, or perhaps with a small crew, and don't carry the expensive overhead of advertising and offices. This is exactly the type of subcontractor I like to hire because they tend to price their services more reasonably than a large company with lots of overhead. You have to be careful, how-ever, to make sure the contractor is going to still be around during the warranty period in case any callback issues arise.

Okay, so if you don't look in the Yellow Pages to find a qual-ified and reliable contractor, then where do you look? I have had the best luck with two primary sources. The first place, and usu-ally the best place, is to ask another subcontractor or supplier. We work with, for example, a large national wholesale building supply company that most people haven't even heard of. Our sales rep works with many other builders and subcontractors and knows who is reliable and does quality work and who is not. He has been a great source for providing our company with quali-fied subcontractors.

Your local lumber company or hardware store will almost surely have a list of contractors they can provide you with. Some even have bulletin boards hung somewhere in the store where contractors can display their business cards. If you decide to take one of the business cards from the board, it's a good idea to ask one of the employees if he knows anything about that particular subcontractor. Usually he can tell you who to call and who to avoid. The employee might even give you a list with three or four names on it stating that while the store policy will not allow them to recommend any one contractor, all three or four are good and warrant a call. This is even better because now instead of just having the name of one subcontractor, you have the names of several, all of whom can provide you with a quote or estimate for the work you want done. In my experience, a personal referral by a supplier or another subcontractor provides the most qualified and reliable results.

Another way to find good subcontractors is by driving around other job sites. For example, you can drive through any new neighborhood where homes are being built and find virtually all types of tradespeople working on the houses. Don't think for a minute that you can't stop and talk to them just because they happen to be working on another job. Subcontractors don't mind taking a moment to talk with you, especially if it might lead to doing business together. Another key advantage of visiting subcontractors on the job site is that you get to see firsthand the quality of work they do. If you are talking to a mason, for instance, observe his crew in action. Is their work neat and do they seem to take pride in what they do? Do they move and work in an almost rhythmic fashion with the flow of bricks being laid? Or do they appear to be moving very slowly, almost dragging, as if they didn't have a care in the world?

So when looking for a qualified subcontractor, be sure to ask people who are in the business and work with contractors every day. A good referral can be worth its weight in gold. Be sure to check other job sites also, as this will give you the opportunity to not only locate subcontractors, but also to evaluate the quality of work they do. As a last resort, you can always check the Yellow Pages or classified ads in your local newspaper.

10: LICENSING, INSURANCE, AND BONDING REQUIREMENTS

Professional contractors should be in full compliance with the licensing, insurance, and bonding requirements of their respective communities. Most of them will tell you that of course they meet all of the requirements of their municipality, but there are a few tricks of the trade you should be aware of. Compliance with licensing laws is usually not a problem because if the subcontractor's license is not current, he cannot pull a permit to do the work. All towns and cities require that before a permit can be issued to a contractor, he must show evidence of having a current license. Usually this is in the form of a pocket license issued to the contractor by the state or other governing body. So when the contractor goes to the building department, he simply presents his pocket license and the permit is issued without further ado.

Providing evidence of insurance is quite another matter. With a reputable subcontractor, this is rarely a problem. There are those, however, who attempt to skirt around the law and operate under the pretense that they carry the required insurance. Before subcontractors do any work for my company, a copy of their insurance is requested. This must be sent directly to us by the issuing agent and should not come from the contractors themselves. I can't tell you how many times I've had subcontractors tell me something like, "Oh yes, of course I carry insurance. I'll have my agent fax a copy of it to you." Several days may go by, and then a week, and then two weeks, and still no insurance, all the while the contractor is promising that "it's on the way." I make it very clear that no payments will be issued to them until we have received the proper evidence of insurance by their agent. This allows the contractor to start the work whether he has the insurance or not (which some builders would not do for liability reasons). We stand firm, however, on our commitment not to pay them until we have received the required insurance documents.

Most professional contractors are bonded, meaning they carry a type of insurance that protects the customer from loss against work not performed by the contractor. For our company, whether or not the subcontractor is bonded or not usually isn't an issue because we don't pay them until the work is completed. If a plumber who is not bonded, for example, only partially completes a job for us, he doesn't get paid—period. We establish from the outset the terms and conditions of payment. If the job is for new construction, the plumber gets paid in two phases—after completing the rough plumbing, and again after completing the finished plumbing. If the plumber gets started on the rough plumbing, but doesn't finish for some reason, he doesn't get paid.

This type of compensation policy renders the requirement to be bonded a moot point. Often for homeowners, however, the payment policy is different. As a builder who can provide a steady flow of business to a contractor, we wield the lever of control. On the other hand, as a homeowner who is hiring a contractor on a onetime basis, it is the contractor who sets the terms and oftentimes an initial payment might be required up front before a job is even started. If you have any reservations whatsoever about the legitimacy of any contractor, ask them to provide you with a copy of the bond issued to them at the same time you request a copy of their insurance. If a contractor is reputable, he will have no reservations about doing so.

11: PROTECT YOURSELF USING THE RIGHT CONTRACTOR AGREEMENTS

One step essential to protecting yourself when hiring a subcontractor is to be sure to "get it in writing." While most professional contractors who have been in business for several years already use their own contract forms, those forms were drafted largely to protect the contractors and do very little to protect you. It is therefore important for you to review the forms to ensure that the contracts also have language sufficient to protect your interests as well. The appendix shows a sample Owner and Subcontractor Agreement that you can review and use to best suit your needs. Outlined in the following text is the substance of the agreement. The heading clearly identifies who the agreement is made between along with its location.

- *Article 1: Scope of Work.* This section covers the scope of work to be performed by the contractor. Include here a complete description of all labor to be performed and materials to be furnished.
- *Article 2: Terms of Payment.* Article 2 identifies the terms of payment to be made by the owner and also lists the total contract amount for the services and materials to be provided.
- *Article 3: Time of Completion.* Article 3 is important because it is used to expressly state the amount of time, or number of days, the contractor has to complete all work. If the work is not completed in the amount of time stated, then the contractor is in default. This section is used to prevent a contractor from starting a job that should only take one week, for example, and dragging it out for several months.
- *Article 4: Change Orders.* Change orders are used to modify the scope of work as the job progresses. Often a homeowner will have a change of mind about one of the details of the home improvement project that is not covered in the original contract. For example, a homeowner might decide she wants the interior of her home painted, and then decide after the contractor has already started the job that she wants the trim painted a different color. This happens all the time and should not be a problem provided that both

parties agree to the change and the appropriate charges for it.

- *Article 5: Clean Up.* This section is used to clarify that the contractor, and *not* the homeowner, will be responsible for the cleanup of a job site after all work has been completed. Although you may be inclined to assume that of course the contractors will clean up after themselves, you would be incorrect to do so. I have seen all too often subcontractors come in during the construction process, do the work they have been contracted to do, and leave the place in an absolute shambles! I am personally very strict about keeping our job sites clean. It provides for a safer and more organized work environment that helps to reduce accidents and provides for a more professional atmosphere. If a subcontractor leaves one of our sites littered with debris, we give that contractor a strong disincentive not to do it again by imposing a stiff back charge. As far as I am concerned, the contractor who makes the mess is the one who gets to clean it up.

- *Article 6: Taxes and Permits.* Article 6 is used to identify who is responsible for the payment of taxes and permit fees related to the work to be performed. If it is the contractor who is pulling the permits and purchasing the materials, then it is the contractor who is usually responsible for paying them. This is another area where you must be careful when comparing quotes or bids from different contractors. Some of them will quote you the lowest price possible to get the job and then attempt to assess additional charges for whatever else they can think of, including permit fees, application fees, and taxes.

- *Article 7: Insurance.* This section states that the subcontractor must maintain a current insurance policy at his own expense during the time that all work is being performed and furthermore, that the homeowner will not be liable for any claims that might arise from the project.

- *Article 8: Liquidated Damages.* This section states the amount of damages to be paid by the subcontractors in the event that the job is not completed on time and as agreed upon. Penalties are typically assessed on a daily basis, so the longer it takes the contractor to finish, the more it costs him.
- *Article 9: Warranty.* Article 9 is essential to any home improvement contract because it identifies what exactly the subcontractor is responsible for, what action will be taken in the event of a defect or problem, as well as the warranty period.
- *Article 10: Hazardous Materials and Waste.* This section is used to clarify who will be responsible for hazardous waste material should any be encountered during the project. Because hazardous waste material, such as asbestos, requires special handling, it is usually the responsibility of the subcontractor to notify the homeowner that such a condition exists, who in turn should notify a qualified and licensed individual capable of handling the material.
- *Article 11: Arbitration of Disputes.* Article 11 states that any claim or dispute that should arise as a result of the work being performed will be resolved and administered through an arbitration body designed to handle such disputes.
- *Article 12: Attorney Fees.* This section is used to identify which party will be responsible for attorney's fees in the event of a dispute. It is most often the prevailing party who will be entitled to reimbursement of reasonable expenditures arising from dispute resolution.
- *Article 13: Acceptance.* Article 13 provides a place for the contracting parties to affix their signature so as to validate the agreement, as well as a place for the date.

12: WARRANTIES

Another important issue that should be taken into consideration when deciding which subcontractor to use is the warranty. Do the subcontractors stand behind their work by offering a warranty on all work performed, and just as important, is the warranty expressed in writing? You may find yourself in a situation where Contractor A, for example, has a lower price than Contractor B, but Contractor A offers a 30-day warranty while Contractor B offers a full one-year warranty. Furthermore, Contractor A states something like, "No, our warranty isn't really anything we have in writing, but if you have any problems, just call me. I always take care of my customers." Meanwhile, along with the initial quote, Contractor B also presents you with a written warranty stating exactly what is covered and what isn't. Although it might be tempting to choose the contractor with the lowest quote, cheaper does not necessarily mean better. In fact, cheaper in the short run can turn into more expensive in the long run. There's a great deal of truth in the adage, "You get what you pay for."

For new residential construction, the subcontractors used by Symphony Homes are required to stand behind their work for a full year. As the builder, we are ultimately responsible, so if one of our subcontractors fails to come out to a homeowner's house for warranty work, we will have the repair taken care of at our cost, but that particular subcontractor will never work for us again. Not only do we provide our clients with a full one-year warranty against defects in workmanship and materials, but we also provide them with a limited ten-year warranty that covers the major structural components of a house. Every home we build is backed by a ten-year warranty at no additional cost to the buyer, and yes, the warranty is in writing. Our willingness to stand behind every home we build for ten years goes a long way with winning the confidence and trust of our customers. In summary, be sure the subcontractor you are dealing with offers a written warranty for any work to be performed.

13: COMPARING AND ACCEPTING PROPOSALS

When comparing proposals by different contractors, there are several things to look for to make sure that you really are getting the best deal for your money. These things include ensuring that the quotes are consistent with each other, outlining the quality of workmanship and materials to be used, whether or not a written warranty will be provided, and the time necessary to complete the task.

A contractor's standard price for quoting work can be very misleading, and many contractors will deliberately and knowingly quote a lower price than their competitors just to get the job. Then they will turn around and add extra charges for whatever they can come up with. Earlier in this chapter, I used the example of concrete and how a contractor's base price can differ greatly from the final price. Another good example is an excavator. For example, you might have two different excavators provide a quote for digging a basement. Excavator A charges $85 per hour and Excavator B charges $75 per hour. Your initial reaction is likely to be, "Great, I'll go with Excavator B and save $10 per hour." If both excavators completed the task in exactly the same amount of time, that would be fine, but guess what? They won't. I've used some excavators who can dig a basement out in less than one day, and others who have taken as long as three days to five days. At $75 to $85 per hour, the difference between one day and five days is quite significant. Rather than have an excavator provide you with an hourly rate, it is better to get a fixed-dollar-amount quote. What you want to know is, "How much will it cost me to have a basement dug?" with no extra charges and no hidden fees. With a fixed quote, you know exactly where you stand.

Also when comparing quotes, you should take into consideration the quality of materials and workmanship that will be used. If the quality of home improvement is poor, then it doesn't matter how much money you think you might be saving. In the end, you really won't be saving anything at all because more money will most likely have to be spent somewhere along the way to repair the initial work. Earlier in this chapter, I used the example of a painter who chose to use a cheaper brand of paint than I had requested. Because contractors have many choices available to them in almost every aspect of home improvement work, it is important to identify from the outset what types of materials will be used to complete the job.

Another factor for consideration when comparing quotes is the issue of warranties that, although previously discussed, bears repeating. If tradespeople are not willing to stand behind their work, you're probably better off not using them to begin with. Several years ago when procuring bids to have an irrigation, or sprinkler, system installed at my personal residence, I had the option of using a cheaper contractor who apparently operated out of his car and, of course, gave me his word that he would stand behind his work. My other option was to use a more expensive contractor who had been established in the area for many years with a physical place of business I could go to should any problems arise, and who also provided a full one-year written warranty on all materials and workmanship. Even though the second company was more expensive, the additional cost was worth it to me for the added peace of mind I had knowing that if anything at all went wrong with my newly installed irrigation system, the company would stand behind their work.

Finally, the factor of time should also be considered when comparing quotes. With all other things being equal, it makes sense (and cents) to use the contractor who can commit to completing the job in the most timely fashion. If your project is more involved, like a room addition for example, you have to be very careful about using tradespeople who may hold up the project for an unnecessary period of time. The contractor's delays will cause additional carrying costs as well.

At the beginning of this last summer, my wife and I noticed that one of the neighbors had hired a subcontractor to build a deck for them. "How nice," we thought, "they're getting a new deck!" A month passed by, and the deck wasn't finished. Then another month passed, and still another month. After four months had passed, the deck was finally finished. "What a shame," my wife and I thought. What should have taken only one week to two weeks to finish had instead taken the entire summer, and then some! The entire summer had passed without the family being able to use their new deck, and summer had now turned to autumn with the days shorter and the nights cooler. In summary, be sure the quotes you are considering are consistent with each other, that the price you have been given is the true price, that the quality of materials and workmanship are high, that a warranty is included, and that the job will be completed in a timely manner.

14: PAYMENTS TO SUBCONTRACTORS

Scheduling payments to your subcontractor will depend on a variety of factors. For a smaller project such as a roof repair or installation of a garage door opener, payment is typically made in full at the completion of the job. Sometimes, however, the contractor may require an initial deposit of up to one half the total amount due just to get started. For moderate to larger home improvement jobs, this is especially true. A subcontractor building a new deck on the back of your house, for example, may require as much as one half the total due to get started. He may give you a reason such as needing the money to purchase the materials. If the contractor is local and well-established, then giving him the required deposit should be okay. But be careful not to get taken by fly-by-nighters who may take the deposit and never bother to return. On a larger project, such as one that may cost $20,000 or more, a much smaller deposit, such as 10 percent, should be all that is required to get started. Other contractors work off what is referred to as a draw schedule, meaning they get paid in a series of payments based on the percentage of the work completed.

Draw schedules such as this are usually divided equally over a series of anywhere from two draws to four draws.

Although payment terms vary widely among contractors, one rule you should always adhere to is to never prepay 100 percent in advance for the work. In fact, I recommend withholding the final payment until the project is fully completed to ensure that all work is finished as agreed upon. What often happens is that tradespeople will finish all but the last little bit of a job and want to get paid in full with the promise that they will return within the next day or so to finish up. I've heard this story so many times that I don't even give contractors a chance to tell it. Before they even start a job, we explain in no uncertain terms that before they are to get paid, the job must be completed in its entirety. If contractors insist on getting paid, you may decide to pay them, but be sure and withhold enough to make sure they come back to finish the work as promised. Usually holding back 10 percent to 20 percent of the total contract price is adequate.

15: MECHANICS' LIENS AND HOW THEY CAN AFFECT YOU

If a dispute arises about the quality of the work performed, or the work was not completed as expected, or any other disagreement arises regarding the work contracted for, you may decide to withhold your payment from the subcontractor. If you were careful enough to outline the terms and conditions of your agreement in a written contract, you may have the legal right to do so. However, you should be aware that most subcontractors are familiar with mechanic's lien laws and the trouble they can cause for the homeowner. If the contractor finishes the work and a customer refuses to pay for whatever reason, the contractor may choose to file a mechanic's lien on the property with the county clerk. A mechanic's lien is a legal document filed with the county clerk against real property as a claim of interest. If a homeowner never intends to move from the residence or refinance the mortgage, then he or she has little to worry about. Sooner or later, though, most people will either move or refinance. In both cases, title insurance must be provided to the lender that indicates that no clouds or encumbrances, such as mechanics' liens, exist on the property.

If a mechanic's lien is found to exist, it must be satisfied before a new mortgage can be placed on the property. Probably your best bet in a case like that is to pay the subcontractor so that you can proceed with the sale or refinancing of your home, and then to work the matter out later in a small claims court or civil court. In any event, you may need to seek the advice of a qualified attorney to represent you.

In summary, educating yourself about the process of working with subcontractors is strongly advised and will be to your advantage. Familiarizing yourself with the pros and cons of working with them will help you to make a decision best suited to your needs. Knowing how to find qualified subcontractors and what to look for when comparing their bids can potentially save you thousands of dollars. Being familiar with subcontractor agreements and warranties can also save you money. Finally, it can certainly be beneficial to know what kind of action to take in the event a mechanic's lien is placed on your property.

P a r t **T** *w o*

EXTERIOR IMPROVEMENTS

4

GENERAL PROPERTY AND GROUNDS

16: GENERAL CLEANUP

One of the most effective, low cost improvements a home-owner can make is to do a good, general cleanup of the exterior around a house. Getting rid of any junk or debris that may have accumulated over the years will do wonders for any house. When prospective buyers drive up to look at a house for sale and see years of junk and debris accumulated in the yard, there's a good chance they may just keep right on driving. There's a great deal of truth in the maxim that refers to "first impressions." Creating a positive first impression is essential to presenting a home in its most favorable light, and cleaning up the junk and throwing out the trash is a great way to start.

If you've lived in your home for several years, there's a good chance that something around the house or in the yard needs to be cleaned up or thrown out. Almost all of us have something in the yard that can be cleaned up. For example, maybe you bought a swing set for your children several years ago that is now no longer used. If it is made of metal, the frame is probably discolored and rusty, the chains supporting the swings may be loose or missing, and the slide is probably dented and falling off. Now let's face it. How much do you suppose that old swing set is really worth? If you're not using it, and your kids aren't using it, what's the point of keeping it around? There's a good chance that your house is worth more by getting rid of it than it is by keeping it. In this case, even though the swing set may be fully paid for, it is certainly more of a liability to you than it is an asset.

You would be surprised by how quickly stuff can accumulate around your house and go unnoticed indefinitely, that is, until someone calls your attention to it. I once bought a house that had a loose gutter that had fallen off before I moved in. The gutter had fallen to the ground and had been carelessly tossed along the side of the house. Even though I had requested that the seller repair the gutter, the day of closing came and still the gutter had not been repaired. I knew it was a simple thing to fix, so I didn't let it hold up the closing. My wife and I had just been blessed with a brand new baby boy and we were anxious to move into what would be a "new" house for us.

The day of closing had come and gone. I thought to myself that as soon as we got moved in, I would fix the gutter by reattaching it to the house. As it turned out, unpacking took longer than expected, the new baby certainly took more time than expected, and before I knew it, old man winter had come to visit for a few months. "Well, okay. I'll wait until the springtime, and then I'll fix the gutter," I thought to myself. Sure enough, spring came just as it always does, and then summer, and then fall, and before I knew it, winter had returned.

A second year passed and that gutter was still on the ground, exactly where it was when I bought the house, only now it had weeds grown up around it and was more unsightly than ever. Along came another baby boy, and two more years had passed, making four years in total, and still that gutter lay exactly where it had since the day we moved in. Before we knew it, it was time to move on to another house. Knowing that creating a good first impression is vital to selling a house, I finally fixed that gutter by reattaching it to the house, which is exactly what I should have done four years earlier.

You can see by this example how easy it is to adjust to something that is out of place or unsightly in the yard. After a while you don't even notice it anymore. It's just there. It's kind of like driving through a neighborhood that's close to an airport and thinking, "How can anyone live here so close to all that noise?" Stop and ask any of the neighbors, though, and they'll probably respond by saying something like, "Oh, the airplanes? We hardly even notice them anymore."

Following is a checklist of items to be on the lookout for in your yard. The list should by no means be considered exhaustive, but it's a good start. Allow common sense to prevail and you'll be in good shape.

- *Bottles, cans, trash.* Clean up any old bottles and cans that may have accumulated in the yard, along with general trash and debris.
- *Tires.* Have you ever purchased a new set of tires but kept the old ones just in case you got a flat in one of the new tires? The old tires, probably stacked on the side of the house or somewhere in the backyard, are probably still there to this day. Get rid of them!
- *Firewood.* Old wood cut up to be used for firewood attracts bugs and insects and is often thrown into a heap. If you're selling a house in the spring or summer, throw it out. At a minimum, stack the firewood neatly and get rid of the loose chips that may be lying around.
- *Dated playground equipment.* I mentioned the worn out and rusty swing set earlier in this section. You may also have some playground equipment made of plastic that when new was bright and colorful but has now become cracked and faded. Throw it out, give it away, or sell it in a garage sale.

- *Lawn clippings and other natural waste.* You may have a spot in the backyard somewhere where the lawn clippings are dumped week after week and have now formed a small mountain, or a spot perhaps where you throw branches broken off of trees by the wind, or even those you have pruned. Get rid of them!
- *Bicycles and other kid's toys.* How many times have you been through a neighborhood and seen old bikes and toys strewn in front of a house? Clean them up!

Impact value: ★★★★★ Strong. The impact value of general cleanup is strong because it will greatly improve the appearance of a home and costs very little to do so. In many cases, the outside of a home can be cleaned up in less than a day and will only cost you your time.

17: LAWNS

Have you ever driven through a neighborhood and noticed one or two lawns that are lush and green and really stand out among all the others, and then find yourself wondering what it is the homeowners are doing to make them that way? One particular family in my neighborhood somehow seems to magically maintain their lawn to near perfection year after year. What's more, I rarely see them outside working on it. It's almost as if a professional lawn crew comes out at night after everyone has gone to sleep and works diligently all night long to beautify the lawn. I happened to be driving by one afternoon and saw the lady who lives there outside, so I decided to stop and ask her what she and her family did to have such a lush looking lawn. She replied that they really didn't do anything special besides water the lawn and fertilize it regularly. I told her that I did the same, but for some reason, my lawn didn't look nearly as good as theirs did. So I asked her what brand of fertilizer she used and she replied that her husband wouldn't use anything but the Scott's brand fertilizer.

After visiting briefly with this lady, I went on about my business, all the while thinking that there couldn't be that much difference between fertilizer brands. In the past, I never bought the Scott's brand because it was too expensive. Being a cost conscious kind of guy, I always opted for the cheaper stuff. Later that week, while at the hardware store, I decided to compare fertilizer brands. As it turned out, even though the Scott's brand was more expensive, it had almost twice the active ingredients as the stuff I had been using. I decided to give it a try for the season, even though I would have to dig a little deeper in my wallet to afford it. I diligently applied the fertilizer several times from spring to fall according to the recommended schedule, along with making sure the lawn got plenty of water. Much to my surprise, my lawn looked every bit as good as my neighbor's!

I share this experience with you as a helpful hint for what you might do to improve your own lawn, not as a glowing testimonial for a particular brand of fertilizer. I don't own stock in the Scott's company, they didn't pay me to write this, and it isn't my intent at all to promote their brand or any other. I'm just letting you know what worked for me. A brand name fertilizer along with ample water did the trick for my lawn.

One additional lawn tip that I'll mention here is that I kept a close watch for any type of lawn disease so that I could treat it immediately if any signs were detected. The type of grass in our area, along with the climate, presents conditions which are conducive to the formation of a disease know as "brown patch" or "dollar patch." When affected, the grass takes on a dead, brown appearance, and the disease spreads in a circular fashion, like a silver dollar. Knowing that this disease struck my lawn indiscriminately year after year, I relented and started to fight back at the first sign of any brown patches. I spent some time familiarizing myself with the products available that are used to specifically treat the disease and purchased a bottle in advance so that I would have it on hand when and if it struck my lawn again. Sure enough, Mr. Brown Patch returned just like he had in the past, but this time I was ready for him. I treated the affected area before it got out of control and within a few days, it was gone. For the first time in a long time, my lawn looked great. It looked so good, in fact, that my neighbors began to notice and before long they were coming to me for advice on how to care for their lawns!

Another note on keeping your lawn looking nice is to keep it mowed, trimmed, and edged regularly. Don't let the grass grow too tall, and make a special effort to get the weed whacker out from time to time. Weeds that grow up along the house, around the mailbox, or anywhere else are very unsightly. It doesn't take much to keep them cut, and it goes a long way to help maintain a pristine and neat appearance of your lawn.

Finally, if you are installing a brand new lawn or replacing part of the lawn, I recommend using sod as opposed to using seed. A seeded lawn usually produces a thinner looking grass and tends to be more susceptible to the growth of weeds. I can drive through our neighborhood and easily tell which houses have sodded lawns and which have seeded lawns. The difference between the two is quite noticeable. The sodded lawns look thicker, fuller, and greener, while the seeded lawns look thinner and not as green. As a new homes builder, we offer only sodded lawns to families who purchase one of our homes. If a family wants to save money be having the lawn seeded, we have them procure the service from someone else because we feel that strongly about the difference in quality between the two.

Impact value: ★★★★★ Strong. The impact value of a green and lush lawn is strong because it will greatly improve the appearance of a home and costs very little. A well-maintained lawn complements the appearance of a home and is part of that positive first impression created when a prospective buyer pulls up in front of the house.

18: LANDSCAPING

Professional landscaping can go a long way toward improving the appearance of a home. If done properly, it can also set your house apart from among all the others on the block and significantly enhance its value. There are several things to keep in mind when planning a landscaping project. They include the type and variety of plants and trees to be used, their quantity and placement, and the many different types of products available to tie it all together.

The type and variety of plants and trees used will vary widely depending on the area or region you live in. For example, in southeast Texas, tall pine trees are quite common because they are found in abundance in the many forests that grow there. In a dryer climate such as New Mexico or Arizona, however, pine trees aren't nearly as common. Most evergreens, on the other hand, would never survive in the southern states and are usually found in the northern regions where the climate is cooler. I recommend checking with your local nursery to determine which types of plants will grow the best in your area. Although I cannot suggest specific plants to use, I do recommend using a balanced variety of plants and trees that will compliment your home. For example, I am especially partial to the beautiful, bluish-green Colorado spruce trees, and in particular, the Fat Alberts, which are known for their vibrant color and almost perfect shape. If it were up to me, I would have nothing but Fat Alberts planted in my yard. However, I know that "variety is the spice of life" and that by using different types of plants, trees, and bushes, a balanced look can be achieved that actually enhances the natural beauty of the spruce trees. Finally, unless you're the type of individual who loves to work in the garden, *and* has the time to do so, I recommend using low maintenance plants that are hardy and require little attention, other than an occasional watering and trimming.

The number of plants and trees used, as well as their placement, is equally as important as their type. On a typical lot, the house is the largest object on the lot and is therefore the primary focal point. Landscaping should be designed to enhance the appearance of a house, not the other way around. If too many trees are used in the front yard, for example, the view of a house can be obstructed. Furthermore, a house can take on an eerie appearance created by overgrown trees and bushes that block the light of the sun and give a shady, dark appearance.

I once purchased a smaller, 22-unit duplex-type apartment complex in which there were large, beautiful trees planted in between each of the driveways. The trees were so overgrown, however, when I bought the property that they had become a real eyesore and were in serious need of pruning. Within a few days of closing on the buildings, I hired a tree-trimming service that promptly alleviated the problem. Within a single day, they had all of the trees trimmed and the branches hauled away. What a tremendous difference such a simple thing made! For the first time in years, the fronts of the duplexes could be seen and the grass that had been starving for sunlight now enjoyed plenty! The entire complex took on a brighter, cheerier look that no longer scared potential tenants away. As a matter of fact, I was even able to increase the rents, due largely in part to the landscaping improvements that I made.

The front of a home is what people see first. As a general rule, one or two large, well-placed oak, maple, or other type of tree is all that is needed in the front yard. Landscaping islands can then be built around the trees with shrubs and bushes, which do not grow as high, to help achieve a balanced look and also to provide some variety. Smaller plants used along the front of a house can also greatly improve its appearance, keeping in mind the same principles to provide balance and symmetry. For example, a slightly taller four-foot to five-foot yew or juniper can be used to accent the corners of a house, balanced by shorter bushes or plants in between the outside corners to provide variety and symmetry.

There are a wide variety of landscaping products available to provide the finishing accents for your plants. They include many different types of wood chips in all sorts of colors, or an equal variety of lava rocks that can be used. Stone, slate, or bricks can be used to create beds or islands to group plants together. Plastic edging material is also available and helps keep the grass from growing into bedding areas. Finally, there are various ponds, pools, fountains, and other accent pieces that can be used to highlight your landscaping. One word of advice is warranted here. If you still have the pink flamingos from the 1960s placed strategically around your house, it's time to ditch them (see Section 16 on general cleanup and debris)!

Impact value: ★★★★ High. The impact value of landscaping improvements is high because making this type of improvement has the ability to greatly improve the appearance of a home. But landscaping can be somewhat expensive. If all of the plants and trees are already there, but just need to be trimmed, the cost is relatively low, but if you are starting from scratch, the cost of plants and accessories can add up quickly, especially if you purchase medium-sized to large-sized trees. For example, depending on the size and type of tree you buy, plan on spending anywhere from $250 to $1,000 per tree, plus another 50 percent or so to have them planted.

19: IRRIGATION SYSTEMS

In Section 17 and Section 18, I discussed the importance of maintaining a beautiful, plush green lawn along with a well-designed and balanced landscaping plan. A big part of maintaining lawns and plants is, of course, ensuring that they have an ample supply of water. An automatic irrigation system, or sprinkler system, is an excellent way of achieving that. There are several points to keep in mind before installing a new sprinkler system. They include the installation process itself, proper water coverage, automation, and winterizing.

A quality, brand-name irrigation system complete with installation can range in cost from about $1,500 to as much as $5,000 or more depending on the number of zones and heads that are required, as well as whether or not you choose to do the work yourself. Installing an irrigation system yourself can save you as much as 50 percent, but before you decide to tackle the job, there are a few things you should know. The technical aspects of hooking up the system, although moderately difficult, can be accomplished by most anyone, especially when using installation guides. The difficult part centers around "pulling the pipe," that is, laying the neoprene or plastic pipe underground that ties the entire system together and through which water flows. One way to do this is by hand-digging a small trench to lay the pipe in. If you only had one trench to dig, that would be no problem, but consider a system with 12 zones and 50 or more sprinkler heads. The pipe has to be run underground to each and every head, and that means numerous trenches would have to be dug to hook the system together. If the soil in your area is soft and pliable, then that may not be much of a problem. My yard happens to be primarily clay and in the summer when it is dry, it practically takes a jack hammer to penetrate the ground!

Professional installers, on the other hand, make the process look easy by using special equipment that cuts a thin trench in the ground while simultaneously pulling and burying the plastic pipe. One of my neighbors, a classic do-it-yourselfer, attempted to tackle the job on his own. He started the project in early spring, and by the end of the summer he had finally finished. I saw the poor old guy out there with his son on many hot summer weekends digging and burying, digging and burying. I have heard that the heavy equipment used to pull the pipe can be rented, but the way I look at it, by the time I purchase the materials, rent the equipment, and spend the time installing the system, I am better off paying a professional to do it right the first time. Furthermore, if there are any problems with the system initially, it will be under warranty and the installers can come back and repair or adjust it as necessary.

Whether you do it yourself or pay a professional installer, another factor to be aware of when putting in an irrigation system is to ensure that you have adequate water coverage. The types of heads that are used vary depending on their location, as well as on what is being watered. For example, rotary heads are typically used for watering lawns, while pop-up heads, or misters, are often used for watering shrubs or bushes. A rotary type of head has a much greater reach and can cover an area from about 10 feet to 20 feet from the head, depending upon the water pressure and the head adjustment. Rotary heads should be evenly spaced in "zones" throughout the yard to provide overlapping coverage in all areas.

If you have several contractors providing bids, you'll be sure to want to compare the total number of heads and zones each contractor is providing so that you can make an accurate comparison of proposals. Some contractors will attempt to use as few heads and zones as possible to reduce their costs thereby enabling them to provide the lowest bid. Beware of such tricks as this! A good irrigation system will have overlapping coverage and provide an ample supply of water to your lawn. Pop-up heads are used around flowers, shrubs, and bushes, and are used to provide a less harsh mist of water so as not to damage them. Once again, overlapping coverage is important to ensure copious amounts of water are available to your plants.

In addition to being aware of the types of heads that can be used and their coverage, it is also important to be aware of the automatic devices that are available to operate an irrigation system. A sprinkler system can be enabled to operate automatically with a centralized timer. With the use of timers, irrigation systems can be programmed to run on specific calendar days, or on specific days of the week, and at specific times of the day. For example, a system can be programmed to run on Sunday, Tuesday, and Friday at 8:00 AM and then on Monday, Wednesday, and Saturday at 12:00 noon. Most systems can be programmed to run at any time you wish using just about any combination of events you could possibly want. One additional item I recommend that is not part of the timer system, but which can easily be integrated into it, is a rain sensing device. A rain sensor does exactly what its name suggests: It senses when it is raining and when it is not. If it has been raining quite a bit, the sensor disengages the timer so that the sprinklers do not come on in the middle of a downpour. A light rain or drizzle, on the other hand, is usually not enough to shut the sprinklers off. A rain sensor usually doesn't cost more than an extra $100 or so and, in my opinion, is well worth it. I can't tell you how many times I've driven by someone's house when it was pouring down rain outside and saw their sprinklers running. Installing a rain sensor is money well spent.

Finally, when installing an automatic irrigation system, you may need to know how to winterize it. This will depend on the climate in your area. In the southern regions where the temperature rarely dips below the freezing point, sprinkler systems do not need to be winterized. In colder climates, however, winterizing is an absolute must. The process is quite easy to do and involves blowing the water out of the lines. This is usually done in the autumn before the cold weather really starts to set in. If the lines are not evacuated, or blown, the water in them will freeze and expand causing damage to the valves and heads. Although the lines should be blown fairly clean of water, don't panic if you don't get 100 percent of the water out. If there is still a little water left in them and the water does freeze, it won't hurt anything because there is plenty of room for expansion. A small air compressor costing between $100 and $200 is all that is needed to blow the lines clear. If you don't have a compressor, most irrigation companies also provide winterizing services at a nominal charge.

Impact value: ★★★ Moderate. The impact value of an automatic sprinkler system has been given a moderate rating, but the value will vary depending on several factors. First and foremost is the climate in your area. If you live, for example, in a southern region where it is hot and dry all the time, then an irrigation system is vital to the health of lawns and landscaping, and the money spent on installing one is likely to represent a good investment. If, on the other hand, you live in an area where the amount of rainfall is above average, then a sprinkler system may not be necessary at all, and the money spent installing one is likely to represent a poor investment. The same principle holds true for the neighborhood in which you live. If the lawns are relatively small, or most of the homes in your neighborhood don't have an irrigation system, then it may not make sense to spend the money on one. You're probably better off using a $10 sprinkler that attaches to a water hose and moving it around from time to time. On the other hand, if you have a larger yard with extensive landscaping, or most of the homes in your neighborhood have sprinkler systems, then it is probably a good idea to invest in a system yourself.

20: OUTDOOR LIGHTING

When properly used, outdoor lighting can be a very cost effective method of enhancing the beauty of most any home. Your first inclination may be to think that prospective buyers never come around at night and will therefore never see your house in the evening, so there is no need to bother with this type of home improvement. Although that may be true for a buyer's first visit, if she liked the house well enough during the daytime, there's a good chance she'll take a drive by in the evening to see what the neighborhood and your house look like at night. It may be on the way home from the grocery store, or after an evening out to dinner, or perhaps after going to see a movie, but if a potential buyer likes your house well enough to consider making an offer on it, she will take the time to drive by at night. This low cost improvement is an opportunity that will allow you to set your house apart from the other houses for sale in your area.

There are a few things to keep in mind before starting your outdoor lighting project. First of all, I recommend buying high-quality, commercial-grade landscaping lights that are available at most any hardware store. They cost about twice as much as the cheaper sets, but they look at least ten times better. I've used both, and I can tell you from personal experience, I would never go back to using the cheaper sets. It's not so much that they don't function as promised, it's just that they look cheap. The commercial grade I am referring to is the low voltage type that is easy to install and usually does not require an electrician to bury lines and does not necessitate pulling a permit.

Secondly, the placement and distribution of lights used is vital to achieving a professional look. If too many lights are used down a sidewalk or driveway, for example, a runway effect is created. With lights spaced closely together on both sides of a walkway, it literally looks like a runway or landing strip for aircraft! If lights are used at all to line drives and walks, be careful not to place them too close together. The same principle holds true when using low-lying lights in bushes and other landscaping areas as well. More is not necessarily better. Use too many lights and it looks like you're decorating for Christmas.

Another factor to keep in mind is the type of lights to use. Lighting should vary by its placement and the desired effect you want to achieve. For example, in shrubs and bushes, the low-lying lights that tend to hug the ground are all that is needed to create a soft glow. To highlight the corners of a house, however, a floodlight can be directed upward against the house. Floodlights can also be used to illuminate the entry area, or a single tree, or even a cluster of trees. When directed upward through the leaves of a tree, floodlights provide a serene and even romantic effect that can really intensify the tree's natural beauty.

You should also be cognizant of the particular brightness of each light used in your outdoor lighting project. If the light is too bright, it creates a harsh look and can even resemble a commercial strip center or a grocery store. Once again, more is not necessarily better. I suggest using lower wattage lighting to give your house a soft glow. For example, a 20-watt bulb is all that is needed for the smaller accent lights used around shrubs, while a 50-watt bulb is plenty for the floodlights used to accent trees and entry ways.

Finally, you'll want to spend a few extra dollars to purchase a timer for the outdoor lighting system. The timer typically plugs into any wall outlet and feeds low voltage power to all of the lights. Timers can be set to turn on and off at any time you desire. I recommend setting them to turn on at dusk and to turn off about the time most people go to bed, usually around ten o'clock or eleven o'clock. If you are concerned about lighting for security purposes, have those security lights adjusted to turn on after your landscaping lights turn off. Lights used for security are much brighter and, if left on during the evening hours while the outdoor lighting system is in use, will greatly detract from the desired effect. In fact, they may as well not even be on.

Impact value: ★★★★ High. The impact value of an outdoor lighting system is high because the appearance of a home can be greatly enhanced during the evening hours for a relatively low cost. Furthermore, this improvement is easy to install and can be done in less than a day.

21: PETS

Owning a pet can be a wonderful thing. Pets can provide companionship to the elderly and others who may be alone, they can provide security to help make a home safe from would be burglars, and they can help teach family members such as children responsibility. If you are improving your home for the purpose of selling, however, you must also be willing to consider the negative factors of having a pet, whether it be an outside pet or an inside pet or any combination thereof.

Setting aside for a moment the love we have for Mr. Fido, the family dog, let's take a minute to examine the negative aspects of having a dog that is kept outside. If Fido is allowed to roam the yard at his leisure, he will dig holes in the landscaping beds where the soil is soft and cool, he will poop in strategic places throughout the yard, and he will bark at each and every prospective buyer who comes to look at your house. Although many of these buyers may feel right at home with Fido because they have dogs themselves, there are just as many buyers who are likely to detest Fido, especially if they have small children. Fido will greet the family by barking incessantly; then he will undoubtedly jump up against the mother's new dress while at the same time putting a run in her hose; and, finally, he'll continue to make a complete nuisance of himself by licking three-year-old Melanie's face. As cute as you may think Fido is, trust me, not everyone else will. If you do happen to have an outdoor pet such as a dog and you are expecting a family over to view your home, I suggest putting him on a leash in the backyard. This way he won't pose a threat to families who are coming over. Even if you think that your little Fido is too gentle and wouldn't hurt a soul, not everybody shares that same sentiment. Be courteous to others by taking a few minutes to put the pooch on a leash or in your backyard if it is fenced.

Indoor pets can create even more problems than outdoor pets. If you're a pet owner, I'm sure I won't be telling you anything new when I say that a lot of dogs and cats will poop and pee wherever and whenever they happen to feel like it. In addition to creating foul and obnoxious odors, these innate habits can ruin expensive flooring. If prospective buyers walk through a house in which the carpets are all stained, they are not going to be thinking about what a nice pet you have, but rather about how much it's going to cost to replace the flooring.

A few years ago in our neighborhood, there was a house for sale in which the homeowner kept a black full-grown Labrador retriever. A real estate agent who happened to be a friend of mine told me about the incredibly horrible damage done to the interior of the home by the dog. When the house first came on the market, she took a prospective buyer to see it unprepared for what was on the inside. The homeowner wasn't there and had put the dog in the backyard, so the real estate agent used the key in the lockbox to let herself and the client in. She told me that when she first opened the door, the stench alone just about knocked her over! As she and her client toured the house, they had to step very carefully so as not to step in anything (if you know what I mean, and I think you do!). The house stank, there was poop and pee everywhere, the walls and doors were marred from scratches, the banister had been chewed on, there was evidence of black hair on just about everything in the house, and last but not least, there were lots of friendly critters, also known as fleas, that served as the welcoming committee for the agent and her client. As you might expect, the house sat on the market for a prolonged period of time and finally sold for about 20 percent below the market value of other homes in the neighborhood.

Impact value: ★★★★ High. The impact value of this improvement, for lack of a better choice of words, is high. If you don't currently own a pet, then you're in good shape and the improvement has cost you nothing. On the other hand, if you happen to be a pet owner, you may have to spend a little bit of money to repair any damage your pet may have caused, and to get rid of any bothersome odors that may be present. The money spent to restore your home to its pre-pet condition represents a solid investment and can potentially make you thousands of dollars. Although there are millions of pet owners throughout the nation, most who dearly love their pets, there are just as many people who don't have pets who may in turn be deterred by the presence of one. Having a pet is like owning a double-edged sword—on the one hand, they can certainly be cute and cuddly, but on the other hand, they can wreak havoc on the exterior or interior of a house.

22: COMBINING GROUNDS IMPROVEMENTS

The following is an experience I shared in *The Complete Guide to Flipping Properties* (New Jersey; John Wiley and Sons; 2003) and illustrates perfectly the kind of value that can be unlocked from a property by making a combination of simple and cost effective improvements. In this example, the combination of improvements included a general cleanup of the property, as well as improvements to the grounds and landscaping.

As an investor who is serious about flipping properties, you *must* be able to look beyond what you see on the surface. In fact, you will come to enjoy driving up to a house that appears to be run down and lacking in care because experience has taught you that these houses are actually diamonds in the rough. While most people see a lump of coal, you will come to recognize it as a diamond that just needs a little polishing. Ideally, you will be able to buy houses at coal-like prices and sell these highly polished gems at diamond-like prices.

This same concept can be applied on a larger scale. For example, I have used it in the apartment business as well as in the new home residential construction business. As a principal for Symphony Homes, I recently took over an entire community that was partially completed with new homes and successfully applied the value play strategy. The community was only about three years old, but the original builder there apparently ran into financial difficulty that caused the progress of new home construction to come to a standstill. As a result, the entranceway and all of the remaining vacant lots became neglected. Weeds and grass went uncut and grew as high as four feet to five feet. Many of the vacant lots were littered with debris left over from the previous builder. In short, the community was a real eyesore! The developer of the subdivision had tried unsuccessfully for over six months to get another builder to come in and take over where the previous builder had left off. No one would touch it. In fact, you would probably be considered foolish to go in and take something like that over. Discussions with the city inspectors led me to believe that even they had written the community off.

My experience has taught me to look beyond what is visible on the surface. Let's take a closer look at the facts of this particular community.

First we'll look at the negatives:

- The entrance into the community was overgrown with weeds.
- The weeds were overgrown on all of the vacant lots.
- Many of the lots were littered with debris left over from the previous builder.
- The residents and city officials were in despair and had given up hope.

Now let's look at the positives:

- Landscaping improvements to the entrance would be quick and easy to make.
- Weeds can be easily cut, and [it] is an inexpensive and quick way to improve a property's appearance.
- Debris is easy to remove.
- The community was ideally situated immediately off of a main road that provided terrific visibility to passersby.
- A brand new post office was located directly across the street, meaning that no less than once or twice a

month, everyone in town would drive by the community and see the improvements being made along with all the new construction activity.

- The community was located only one half mile from a major state road that was heavily traveled, and only a mile or so from a major interstate highway. Both of these roads served as major traffic arteries for commuters and would be easily accessible from the community.
- The homes in the community were only three years old or less, meaning that our new homes would fit in perfectly.

As it turned out, our company was able to negotiate a very favorable price and subsequently took over the remaining lots. As a condition for doing so, the developer agreed at his expense to have all of the vacant lots mowed, the debris removed, and the entranceway cleaned up immediately upon closing. Within one week, the community was cleaned up and a sense of pride was restored to the residents who lived there. In fact, the existing residents'. . . sincere expression of gratitude toward us meant a great deal and was certainly appreciated by the Symphony Homes team. Our ability to envision the hidden potential in that community has allowed us to enjoy a substantially higher profit margin on a per unit basis than we otherwise would have.

In summary, don't underestimate the power of the value play strategy. It is indisputably one of the most effective means available to you to create wealth and to enjoy a fuller and more rewarding life.

5

EXTERIOR STRUCTURES

23: DECKS

Out of all the improvements available to homeowners, decks are one of the most popular choices. They are typically designed to accommodate easy access through the rear of a house, for instance, either through a sliding glass door or a standard door. They are often located off of the kitchen or family room, but they can also be situated off of a bedroom, such as the master. Decks provide a perfect place for the family grill, as well as a place to entertain. They can be designed to overlook a peaceful and serene lake, or to provide a panoramic view of a majestic mountainside. Whatever their use, decks continue to be a preferred choice among homeowners. There are several items to be aware of, however, before embarking on your next home improvement project.

While there are many types of materials that can be used to build a deck, the most common is some type of wood product, usually either pine or cedar. If pine is used, be sure it is "treated," meaning the lumber has been specially treated with a chemical agent that enables it to withstand nature's elements better, such as the wind, rain, and sun. If the wood is not treated, it will deteriorate over a period of a few years and begin to rot. One primary advantage of using treated wood is that it can be painted, so if you're thinking about painting a deck rather than staining it, using treated lumber is the better choice because it is less expensive than cedar. On the other hand, if you're thinking about staining a deck, then cedar is the better choice. Cedar wood has a naturally red color to it, and stain enhances its natural beauty to make it look absolutely stunning! The primary disadvantage to staining is that it lasts only one year to two years, depending on how harsh the climate is in your area. The staining process is not expensive; an average sized deck will require only three gallons to five gallons of stain. But staining can be time consuming. Before a deck is restained, it's a good idea to first clean it with a power washer and a cleaning solution designed especially for decks and available at most hardware stores. So if you don't want to deal with the periodic maintenance and upkeep of a stained deck, a painted deck may be a better choice for you.

I personally prefer the beauty of stained cedar wood decks. Our home sits up high because it is built on what is referred to as a daylight basement. So the deck sits up a full level from the ground and has two stairways uniquely designed to angle around the front and side of it. Every winter our deck takes a severe beating because it is subjected to subzero temperatures while being pounded with snow and sometimes ice, and every spring, your humble author spends one day cleaning, scrubbing, and power washing, and another day staining and finishing. I have to keep reminding myself after several hours in the sun that it will all be worth it when I am finished. It generally takes a few days for my body to recuperate, but as I sit on the newly stained deck with my family enjoying hamburgers and hot dogs hot off the grill, I have no regrets about my preference for the beautiful, rich cedar wood.

(Also see "41: Adding a Porch to Your Home.")

Impact value: ★★★★ High. The impact value of this improvement is high because decks remain quite popular among homeowners. Costs vary somewhat among the choices that are available, such as whether treated lumber or cedar is used, and also on how elaborate the design is. I recommend building and budgeting for a deck that is consistent with those in your immediate neighborhood. If you live in a community where homes are moderately priced, it's best to stay with a moderately priced deck. On the other hand, if you live in a more expensive, high-end community, then you're better off spending a little more and building a deck that will truly complement your home and neighborhood.

24: PATIOS

While serving a similar function as that of decks, patios achieve much the same purpose but provide an altogether different look. They are most commonly made of cement but can also be made using brick pavers. Another method used to create patios is referred to as "stamping." Stamping is a process that utilizes the less expensive cement and adds color and patterns to it. This allows users to achieve a look similar to stone, or even brick, without the expense. It can also be used to create walkways. I recently had a sidewalk that had settled somewhat at a model home in one of our communities replaced with a more decorative stamped walkway. It turned out to be a good choice because many of our guests have made favorable comments about it.

One primary limitation of patios is that they must be built at the ground level. So if you are trying to achieve several feet of height, building a patio is not a likely option. Height can be more easily achieved with decks than with patios. One advantage of building a patio instead of a deck, however, is that there is no painting or staining required. Once the patio is in, the only maintenance needed is an occasional sweeping or washing with a water hose. Patios can also be designed in most any shape or size, limited only by your imagination. The neighbors next door to us have a beautiful patio made of bricks that were arranged in a circular pattern and with various levels providing for a rich, elegant appearance.

Impact value: ★★★★ High. The impact value of this improvement is high because patios, like decks, remain popular among homeowners. Costs vary widely among the many choices that are available. A no-frills cement patio, for example, should cost no more than $2 to $4 per square foot, while the more elaborate brick patios can easily cost $20 per square foot and more. The same reasoning applies when building and budgeting for a patio as does for a deck, which is to build something that is consistent with those in your immediate neighborhood. A good rule of thumb is to not try to outspend your neighbors by having the most expensive and elaborate patio in the community.

25: GAZEBOS

Although adding a gazebo to a backyard isn't nearly as common as building a deck or patio, a gazebo can help create an aura of romantic charm like no other outdoor structure can. Gazebos have been and are known by many different names. For example, they are sometimes referred to as summerhouses, kiosks, alcoves, and even garden temples. The word "gazebo" stems from the phrase to "gaze about" or to "look out." A seventeenth-century philosopher named Francis Bacon referred to gazebos as "the summerhouse on the summit of a garden." Early gazebos were similar to small temples and were built all over Greece and Rome. They were typically made of an intricately detailed marble. Furthermore, because of their elegant beauty, gazebos often became the central focal point in homes as well as in public places.

Depending on the size of a gazebo, its useful function will vary. A smaller gazebo might provide just enough room to sip a glass of lemonade with a few friends seated at a table on its deck, while a larger one may provide enough room to entertain several people, and perhaps host an outdoor dinner. A gazebo, which has been well cared for, can also make a highly decorative accent piece in a backyard and, just as in Greece and Rome, may become the central focal point for both family members and guests alike.

A gazebo can also provide a wonderfully romantic setting where couples can share their innermost secrets and can dream the dreams of a life of love and happiness together. The one gazebo memory that I am especially fond of is that of the beautiful young woman to whom I was about to propose. I had arranged to take Nancy, driven by a chauffeur in a limousine, to one of Houston's finest restaurants. Behind the restaurant was a magnificent garden, complete with peacocks strutting proudly in all their splendor and glory. A wooden bridge draped gently across a quiet brook led to a softly lit gazebo. It was there on the steps of the gazebo that Nancy and I whispered our own sweet nothings to each other. Then, when the moment was just right, the evening sky clothed with the angels of heaven, on bended knee I asked for my sweet Nancy's hand in marriage. Several years and three children later, we are still very much in love with each other.

Impact value: ★★★★ High. The impact value of this improvement is high for three reasons. The first reason is that the cost to build a gazebo is comparable to that of a deck or patio, depending on its design, size, and the materials used to build it. The second reason is that although a gazebo is not as common as other improvements, its uniqueness makes it all the more appealing. Finally, gazebos can add an element of charm to any backyard that can ignite the flames of romance in most any relationship.

26: POOLS

Because installing an inground swimming pool is one of the most expensive improvements a homeowner can make, the decision to do so must be carefully weighed before proceeding. Consider that even a small, no-frills swimming pool can easily cost $40,000 or more. How much is a swim in the backyard really worth? Because most homeowners finance large improvements such as this, is an occasional dip in the pool worth an extra $300 per month each and every month for the next 20 years? For $300 per month, you could buy one heck of a membership at an exclusive fitness center, complete with a heated indoor pool, weight lifting program, and personal trainer. The investment made to install a swimming pool is rarely recouped at 100 percent. In most cases, the only way an investment in a pool can be justified is if the home is located in a predominantly warmer climate, such as in the south, and in a more expensive neighborhood where swimming pools tend to be the norm.

In addition to being expensive to install, pools are also expensive to operate and maintain. There are chemicals to buy, special equipment to acquire, water to fill the pool, electricity to operate the pumps, and gas to warm it if the pool is heated. Those costs can easily add another $100 to $150 per month to the cost of taking that refreshing dip. Keep in mind that these are just the costs of operating and maintaining the pool. Heaven forbid that anything should go wrong with the pool! Common problems affecting swimming pools are cracks in the surface along the bottom or sides, faulty electrical wiring that can lead to electrocution, inadequate treatment of the water that results in a cloudy appearance initially and progressively worsens as algae forms, and inoperable pumps along with dirty or clogged filters both of which are expensive to replace. Adding in the operating and maintenance costs can easily bring the total cost of pool ownership to $500 per month or more. That personal trainer and heated pool at the health club are sounding better all the time.

In addition to the initial cost of installing a pool and the ongoing cost of maintenance and repairs, there are also liability issues to be mindful of. First of all, the law mandates that a fence must be erected around inground pools for obvious safety reasons. Without a fence, a small child could easily fall into the pool and drown, and sometimes even with a fence, children can still get in, through an open gate, for example. Any child falling into the pool and not knowing how to swim could prove to be tragic, perhaps even fatal. The accidental death of a child is a difficult cross to bear for anyone, especially a parent. Many families with small children will automatically rule out a house with a swimming pool for that very reason. They don't want to take any chances with the safety of their little ones.

Although pools offer cool and refreshing enjoyment in the summertime, they are virtually worthless in the autumn and winter seasons, especially in the northern regions. Unless it is an indoor heated pool, of which very few are, most people are lucky to get even six months use out if it. Remember that our $500 per month cost of ownership for a pool was based upon a full 12 months of use. If the total annual cost was divided over the number of months a pool actually got used, the monthly rate increases to a phenomenal $1,000 per month! Wow, that health club is really sounding good now!

Impact value: ★★ Low. The impact value of this improvement is low due to the large investment required to install a swimming pool, along with the cost of operating and maintaining it month after month. It is highly unlikely that you will recoup the full cost of a swimming pool when your house is sold. In fact, a pool may even be considered a liability rather than an asset, especially to a family with small children who wouldn't dare take a chance on the accidental drowning of a child. If you're the type who really enjoys swimming on a regular basis, my advice is to either (1) spend the money instead on a membership at a local health club, or (2) get to know one of your neighbors who already has a pool.

27: HOT TUBS AND SPAS

Hot tubs and spas provide homeowners with an enjoyable and relaxing alternative to the larger and more expensive swimming pool. Rather than taking a refreshing dip as you would in a pool, hot tubs are designed with the sole purpose of relaxation in mind. The water in them is typically heated to a warmer temperature than in a swimming pool (hence the name "hot tub") ranging from about 100° to 110° Fahrenheit and is circulated through jets operated by a pump device. Many options are available today that can enhance the hot tub experience, such as built-in DVD and CD players, swirling jets that can be adjusted at various angles and speeds, and built-in compartments that hold ice to keep beverages cold.

The cost of a hot tub can vary quite a bit and will depend on the type of tub installed, its size, and the options purchased with it. Like swimming pools, hot tubs come in two basic types—aboveground and inground. An aboveground tub is typically much less expensive that its counterpart, the inground tub. The tub itself is usually made of fiberglass and is supported by an enclosure made of wood, often cedar. In addition to providing support for the shell, the enclosure also houses the equipment necessary to operate the tub, such as the pump and wiring. Besides being less expensive than an inground system, aboveground tubs can be set up and ready to enjoy in less than a day. Aboveground systems are portable also, meaning that if you later get tired of your hot tub, you can always sell it. Furthermore, if you decide to move, you have the option of taking it with you.

The process for installing an inground spa is much like that of putting in a swimming pool, only on a smaller scale. Not only are inground systems more expensive than aboveground hot tubs, they are, of course, more permanent and do not offer the same portability. Once they are in, there's no changing your mind unless you're prepared to spend a lot of money. One primary advantage of an inground spa, however, is the degree to which they can be customized. A spa can be designed to take on most any shape or size, and it can accommodate as few as 2 people or as many as 20 people or more. Hot tubs, on the other hand, are typically not rated to hold more than 10 people to 12 people at a maximum, with 4 to 8 being the average. Although most commonly built as outdoor systems, hot tubs and spas can be designed for indoor use as well, especially if you have a basement. They can also be enclosed in a sunroom or an all-seasons room, or even built into a gazebo or deck. Their design and placement is limited only by your imagination.

Just as a swimming pool must be treated regularly with chemicals and cleaning agents, so must a hot tub or spa. The primary difference between them is the volume of water. Swimming pools can easily hold 10,000 gallons to 20,000 gallons of water or more, while the average hot tub may only hold 400 gallons to 500 gallons. Consequently, a swimming pool requires more chemicals to keep the water clean, resulting in higher maintenance costs. You should also be aware that maintaining the proper pH levels in a hot tub requires close monitoring because the volume of water in them is much less than in a pool. With a smaller quantity of water, a little more effort is required to achieve just the right pH level in hot tubs and spas, so again careful attention must be paid to monitoring these levels.

Impact value: ★★★ Moderate. The impact value of adding a hot tub or spa as a home improvement is moderate. Although much less expensive than a swimming pool, hot tubs and spas typically rank only somewhat higher in the expected return on investment. On average, a homeowner can probably expect to recoup most of the money invested in a hot tub or spa, but don't expect to command a premium for it. Another factor to keep in mind before spending money on a spa is its relative demand in your area, which will vary depending on what part of the country you live in. If you will be the only hot tub owner in town, chances are there's not much demand in your area for such items. But if many of your neighbors already have a hot tub, then the tubs have already proven themselves in the marketplace of supply and demand. Finally, the money invested in a hot tub should not exceed that of others in your neighborhood. In other words, don't go all out on an expensive system in a neighborhood where home values are at or below the median selling price. Larger and more elaborate spas should be reserved for higher end luxury homes.

28: STORAGE SHEDS

Adding a storage shed in your backyard is a great way to increase the desirability of your property, especially among men, because they often have items such as lawn equipment and tools to store. Although sheds are available in cheaper materials such as plastic or a light-gauge metal, I recommend a structure made of wood painted to match your house. If possible, the shingles should match the house as well. In *The Complete Guide to Investing in Rental Properties* (New York; McGraw Hill; 2004), I wrote about the importance of storage sheds as follows:

Believe it or not, increasing the amount of available storage space a rental property has can justify an increase in rents. Everybody needs a place to put their stuff, including tenants. The more space they have to put it, the happier they are. I know of two brand new condominium units that sat on the market unsold for almost two years primarily because they lacked adequate storage space. After looking at the units, both of which were very nice on the inside, I asked the sales agent why they hadn't sold yet. She replied that almost without fail, the negative feedback she received was directed at the lack of closets and additional storage areas, such as a garage, attic, or basement.

Creating additional storage space is very easy to do, especially on the outside. You can purchase a ready made shed or storage closet, for example, from almost any home improvement store to instantly add space. Or if you prefer, a more permanent storage shed such as one made from wood products can be constructed. These types of sheds can also be designed to match the color scheme of the house. Some homeowner's association may restrict the usage of outside storage sheds, so be sure to check with them before spending any money. Sheds like these are especially popular with men, because they tend to own things like ladders and shovels, or lawn mowing equipment. After having shown numerous houses to couples, I can tell you that one of the first things men like to look at is the garage, and running a close second is some type of storage shed. Most women, on the other hand, prefer to look at the kitchen, and in particular, the cabinets. In both instances, couples are looking to see if there is enough space to store their belongings. So whether people are looking to buy a house or to rent it doesn't matter, and whether it's a man or a woman doesn't matter either. They all want a place to put their stuff.

One additional idea to consider to increase the revenue stream of your rental property is to create storage space with the idea of renting it out. That's right. Rather than just give the space away to the existing tenant, you agree to rent it out at an additional charge. The idea is to build a storage shed or building large enough to store items of value such as a boat, camper, or recreational vehicle (RV). This will depend upon the neighborhood your rental property is in and whether or not the association bylaws will allow storage facilities such as these. It will also depend upon the size of your lot and whether or not there is room to put a building on it. If the tenant living in the house isn't interested in renting the building, don't let that stop you from putting up a building and leasing it to someone else. Your tenant is not likely to object because people who store boats and RVs usually get them out of storage only every now and then. Even if they do, too bad. The property is yours to do with as you wish so long as it complies with all the local laws and ordinances.

So there you have it. If a storage shed is good enough for a rental property, it is certainly good enough for that of a homeowner's, and in particular, men. Once again, I suggest spending a little more on a quality built wooden structure that will complement your house rather than the cheaper plastic or sheet-metal type.

Impact value: ★★★★ High. The impact value of adding a storage shed as a home improvement is high due to its perceived value, especially among men, provided that the shed is built as a more permanent structure as opposed to a temporary one. It isn't so much that you will be able to command a large premium for having a shed in your backyard, but rather that you will be able to increase the marketability of your home as a result of having the additional storage space available to a prospective buyer.

29: GARAGES

Although most homes today already have either an attached or detached garage, there are several things that can be done to improve its value. These include cleaning the garage up, organizing its contents, and adding drywall and paint. A garage is much like a storage shed in the sense that everyone wants a place to store their stuff. The problem is, the more space we have, the more stuff we accumulate.

If you are getting ready to place your home on the market to sell, be sure to take time to clean out of your garage all of the junk and clutter that has accumulated over the past several years. It's amazing how fast old and worthless stuff collects over such a seemingly short period of time. If your garage is anything like mine, I'm sure there are things in it that have been there so long, you've probably forgotten they were even there. If you haven't used any of the following items in the past three or more years, it may be time to throw them out. I know that's a hard thing for many of you to do, but I have faith in you that if you really put your mind to it, you can do it. Let's take a look at some of the things that can be disposed of:

- Partially full or empty containers such as paint cans, lubricants, old jars, and bottles
- Worn out toys such as bikes, wagons, and games
- Lawn equipment in disrepair such as mowers and yard tools
- Miscellaneous items such as empty boxes and pink flamingo yard ornaments

Once you get all of the old stuff cleaned out of your garage, the next thing to do is to organize it. There are many fairly inexpensive options available today for organizing and arranging a garage. Some of these include cabinets that can be hung or mounted on the walls, various types of plastic or steel shelving, and special racks that can be used for hanging bicycles and sports equipment. Depending on the height of your garage, you may also be able to build in some overhead storage racks, shelves, or hangers.

Another improvement that can make a big difference in the appearance of a garage is drywall. Many older garages and even some newer ones have been constructed without drywall hung on the interior of the studs; consequently, what is visible on the inside of the garage are wooden studs, black colored paper, and electrical wiring. Hanging drywall throughout the garage will greatly improve and modernize its appearance. After hanging the drywall, the seams should then be taped and floated. To finish the garage properly, I suggest painting the walls a light, neutral color after all the sanding of the seams has been completed.

Impact value: ★★★★ High. The impact value of this home improvement is high because cleaning and organizing costs very little relative to its potential impact. Cabinets, shelving, and paint are all fairly inexpensive. Although drywall costs somewhat more, it provides a garage with a finished look. Furthermore, once the drywall has been hung, cabinets and shelving can then be attached to it.

30: PLAYGROUND EQUIPMENT

The types of playground equipment on the market today for families with children is truly amazing. There are all types of play structures, some with swings and slides, some with monkey bars and tree houses, and some even with tubes to climb through or even simulated rock climbing structures. Some are made from cedar or redwood and are built to last a lifetime, while others are made from plastic or galvanized metal and have a much shorter life span. Parents all across the nation purchase playground equipment in hopes of bringing an added measure of happiness and joy to their children.

Play structures that are made of heavy six inch by four inch, or four inch by four inch, wooden timbers are designed to last many years and to withstand heavy use. These play structures are most often made from cedar or redwood. Before installing this type of system, the ground where the play structure will be positioned must be properly prepared by leveling it to ensure the children using it will have an even footing.

Often if the equipment is used in a commercial or public area, further preparation is required. A layer of heavy plastic is laid down on the area where the system will go to prevent any grass or weeds from growing up through it, and then a layer of bark mulch or small stones is laid on top of that to provide a cushioning effect in case someone falls. This type of preparation is not limited to commercial or public use only; homeowners will sometimes elect to provide this added measure of protection for their children.

After the initial installation of the system, it is highly recommended that all of the wooden surfaces be treated with a sealer that will help protect and preserve the beauty of the wood. Sealers are also available with various colors of stains mixed in with them to further enrich the wood's natural colors. Once these play structures have been installed, very little maintenance is required because the systems are solidly built to withstand even the heaviest of abuse.

Just as a cedar or redwood deck requires periodic cleaning and sealing, however, so does a play structure. Rain, snow, ice, and sun all take their toll on any type of wood surfaces and must be resealed either annually, or every other year at a minimum. The process is fairly inexpensive and can usually be done in less than a day. These durable play structures can enhance the appearance of most any backyard and, when properly cared for, will most likely outlast your children's youthful play years.

Play structures made from plastic are much less expensive than their more permanent wooden counterparts. While they are also not built to last as long, they do come is a variety of bright and colorful shapes and sizes. Unlike the more permanent wooden structures, very little, if any, surface preparation is required to install play sets made from plastic. Furthermore, no periodic or ongoing maintenance is required other than an occasional cleaning. Finally, the sets can easily be moved around from place to place in a yard if desired. Some disadvantages of plastic play sets include cracking, discoloration from the sun, and bees. Yes, bees. In the warmer summer months, bees like to make their nests in between the walls of the plastic, entering in through either drainage and vent holes or cracks that have occurred from wear.

Swing sets made from galvanized metal were quite common once upon a time. These sets were often painted and consisted mostly of a few swings and a slide. Although for residential use, galvanized sets have lost market share to the more preferred wooden playground equipment and plastic play sets, they are frequently used for both commercial and public purposes, such as at a park. The galvanized metal used in these park areas is a much heavier gauge and is designed to withstand even the heaviest abuse. The paint applied to these systems is referred to as a "powder coat" and is also designed to withstand heavy usage.

Impact value: ★★ Low. The impact value of playground equipment as an improvement is low because most people are not willing to pay extra for it, especially if it is made of the less expensive plastic or metal. Prospective buyers would probably even expect that the cheaper play structures be removed from the yard depending on whether or not they have small children who would benefit from it. In general, don't expect to recoup your investment at the time of resale for any money spent on playground equipment. Your best bet is to either take it with you, give it away to another family, or sell it in a garage sale.

6

GENERAL EXTERIOR

31: PAINTING

One of the most cost effective ways you can improve the appearance of a house is by giving it a fresh coat of paint. Although painting a house is somewhat labor intensive, if you want to save money, it's a job that just about anyone can do. On the other hand, if you prefer not to paint or don't have the time, the work can be hired out fairly inexpensively. I suggest you take the time to shop around, though, because labor prices vary widely. There was a time when I didn't think twice about grabbing a paint brush and roller and tackling a painting job myself. Now that I'm a little older, however, I don't think twice about calling a painter to hire the work out. The primary advantages of painting a house are that it doesn't cost very much, paint is easy to apply, and usually the work can be done in less than a week. A fresh coat of paint can transform a house from being the ugly duckling on the street to being the most beautiful swan.

Whether you paint the house yourself or hire someone else to do it, there are a few things you should be aware of before you get started. First of all, the exterior of a house must be properly prepared before it can be painted. If the paint is peeling, the surface will need to be scraped to remove the paint that is flaking off. Depending on how severely the paint is peeling, you may be able to get by with using just a scraper. However, if the paint is peeling excessively, you may need to use a power washer to blast the chipped and flaking paint off. After scraping or power washing the surface, some of the areas may require sanding to smooth out the surface area. The exterior of the house should be washed with a mild solution of soap and water after scraping is completed. The next step in properly preparing the surface of a house is to paint it with a primer, especially those surface areas that have been scraped down to the bare wood. In addition, most primers contain chemicals that effectively kill any mildew that may be present.

One of the most important decisions you'll need to make when painting your house is the selection of the colors. First of all, you'll want to ensure that the colors chosen are consistent with those in your neighborhood, especially those properties that have been painted within the last few years. If most of the homes in your neighborhood have not yet been painted, I recommend driving through newer communities where the colors are not dated. In an older neighborhood, for example, the majority of houses may be painted colors that are dated and no longer in style. In many areas, earth tone colors such as tan or beige are the preferred colors of choice. Not that long ago, dark brown colors were predominant in many neighborhoods but are now considered dated. In some coastal areas such as Florida, brighter colors such as peaches and pinks are used.

Because the color selection process can be a little tricky, be careful before you go out and buy 10 or 20 gallons of paint thinking you've found just the right color. You may be sorry if you do. Just because you find a color you like on a color sample at the paint store doesn't mean you will like that color once it has been applied to the surface of your house.

Speaking from experience, my wife, Nancy, and I made that very mistake on one of the first homes we lived in. We wanted to paint our home a taupe color and, according to the color sample, thought we had found just the right color. After about half an hour of applying the paint to the house, we discovered that the color didn't match the sample at all. Instead of the taupe we were hoping for, the paint looked more like a flamingo pink. Because we weren't living on the coast of Florida at the time, the color was not a good match for our community. Nancy and I went back to the paint store to look for a slightly darker color. Thinking once again that we had found just the right color, we started painting, only to discover this time that the paint was too dark and almost looked purple. Okay, so we went from flamingo pink to passionate purple. Once again, we returned to the paint store in search of just the right color, and this time found it. It was the taupe we thought we were getting all along.

One additional item to be aware of when checking the paint color is to be sure to wait long enough for it to dry completely. Paints tend to appear darker when they are wet and lighter after having dried, so be sure to allow ample drying time to check their true color. You'll also want to check the color in the sunlight, as well as in the shade, as variations of natural light cause colors to appear differently as well.

Impact value: ★★★★★ Strong. The impact value of this home improvement is strong because paint can do a great deal to improve the appearance of a house at a relatively low cost. If you're willing to apply a little elbow grease, you can save even more by doing the work yourself. Either way, whether your house happens to be an ugly duckling, or just needs a little freshening up, applying a fresh coat of paint will go a long way toward transforming it into a beautiful swan.

32: SIDING

Most houses have some type of siding on them, especially those located in median-priced to lower-priced communities. This is because siding is a cheaper alternative than other materials such as brick or stucco. There are three primary types of siding available today, each one made from a different type of material and each one offering its own unique advantages and disadvantages: wood, vinyl, or cement board.

Wood siding has been around for many years and at one time was the most common type of siding used. It comes in various patterns, widths, and styles, and although easy to install, it must be installed properly to ensure that each piece is level and overlaps the other pieces correctly. One primary advantage of using wood siding is that it is the least expensive of the three types of siding most commonly used.

Another advantage of wood siding is that it can be painted any color you want. In ten years, if you get tired of dark brown (or the color has become outdated), you can easily change it by painting the siding a newer and more popular color. The fact that wood siding must be painted, however, is just as much of a disadvantage as it is an advantage. Because the elements, such as wind, sun, rain, snow, and ice, all take their toll on painted surfaces, those surfaces demand to be painted. In other words, the paint on wood siding eventually wears out leaving you with no choice but to repaint. It is no longer a matter of choice but necessity. Depending on the quality of paint used, a homeowner can expect to have to repaint every ten years or so.

Vinyl siding has become increasingly popular among homeowners in recent years and is commonly used in new construction. For example, vinyl siding is the material of choice for my company, Symphony Homes, for several reasons. First of all, although vinyl siding is approximately one and a half to two times more expensive than wood siding, it offers several advantages that wood siding does not. For example, vinyl siding comes in almost any color you can imagine, so it doesn't have to be painted.

Maintenance requirements for vinyl siding are not as great as for wood siding either. Rather than having to repaint every so often, a mild solution of soap and water is usually all that is needed to clean its surface. If signs of mildew are present, I recommend adding a little bit of bleach to the water because bleach is very effective at killing it.

Another advantage of using vinyl siding is that because the color is incorporated directly into the material, it is permanent and will last much longer than a painted surface. So, unlike its wooden counterpart, it will not require painting on a periodic basis. This can potentially be a disadvantage, however, because if the color chosen today becomes outdated in 10 years or 20 years, you will not have the option of changing it by simply applying a coat of paint.

One additional factor you should be aware of when considering using vinyl siding for the exterior of your home is its relative thickness. If you are obtaining quotes from several siding contractors, a key difference in their quotes will be the quality of the siding they are using. For example, although Contractor A might have the cheapest quote, he may be using a thinner and inferior 36 mil product. Because vinyl siding is measured in millimeters of thickness, the higher the number, the better the quality. Contractor B meanwhile may provide you with a higher quote because she is using a better grade of vinyl, such as a 42 mil or 44 mil product. I recommend using a minimum of 40 mils because the thinner products tend to look wavy and uneven when attached to the surface of a house.

Cement board has been available for several years now and is also growing in preference as a replacement for wood siding, especially in coastal regions where the average moisture or humidity levels are much higher than in other areas. One primary advantage of cement board is that it is extremely durable. Some brands are designed to last for up to 100 years or more. Like wood siding, cement board must also be painted, so virtually any color can be used to achieve the look you want.

A primary disadvantage of using cement board is its cost; it is typically more expensive than even vinyl siding. The labor costs to install cement board is high in large part due to the difficulty of working with the material. Although it can be cut just like wood siding can, cement board is much heavier than wood siding or vinyl siding and is therefore more difficult to hang. Another cost component of cement board, once it is hung, is the cost to paint it. If it is strength and durability you are looking for though, the cement board products are your best choice.

Impact value: ★★★★ High. The impact value of installing any one of the three siding products is high because doing so will significantly improve the appearance of a home. While replacing or installing siding on a house is more expensive than repainting one, it nevertheless represents a terrific value due to its ability to greatly enhance a house's appearance.

33: ROOF REPLACEMENT

If it's been 20 or more years since your roof has been replaced, it may be time for replacement, especially if any evidence of leaking is present. A leaky roof is usually fairly easy to detect by a simple inspection of the ceilings in your house. If any staining or water spots are visible on the ceiling, then there's a good chance you may have a leak. In some cases, the source of a leak can be located and patched. In other cases, if the leak is too severe and the roof is worn out anyway, then the roof will need to be replaced.

The cost to replace a roof can vary widely with age and condition. Most composition shingles have a minimum life of 25 years, so if the existing shingles are less than 15 years old, it's a pretty safe bet that any repairs required will be minimal. After 15 years, the shingles can begin curling up and wearing to the point where leaks may begin to develop.

If a new roof is needed, the cost to replace it is usually not prohibitive. If, for example, a new layer of shingles can be applied over the existing layer, the cost is less and time involved is shorter than if two or three layers of shingles already exist that need their removal. This can effectively double the price of a new roof because the labor required for the tear-off can be quite expensive due to the additional time and labor required.

Furthermore, older homes that already have several layers of shingles on them may require work in addition to removing the old shingles. For example, the deck of the roof may be damaged as a result of water leaks that have occurred over time. If the house needs to be completely redecked, the cost will certainly increase.

I recently purchased an investment property in which the entire roof, including the underlying deck, had to be stripped off and replaced. Unlike newer decks that are often made of plywood, the deck on this roof was made of wooden planks that had seen their better days. Once the planks were removed, the attic area of the roof became exposed because there was nothing at all on the top to protect the house. In a situation like this, your roofer must be prepared to act quickly so that no water damage occurs in the event that it begins to rain while the attic area is exposed. If rain poses a threat, the roof can be draped with a tarp to prevent any water from damaging the attic area, as well as the rest of the house.

Roofing shingles are available in many types and styles, including those made of asphalt, wood, and even ceramic. The most common and the least expensive of these are composition shingles. Composition shingles are available in a variety of colors and come in several styles, including the standard three tab and the slightly more expensive dimensional shingle. I personally prefer the dimensional shingle because it provides a more uniform and upscale appearance. When selecting the type and style of shingle to use, it's best to be consistent with what the other houses in your neighborhood have. If all the other houses have composition shingles, for example, then you'll most likely want to invest in a comparable shingle as well.

Impact value: ★★★ Moderate. The impact value of replacing existing roofing is moderate because the cost to do so can be somewhat substantial relative to the improvement in appearance that will result. If the appearance of your existing roof is acceptable, then you'll probably want to leave it alone and save your money for another type of improvement that will make more of an impact on value. This is, of course, assuming that your existing roof is still in good repair and does not leak.

34: ROOF CLEANING

One of the roofing industry's best kept secrets is the little known fact that roofs with asphalt shingles on them can be cleaned and made to look like new again. That's right. The color in composition shingles can be restored to look as good as new. In my experience, I have not found many people who are aware of this. I suppose this is because most roofing companies are in business to replace old roofs with brand new ones. It is quite common to see advertising for plumbers, electricians, and certainly roofers, but when is the last time you saw an ad for a roof cleaning service? Probably never.

In *The Complete Guide to Investing in Rental Properties* (New York; McGraw-Hill; 2004), I wrote about composition shingles and how they can be cleaned, as follows:

> Cleaning asphalt shingles on a roof can also go a long way to improving the appearance of a house. Contrary to what most roofing companies would have you believe, when an asphalt roof is several years old and begins to look dirty, it can be easily cleaned with a solution sold in most hardware stores. Most shingles have a minimum of a 20-year life, and some are guaranteed to last for up to 30

years. After as few as 3 to 4 years, however, the shingles can begin to build up a deposit of mildew that, from the ground, makes them appear old and worn. At first glance, you may think they need to be replaced. If the shingles are not more than 10 years old or so, chances are they only need to be cleaned, provided of course that the roof is not leaking.

I once owned a 24-unit apartment building in which the roof top looked like it needed replacing when I first bought it. There were several large trees around the apartment building that also contributed to the buildup of deposits on it. I asked the seller how old the roof was. He stated that the shingles were only 5 to 7 years old or so and that they had a 25-year life. I determined that I could get by with cleaning the roof rather than replacing it. As I recall, I spent around $1,000 to have the roof professionally cleaned. To have it replaced would have cost me ten times that much. This was the first time I had ever done this, but I must tell you, I was very impressed with the outcome. The roof looked like brand new at a fraction of the cost of replacing it!

So there you have it. If your roof looks old and worn out, it may just need to be cleaned, especially if it is only a few years old. You can either clean the roof yourself by purchasing the cleaning solution at your local hardware store, or you can check the Yellow Pages for a company that provides this service. As previously stated, roofing companies that provide this type of cleaning service may be hard to find. I was able to locate the company that did my apartment building through a commercial roofing service. Because it was a larger job, they were eager to do the work.

Impact value: ★★★★★ Strong. The impact value of this home improvement is strong because the process of cleaning a roof does not cost very much relative to its impact on improving its appearance. If you do the work yourself, roofing can look almost like new for less than $50, which is certainly much cheaper than replacing it.

35: RAIN GUTTERS

Buildings or houses with a pitched roof have a variety of drainage systems. If a building structure's overhang is wide enough, water can drain directly to the ground without the use of gutters. Most building structures today, however, have some type of drainage system incorporated into their design. Believe it or not, rain gutters have been around for thousands of years. Archeologists have discovered ancient dwellings with elaborate collection systems incorporated into their design that were used to channel rainwater into storage cisterns that could then be used for drinking water, as well as for bathing.

The use of gutters was also quite common in most of Europe and, at one time, were actually built into the eaves of the roof itself. They were known at that time as "box cutters." As construction methods developed over the years and gutters were moved to the outside of the eaves, their use became even more prevalent. Although gutters are still used today in some third-world countries to capture and contain water for drinking and bathing purposes, their primary use in the United States is to channel water through a series of troughs and down spouts to direct it in controlled drainage paths away from a house.

If your house doesn't have rain gutters, you may want to consider the following facts. Gutters are an important component of every house because they serve to channel water away from it, thereby extending the life of its exterior. Without gutters, water is free to run down the roof, back across and under the eaves, and down the sides of the house eventually causing water damage. Furthermore, the runoff from the roof can seep in around windows over time, potentially causing water damage to the interior of a home.

Finally, water running off of a roof with no rain gutters onto a cement driveway will eventually cause a channel to be formed in the driveway itself through the process of erosion. This is especially true if the concrete is freshly poured and has not had time to fully cure. The next time you happen to notice a house with no gutters on it, take a look at the driveway and examine it for signs of erosion at the point where the water runs off and makes initial contact with the cement and you'll see what I mean about erosion forming channels in it.

Rain gutter systems are most commonly made from galvanized steel, aluminum, copper, and even plastic. In addition, gutters are available in a wide variety of colors, so painting them is often not necessary. If you decide to install a gutter system yourself, the materials can be purchased in precut lengths from your local hardware store and then trimmed on site to the exact length needed. Down spouts and hangers are readily available, too. Gutters are fairly inexpensive, and for several hundred dollars, you should be able to install a complete system.

When installing the gutters, you should make sure that they are hung properly. The front edge should be about one-half inch below the back edge, there should not be any low areas that can collect water, and all of the joints should be sealed properly to ensure that the water flows through the gutters and to the down spouts rather than dripping through the joints. Finally, if the gutters have a cover screen or similar device used to keep them free of debris, be sure to check them periodically to ensure that they do not become clogged with leaves that would result in water flowing over them and thereby rendering the gutters useless.

For about a $1,000, you can hire a professional to install a complete rain-gutter system. Even though the initial cost is more than if you did the work yourself, to me it is well worth it. By having a professional install the gutters, you can usually depend on them to be hung properly with everything functioning as designed. Most companies have a supply of material on their truck that is measured and custom fit to the exact specifications of your house.

If there are any problems with the gutters, reputable companies will often provide a minimum 90-day warranty on the complete system and will come back to make adjustments if necessary. Another point to keep in mind is that the majority of the installation process takes place on ladders. If you're not comfortable working from a ladder, especially if you have a two-story home, it's best to leave the installation of rain gutters to a professional.

Impact value: ★★★★ High. The impact value of this home improvement is high because gutters are relatively inexpensive to install, serve a very important purpose, and will enhance the appearance of most any home by providing a clean and finished look to the eaves and corners of the house.

36: BRICK AND MASONRY

Brick has long been used in the construction of new homes and can be used to cover the entire exterior of a home. It can also be used in conjunction with other types of exterior facades, such as vinyl or wood siding, stucco, stone, and most any other type of covering. Although some homeowners prefer to have 100 percent brick on their house, it's also a good idea to complement the brick with another type of exterior covering, such as vinyl siding. Using a solid-color siding to provide contrast to the brick will help add dimension to the appearance of a house. It can further be complemented by using a darker accent color on the trim and shutters of a house if it has them. Brick is sometimes used to create a "belt" or "band" down the side of a house, which is typically about three feet high or so. Siding is then used on the upper portion of the house. Using a combination of brick and siding is much less expensive than using all brick and makes the use of brick more affordable.

If you're thinking about adding brick to your existing home, you'll first need to determine whether or not it can be added. Whether your house has a slab foundation or a basement foundation, a "brick ledge" is needed to support the brick. A *brick ledge* is the portion of the foundation located on the outside edge that is formed at the time the foundation is poured and that supports the weight of the brick. If there is no brick ledge, then there is no way to support the brick. The brick ledge is sometimes not visible because it often lies just beneath the soil. To determine if your house has a brick ledge, take a small shovel and dig down several inches by the edge of the house so that the foundation is exposed. Look for a small ledge approximately four inches in width that runs down the length of the foundation. If you find a brick ledge, then you're in good shape, otherwise, you'll have to pass on this home improvement.

Because brick is available in so many colors and styles, it's sometimes very difficult to determine which color is right for you. Most brick companies have a showroom with samples of all the different types of brick they offer, which is a great place to start. What you have to be very careful of, however, is that what you see on a small sample board is not truly representative of what it will look like on the house. One reason is that fluorescent lighting in the showroom is not the same as natural light from the sun, so the color of the brick will vary. Furthermore, this color difference is greatly magnified when the color reflected by fluorescent light on a small sample is compared with the color reflected by natural light on an entire house.

Another factor that affects the appearance of the brick is the color of the mortar. If no dye is added to the mortar, which is the way most houses with brick are built, the mortar takes on a light gray appearance. Dye can be added to the mortar, however, to give the brick a completely different look. You may not think coloring the mortar would make that much difference, but I can tell you from experience that it makes a significant difference in the appearance of brick.

I once built a house using a traditional roman red brick on it. It just so happened that my next door neighbor, as well as the neighbor directly across the street from me, used the exact same brick. I could have selected a different color of brick to provide some variety, but I really liked the roman red, especially on the type of house I was building. As it turned out, one neighbor did not use any dye in the mortar at all, leaving it a light gray color, while the other neighbor used a red dye in the mortar, which gave it a light red appearance. I decided to darken the mortar on my house by using a black dye, resulting in a dark-gray mortar.

After the houses were completed, the average passerby would never know that the same brick was used on all three of them. One point to be aware of when using dye is that if it isn't mixed properly with each batch of mortar, the color of the mortar will not be the same, causing inconsistencies in the appearance of the brick.

So while the showroom is a good place to start the selection process for brick, I recommend carrying your research one step farther. Most brick companies maintain a list of houses that have used all the various types of brick they've sold over the years and will gladly provide you with a street address so that you can drive by and see what the finished product will look like. Select the two or three brick colors you like best and then spend an hour or two driving around looking at houses before making your final decision.

If your home already has brick on it, but the brick has begun to look a bit worn and weathered, you'll be happy to learn there are several things you can do to improve its appearance. First of all, if the brick is discolored from dirt or mold, or if it has taken on a chalky appearance, it can be cleaned with an acid-based product known as "muriatic acid," which is a form of hydrochloric acid. Muriatic acid is typically diluted with water at the prescribed ratio and then applied with a scrub brush to clean the brick. While the acid is fairly inexpensive, it does a terrific job of cleaning brick and can restore it to look like new.

If the brick only has a buildup of dirt on it, there's a good chance you can get by with a solution of just soap and water. Once again, I recommend applying the solution with a scrub brush and then rinsing it with a low pressure garden hose. Do *not* use a power washer or high-pressure washer to clean the brick because by doing so you run the risk of leaving wand marks on it. The high pressure from a power washer will literally leave marks or streaks on the surface of a brick wall because it washes a portion of the brick surface away. Please take my word for it; I've seen the damage that can result from using power washers all too many times.

Finally, if you observe any cracks or separation in the mortar, it can usually be made to look like new again. Most hardware stores sell a mortar-like filler that can be applied with a caulk gun to fill in any cracks or crevices that may be present. If the mortar has severe areas of separation that extend several inches, or worse yet, several feet, the house may have a foundation problem. Unfortunately, if that turns out to be the case, it's going to take a lot more than a tube of caulk to rectify the problem.

Impact value: ★★★★ High. The impact value of adding brick to a house as a home improvement is high, even though the cost of brick itself is somewhat expensive. In most areas of the country, the use of brick as an external covering is quite desirable, although not always affordable. Most people are willing to pay more, when they can afford it, for a house having brick on it than for an identical house having no brick.

37: EXTERIOR DOORS

Have you ever driven through a neighborhood and seen a house that had a front door that was so stunning it made you stop your car, or at least slow down, so as to get a better look? When I see magnificent looking front doors, the ones that are real showstoppers, I can't help but slow down to more fully appreciate their beauty. A beautiful front door can really accentuate the appearance of a house in a very positive way and helps set the tone for guests who may be visiting, as well as for those prospective buyers coming to look at your house.

Front doors are available in a variety of shapes and sizes and are most often made from either metal or wood. Some doors feature a single side panel, while others offer a double side panel. A single side panel can be placed on either side of the door and, in most cases, is determined only by your preference as to which way the door will open. Side panels usually have windows in them ranging anywhere from ¼ to ½ to ¾ the length of the panel leaving enough room for a solid panel at the bottom.

The glass used in doors and sidelights can be a standard clear glass, a leaded glass, or even a stained glass. Numerous intricate designs can be created using the latter two types to provide for a beautiful, elegant look. Furthermore, leaded and stained glass windows provide a measure of privacy while still allowing some light in. So, although the clear windows are less expensive, they do not provide the same beautifying effect that the other choices do. Furthermore, depending on the size and placement of the window, it may be necessary to cover clear glass with a shade, blind, or curtain to prevent others from peering in.

The majority of less expensive doors are most often made of metal and can be painted to suit your needs. Although some metal doors are constructed as a hollow core type, I strongly recommend that you spend a little more money and invest in an insulated door, most of which have a foam core as the insulating barrier. You can purchase a quality foam-core, steel, insulated door starting at about $200 or so. If leaded or stained glass windows are added, the price can quickly increase to $1,000 or more.

Insulated steel doors require little maintenance and are designed to last for as long as 20 years. Doors made from wood products are typically more expensive than steel doors, especially if they are made from wood such as oak, cherry, or mahogany.

The cost of a wooden door starts around $500 and can easily be as much as $5,000. Wooden doors can be of the flat panel type with no design or window, or they can be made with a most elaborate and intricate detail that highlights the natural beauty of the wood.

The more expensive doors are usually made of solid cherry or mahogany wood and are designed with beautiful leaded glass windows in them. A variety of stain colors are available for these doors that will bring out the rich colors of the wood. The beautiful red mahogany is my personal favorite. Wax sealers are also available and recommended for wooden doors to protect them from the elements such as wind and rain, but especially from the damaging UV rays emitted by the sun.

Wood doors require more maintenance than steel doors and must be refinished and sealed every few years to preserve and extend their useful life. But it is the doors made from wood that are the real showstoppers.

Impact value: ★★★★ High. The impact value of this home improvement is high provided that your current front door is replaced with one that is superior in appearance, quality, and its ability to seal out the elements than the one you currently have. For example, if you replace a plain, no-frills door with a new, plain, no-frills door, you're not any better off value wise than you were before you started. On the other hand, if you upgrade your current door with a stunning, showstopping mahogany door, you'll make a first impression to guests that says Wow!

38: WINDOWS

Installing new windows in a house is a great way to update and improve the appearance of a home, especially if the existing windows are 15 years old or older. Furthermore, most new windows are constructed with double-paned glass and are much more energy efficient than those made even a few years ago. The windows in my house are only five years old, and I'm already thinking about replacing them, as I'll explain later.

Depending on the size, style, and type of construction, the cost of a window can range anywhere from $100 to $500, and even much more for larger picture windows. Replacing your windows can generally be done in one day to two days, especially if a professional window company is replacing them. There are a wide range of options you should be aware of before making a purchase decision, including color and style, insulating values, and the actual construction of the window itself.

Although windows are available in almost any color you want, the most common color is white, followed by tan or beige, because these colors will go with just about any color that may be used on the rest of the house. White windows especially provide a clean and pristine appearance that will go with any other color used on a house.

Window panes can be used to dress up the front of a house, but they are often avoided in the back of a house. This is because using individual panes in a window partially obstructs the view and also because this type of window costs a little more than those without the smaller panes. Many families spend much of their time in the back portion of their home where the family room and kitchen typically are. Using windows without the smaller panes allows them to view the outdoors more clearly. Windows with curves or arches in them can also be used to dress up your home and are not that much more expensive than ordinary rectangular windows.

Another factor to keep in mind when replacing windows is their insulating value. While most windows 15 years or older were built using single-pane construction, most newer windows are built using double-pane construction (sometimes referred to as "double glazed"). The new double-paned windows have much higher insulating values, seal better, and allow less air infiltration than their older predecessors. If your house feels cold and drafty when the wind blows outside, it's a good indicator that it's time to replace the windows. Installing new windows in a house can easily save you 20 percent or more on your utility bill, both in the summer and in the winter. That can easily result in a savings of $400 to $500 per year depending on your average bill.

Windows are most often constructed of one of three types of material, each offering their advantages and disadvantages. They include aluminum or steel, wood, and plastic or vinyl. Windows made with an aluminum type construction are the least expensive compared to the other types. The primary drawback of aluminum and steel windows is that they will begin to oxidize or rust over time. Furthermore, the frames do not hold up very well and tend to stick.

Windows made with wood framing are often the most expensive and considered by some to be a much desired upgrade. They can be purchased prepainted or natural and then painted any color you like. Wood is also a better insulator than metal or vinyl, so they should keep your house warmer, right? Not necessarily. I mentioned at the beginning of this segment that although the windows in my house are only four-years to five-years old, I am already thinking very seriously about replacing them. It just so happens the frames are made of wood.

When the windows were first installed, they were natural wood and therefore needed to be painted. The combination of paint and wood caused the windows to stick from the very beginning. Then when it was time to open the windows in the spring after being closed all winter, I thought I would surely end up with a hernia from the strain of trying to open them. Almost every window in the house was stuck closed.

To this day the windows do not operate well and most everyone of them sticks. Furthermore, they don't seal very well either. As I write these very words, strong Canadian winds are blowing in from the north and gusting up to 40 miles per hour and more. The windows do such a poor sealing job that the blinds covering them actually move slightly when the wind blows. As you have probably guessed, I'm not a big fan of windows made from wood.

Vinyl or plastic windows, on the other hand, do everything my wooden windows are supposed to. In the new homes built by Symphony Homes, all windows installed are made from vinyl, unless a homeowner requests otherwise. Not only are vinyl windows less expensive than those made from wood, they are in my opinion far superior in operation and insulating qualities as well. Vinyl windows tend to seal very well and are very effective at minimizing air infiltration. In addition, they are not prone to stick like the other types, but they generally provide very smooth operation year after year. When I eventually replace the windows in my home, it will be with a set made of vinyl.

Impact value: ★★★★ High. The impact value of replacing windows is high for two reasons. First of all, installing new windows in a house is akin to a person getting a facelift. New windows will definitely brighten up the appearance of a house, and will look even better if the house has been newly painted. Second of all, new windows add value because they will save you money month after month, year after year, and will provide for a more comfortable living environment.

39: FENCES

If you're thinking about installing a fence, you're fortunate in that there are many options available. A fence can be made out of chain link, wrought iron, or cedar. Fences can also be made out of natural barriers such as a row of trees or bushes. Believe it or not, some fences are even invisible. That's right. Invisible. The type of fence you choose will depend largely upon the purpose for which it is being erected. Some people put up fences to keep the neighbors' kids out of their yard, while other people put up fences to keep their own kids in their yard (especially with small children). Some people may just want a little more privacy and aren't really concerned with keeping anyone in or out. While there are many reasons for erecting a fence, you should be aware of the advantages and disadvantages of each fencing type.

While chain-link fences, for example, tend to be less expensive than other types, they tend to be less aesthetically appealing than other types. Wrought-iron fences, on the other hand, are nicer looking than chain-link fences and are available in a variety of colors. They are also more expensive than chain-link fences and offer about the same degree of privacy, which isn't very much because you can see right through both types.

Cedar fences are very attractive, cost a little more, and offer much more privacy than do chain-link fences and wrought-iron fences; however, they also require periodic maintenance similar to decks. To keep a cedar fence looking new, you should power-wash and treat it with a sealer every other year or so.

If the bylaws in your neighborhood don't allow human-made fences such as these, you may want to consider installing a fence using a natural barrier, such as a row of trees or bushes.

Finally, there's the invisible fence that I mentioned earlier. Invisible fences are most often used in neighborhoods that do not allow the more traditional type of fence such as a chain-link fence or cedar fence. Invisible fences are used to contain pets, and more particularly, dogs. The fence is actually a wire or cable that is buried just beneath the surface of the ground. If a pet gets too close to the cable, usually within five feet to ten feet, a signal is transmitted to a device worn around the pet's neck on its collar that emits a small electric shock. The closer the pet gets to the invisible fence, the greater the intensity of the shock is. It doesn't take long for a pet to learn exactly where the barrier is and to avoid getting too close to it so as not to get shocked. In some regions, invisible fences are practically unheard of, but in other areas, they are quite common. Two of my three immediate neighbors actually have invisible fences that they use to keep their dogs contained.

In *The Complete Guide to Investing in Rental Properties* (New York, McGraw-Hill, 2004), I wrote the following about fences in a section entitled "Fancy Fencing":

> Improvements to fencing can also go a long way toward enhancing not only the appearance of a rental property, but the functionality of it as well. Although not all houses have fences, there are many areas in which every house in an entire neighborhood is built with a fence. This is especially true of new construction. Again, the prevalence of fencing will vary by area. I lived in areas where every house in the neighborhood has had a fenced yard, and I've also lived in neighborhoods where fences weren't allowed at all with the exception of those required by law for swimming pools. If the fence is made of a wood product such as cedar, for example, after many years they begin to look worn and run down. If the wood is still in good condition and is made from cedar, the fence can be power washed and then stained to make it look like new again. This process is very inexpensive and can make the fence look like new for years to come. Other fences made of wood can be painted to achieve similar results. Decorative slats and accessories are also available if you choose to go with the "fancy fencing" look.
>
> If the wood is beginning to show signs of deterioration, it may be time to replace it. Replacing a fence made of cedar or a similar wood product is much more expensive than painting or power washing. If the fence has deteriorated to the point to where it is no longer usable and you cannot justify the expense of replacing it, tearing it down and hauling off the debris is another inexpensive alternative. Whether you choose to remove the fence all together or replace it will in part depend on what is the norm in that particular neighborhood. If all the surround-

ing houses have fences, chances are yours will have to be replaced to comply with the association rules and bylaws.

Before installing your own fence, you'll need to carefully weigh all of the many options available. Primary factors which determine the type used are cost, style, purpose, and the bylaws in your neighborhood.

Impact value: ★★★ Moderate. The impact value of erecting a fence is moderate because it is not expected to enhance the value of a house any more than the cost of the fence itself. If the fence is old or in disrepair, it can actually detract from the value of a home because it will cost money to remove it and replace it with a new one.

40: IMPROVE AN EXISTING PORCH

A well-designed porch has a way of giving a house that special country charm look, depending, of course, on the type of home it is on. Porches provide an outdoor area to enjoy relaxing activities such as reading a book, visiting with family members, or perhaps even taking a little siesta. Kids love porches, too, because they find it is a great place to play with cars or dolls or even small bikes, and let's not forget the pets, especially when it happens to be raining. There's nothing like an afternoon nap for the family cat curled up on the front porch during a summer rain shower. If your house already has a porch, there are several low cost improvements that can be made that will help to adorn its appearance.

First and foremost among improvements is painting. If it's been several years since your porch has seen a fresh coat of paint, it's probably time to get out the brushes. I once owned an investment property that had a small porch on the front of it. The porch, sorely in need of painting, was made to look like new in just one afternoon and with only a few gallons of paint. So with an investment of less than $100, the overall appearance of that house was significantly improved. Porches stand out better when using lighter colors such as white or a light earth tone. Keep your porch bright and cheery and stay away from dark colors such as brown.

Porches can also be dressed up by using inexpensive pieces of decorative trim. Trim material, available in a variety of styles, can be used along the lower portion of the roof, to replace existing railing and posts, or to accent the existing columns, railing, or trim already in place. These decorative trim pieces are available at most hardware stores and require only a minimum level of skill to install. Once the trim is in place, all that is needed to complete the job is to paint them to match the existing color of the porch.

Finally, you may want to consider enclosing your porch by screening it in and then securing it with a door. Although porches are designed to enable you to enjoy the fresh outdoor air, sometimes that's difficult to do because of pesky pests such as mosquitos. Screening in a porch and installing a door is fairly easy to do and represents a low cost way to increase the level of comfort while relaxing outdoors on a cool autumn evening.

Impact value: ★★★★★ Strong. The impact value of this home improvement is strong. Painting a porch, decorating it with trim, and screening it in to increase comfort are all low-cost methods of improving your house. What's more, the improvements are quick and easy to do and in most cases can be done in less than a day.

41: ADDING A PORCH TO YOUR HOME

In Section 40, we discussed ways to improve an existing porch if your house already happens to have one. If your house does not have a porch, however, you may be able to add one if desired. There are several factors that will affect your decision to add a porch and determine whether or not it is actually feasible. They include complying with current setback requirements, understanding your area's frost laws, and designing the porch so it compliments the house's existing style and construction.

Before getting started on your porch addition, you'll need to know what the setback requirements are for your lot. The building line, or setback line, is defined in the Glossary of this book as "Distances from the ends and/or sides of the lot beyond which construction may not extend. The building line may be established by a filed plat of subdivision, by restrictive covenants in deeds or leases, by building codes, or by zoning ordinances." In other words, the setback line represents the minimum distance from a fixed point in which a house or building may be constructed.

A typical front yard setback line may be, for example, 25 feet or 30 feet from either the edge of the road or from the utility easement that runs across the front of the property if there is one. A simple examination of the property's survey, which you should have received when you purchased your home, will show where the setback lines are. If you don't have a copy of your survey, you should be able to contact your local municipality to determine what they are. Adding a porch to the front of your home may not be feasible because most houses are built right up against the front setback line. The reason builders do this is to save money in the construction costs of the home. The closer the house is to the road, the less expensive it is to build. The cost savings result from less concrete required in the shorter driveway, less trenching or digging to lay underground utilities, and fewer materials used when laying them.

If a porch cannot be built onto the front of your home, there may be a way to incorporate its design to wrap either around or on the side of the home. Once again, though, you'll need to be familiar with the setback requirements that affect the side yard. In many communities where there exists a very tight lot configuration, builders construct homes in a manner that pushes houses right up against the building lines, so there may not be any room to accommodate a porch addition. Homes built on larger lots, such as a half acre or more, often do have ample room for porch additions and may or may not be pushed up against the building lines. Finally, because houses tend to be pushed up against the front building lines to save money on smaller lots, there is almost always room in the back to add a porch. So if you aren't able to add a porch to the front or to the side of your house, you will more than likely be able to do so in the back.

After you have determined the feasibility of adding a porch, wherever it happens to be located, you will want to check with your local building authority to determine how the frost laws will affect its design and construction. In the warmer climates where the average winter temperature rarely dips below freezing, for example, the ground can be prepped to have concrete poured directly on to it with very little thought given to changes in temperature. Whether the porch is designed with a floor made from treated lumber, plastic, cedar, or concrete, footings will need to be poured to support its weight, but with no consideration given to frost laws because they do not apply in the warmer climates.

In the northern climates, however, special attention must be given to the construction of the foundation that will support the porch. The "frost laws," as they are referred to, determine the minimum depth the foundation or footings must be poured to ensure that the foundation does not move as the ground freezes during the winter months and then thaws during the spring and summer months.

Depending on where you live, the frost laws may require a minimum depth of three feet to six feet for the support walls or footings. These foundation walls, which are typically a minimum of eight-inches thick, will significantly impact the cost of building a porch. That, along with ensuring the construction methods used are adequate, is why it is so important to understand what the laws are that affect your project. As we have just seen, it is less expensive to add a porch to your house in the southern regions than it is in the northern regions.

After determining that adding a porch is feasible, the next step will be to design it in a manner which complements your home. In other words, the style of the porch should be made to fit the style of the house, including the materials used to build it. For example, the composition of the porch's roof should match that of the house, the wood used should be of similar type and appearance, and the colors used should match or accent the existing colors of the house. In addition, there are a variety of decorative posts and columns available that can be used to give the porch character. To save money, posts can be built of treated lumber wrapped with cedar, and painted. Treated lumber can also be used to make the hand railing and posts that go in between, and then painted or stained to match the house.

Adding a porch to your home requires precise planning and may quite possibly include working with or hiring a professional contractor to ensure that the work is done properly. In addition, be sure to check with your local building inspection department to determine whether or not a building permit will be required. In most areas, a permit is likely to be required to add a porch, especially if a poured-wall foundation is needed or any electrical work for outlets or lighting is done.

Impact value: ★★★ Moderate. The impact value of adding a porch to a house is moderate because the cost can run several thousand dollars depending on the materials used and the type of construction required to build it. In general, you should be able to recover any money invested in a porch addition, but the improvement will not necessarily earn a return greater than your invested dollars.

42: SIDEWALK AND DRIVEWAY IMPROVEMENTS

There are many ways to improve a sidewalk or driveway, several of which will fit even the most budget minded individual's needs. They include upgrading from existing materials to newer or better materials, using landscaping as an accent, and using brick pavers to enhance the look of drives and walks. The possibilities are limited only by your imagination.

Walks and drives are made most often from one of four common elements. They are gravel, asphalt, cement, and brick. While gravel drives were once the prevailing method of putting in a driveway, they have been gradually replaced most often by either asphalt or cement driveways. Gravel driveways are rarely used in new construction, except perhaps in rural areas. They are the least expensive of the four types listed here, and for good reason, because they tend to give way to rain, snow, and ice, resulting in potholes and unevenness. Furthermore, when it is hot and dry, they can generate a lot of dust.

Asphalt drives are the next step up from gravel in cost and are much more durable. If you currently have a gravel drive and want to improve it in the least expensive way, putting in an asphalt drive is a good way to do it.

Cement drives are the next step up from asphalt in both cost and durability and are often found in newly constructed communities. Cement driveways typically cost about twice as much as asphalt drives.

Finally, if you want to really upgrade and improve your existing driveway, you can have one made entirely of brick. Brick is available in many colors and patterns and is likely to cost about five times as much as a cement drive.

Regardless of what your walks and drives are currently made of, they can be beautified by lining them with a row of flowers, hedges, or small trees. In addition, the beds of the plants can include bark mulch, lava rock, or other substances to add color and variety. Using plants to accent drives and walks is a terrific, low cost way to really dress them up.

Bricks, or brick pavers as they are known, can also be used to enhance the look of a driveway or sidewalk. A single or double row of brick pavers can be used to line walks and drives to create a rich and attractive look without breaking the bank. Finally, you may also want to consider using a combination of plants and brick pavers to really beautify a driveway. Shortly after moving in, my neighbor had a row of brick pavers laid along the sides of her driveway and sidewalk, and then had a professional landscaper plant a variety of plants all the way down the drive. The landscaper then created scalloped beds with plants around the sidewalk that were filled with a red colored mulch. By the time my neighbor finished with this simple project, she had created a powerful first impression to anyone who happened to pass by.

Impact value: ★★★ Moderate. The impact value of driveway improvements is moderate because there is such a wide range of the types of improvements that can be made as well as their respective costs. On the lower end of the return on invested dollars in an average community is upgrading an existing driveway to one that is all brick because the cost to do so could easily surpass $15,000. The cost of a comparable cement driveway would be about $3,000.

As a builder, I know from experience that people purchasing a new home would prefer to spend their money wisely on the many different upgrades and options that are available to them. An all-brick drive is far down on the list of preferences in median-priced and affordable-priced housing. On the upper end of the return on invested dollars is using landscaping to line walks and drives. Shrubs and bushes are much more affordable and when done properly, can help create a very positive impression of your home.

43: SIDEWALK AND DRIVEWAY REPAIRS

If you're satisfied with your existing driveway and have decided that improvements to it are not warranted, you'll still want to examine it for wear and tear. While concrete drives are known to settle, shift, and crack, asphalt drives tend to develop holes and become worn looking. If you've ever pulled into a driveway that's cracked or full of potholes, I think you'll agree with me that it's an immediate turnoff, especially to prospective buyers.

If a buyer pulls up to look at your house and is greeted by a large crack in the driveway, she may begin to wonder what else is wrong with the house. Logical reasoning could lead her to conclude that if the driveway is cracked, the foundation of the house is likely to be cracked as well. As the buyer walks into your house for further examination, she is entering with the preconceived notion that not only does the house have problems, but that it may in fact have serious problems. Although your house may be immaculate on the inside, the bad seed has already been planted in the buyer's mind, so as she enters and walks through your home, it is difficult to see how beautiful it is because she is asking herself: "What else is wrong with this house?" Your best bet is to repair any such problems before initiating the sales process.

Driveways can crack or settle for any number of reasons. One such reason is that if there is a large tree planted close to the drive, it's quite possible that the root system from the tree has grown underneath it for years and years all the while remaining undetected until one day you begin to notice a separation in it. Before you know it, the separation has turned into a large crack, and the roots are finally pushing a portion of the concrete up. To repair this type of problem, the concrete will, of course, need to be replaced and the roots that have grown up under the drive will need to be cut out. It may even be necessary to move the tree that has caused the problem to begin with to another location in your yard, if possible, or to cut it down for firewood.

Other problems that can affect drives and walks, especially in newly built homes, are the water and sewer lines that run underneath them. In new construction, before the driveway is ever poured, the ground must be properly prepared by compressing and compacting the soil as much as possible with a bulldozer or grader, followed by adding a layer of sand several inches thick to provide a stable base for the concrete. It also helps to have a good, heavy rainfall before pouring the driveway because this will enable the soil to become more fully compacted.

If water or sewer lines run beneath any areas that are to be covered with cement, special care must be taken to ensure that the trenches that they are buried in are completely filled in. If they are not, after several rain showers, the soil above the lines and trenches will settle down into the voids. Sometimes the settling can be so severe that the surface ground sinks several inches. If the sinking occurs under the driveway, then the driveway itself will eventually give way, too.

Chances are if you have moved into a brand new home and see an area that appears to be unusually depressed, it's most likely related to underground utility lines. If your home is still in its warranty period, then your builder should cover the cost to repair the depressed area, including any drives or walks that may have been damaged as a result.

If the crack or damage to your concrete is severe, it may need to be replaced. For smaller cracks, most hardware stores sell a concrete filler that can be purchased in a tube similar to caulk. The filler is then used to fill in the cracks and helps to reduce their visibility. If the concrete needs to be replaced, it will certainly be more costly because the old concrete must be broken out, then hauled away, and then properly disposed of. The cost to replace concrete that requires a tear out can run three to four times that of a normal pour job. If it's noticeable enough to affect a prospective buyer's first impression, however, you should go ahead and have the concrete replaced so that you can sell your house.

Unlike driveways made of cement, driveways made of asphalt rarely require a complete tear out and replacement. If an asphalt drive becomes damaged or settles a little, it can usually be repaired by filling in the affected area with more asphalt. Drives made from asphalt also require periodic maintenance. There is an inexpensive process referred to as "seal coating" in which a driveway is coated with a black substance similar to tar that has been liquefied. Once the coating has dried, the driveway looks brand new again. The process is similar to painting a house. Once the house gets a fresh coat of paint, it is made to look like new again.

Finally, your driveway may just need to be cleaned. If oil deposits, grease, or other undesirable elements have collected on the surface of the drive, then the drive may just need a good cleaning. This is especially true if the driveway has never been cleaned before. Special chemical cleansers designed for this very purpose are available at most hardware stores. If the chemical agents don't work, then you may need to power wash the stained area in addition to using the chemicals. Be careful not to use too strong of a setting on the power washer as it could actually end up damaging the driveway.

Impact value: ★★★★ High. The impact value of driveway repairs is high because the cost to repair a driveway is usually minimal. Even if a section of the drive must be replaced, it is not cost prohibitive and will make a substantial difference on a prospective buyer's first impression of your home.

44: JUNKY CARS, BOATS, AND RVS

Getting rid of junky cars, boats, and RVs is by far one of the easiest and least expensive improvements that can be made to produce immediate economic results. I like to compare it to buying a used car. If a car is dirty on the outside and even dirtier on the inside, there's a good chance the customer may not be interested in buying it. In fact, you may have a hard time getting someone to even look at it. If, on the other hand, the car has been cleaned inside and out, the owner will have a much better chance of selling it.

Even if the car has a minor problem or two, the owner's odds of selling her car will be greatly improved just because of its clean appearance. A potential buyer may easily infer from a dirty car's unkempt appearance that perhaps the car hasn't been taken care of very well over the years. The same buyer may also infer from a car that is nice and clean that it has been well maintained. This same principle is just as true for homebuyers as it is for car buyers. If prospective buyers show up to look at a house and see cars up on blocks and old boats in the yard, they may not even bother to stop, regardless of what kind of condition the house is actually in.

Cleaning up trash and debris from a property is easy to do and doesn't cost very much either. If there are junk cars, old motorcycles, or engine blocks lying around, throw them out! Get rid of all of that unsightly junk! You want the outside of the property to be inviting. A lot of stuff lying around the outside is a poor reflection on the entire property and will surely create a very negative first impression on prospective buyers. Paying attention to appearance in every aspect of improving your home is the key to increasing its value.

Impact value: ★★★★★ Strong. The impact value of this home improvement is strong. Disposing of old cars, trucks, boats, engine parts, campers, and other useless junk provides homeowners with a low cost method to really make a difference in the appearance of their home.

45: COMBINING EXTERIOR IMPROVEMENTS

In *The Complete Guide to Buying and Selling Apartment Buildings* (New Jersey; Wiley; 2002), I tell the story about a property inspection I did on an apartment complex. I flew down to Texas to meet with one of my property managers, Richard, and the real estate agent to inspect an apartment complex that I was thinking about buying. Following is an excerpt taken from that story as it relates to a combination of needed improvements:

Through contacts of mine in the Texas market, I had identified two separate apartment buildings available for sale by the same owner. One was a 25-unit complex and the other was a 36-unit complex. The two properties were located about a mile apart and could be operated by the same manager. On the surface, the deal appeared to be priced right and offered some upside potential. I was very knowledgeable about that specific market because I owned a 98-unit building approximately five minutes away from these two. Both buildings were rented out as "all bills paid" (master metered), but surprisingly, both buildings had been wired with individual meters. The current owner was absorbing that unnecessary expense out of his income. That was fine with me, however, because that represented an opportunity to create value. . . . So far, things were looking pretty good. The two apartment complexes had all the makings of a good value play. According to the real estate broker representing the seller, both buildings were in fair condition, but did need a little work. That was okay with me because I am used to buying them that way. As I've already described, that's one of the key ways to create value. Because I lived out of state from where the apartments were located, I could only go by what the broker told me over the phone and also by a couple of photos he sent me. The photos looked good, and the broker assured me the properties were in fair condition, so I put the deal under contract.

I had a 30-day feasibility period for due diligence and property inspections, so that gave me ample time to arrange a flight to Texas to view the properties. Before I go any further with my story, let me say a word or two about real estate brokers. Their job is to sell, and part of that selling process includes presenting a property in its most favorable light. The real estate broker in this case was not dishonest with me, he simply presented the deal to me in the best possible light. This is certainly not to imply that all brokers are the same, it's just to say that some are more forthcoming than others. Now on with the story. I had already seen the 25-unit building on a previous trip and knew it needed quite a bit of work. It needed to be painted, which wasn't a big deal, but it also needed a new roof, extensive interior repairs, and the parking lot needed to be resurfaced. I was aware of these facts before ever entering into an agreement with the seller and an offsetting adjustment was reflected in the contract price.

Because I had already seen the first building, I met the broker at the second building, which was the 36-unit. I also had an associate of mine, Richard, who was a property manager, meet us there. His experience from an operational and maintenance standpoint have proven to be invaluable to me. My first impression of the apartments from the outside was somewhat favorable. They obviously needed to be painted, they looked a little dumpy, and there was definitely room for improvement with the lawn care and landscaping. That was all fine with me because those are the kinds of deals I like, the ones that need aesthetic improvements, just a little face-lift. A closer inspection of the interiors was about to reveal much, much more than I had bargained for, as you shall see. . . . On to the next unit. The broker knocked on the tenant's door and a young lady of about 20 or so answered. We told her we were there to do a quick walk-through inspection and would only be a minute. She was very accommodating and invited us in. When I first stepped into the apartment, I couldn't believe my eyes. Parked right in the middle of the living room was an old, broken down Harley Davidson motorcycle! Somewhat jokingly, I asked the lady if the motorcycle came with the apartment. She replied, "No, it's just my boyfriend's." I wanted to ask her if the oil dripping out of the bottom of it and all over the carpet was her boyfriend's, too, but I held my tongue. Even though I had not seen a truly representative sample yet, I was already beginning to get a good feel for the tenant mix, as well as the property's management. Richard scribbled another note on his pad, "motorcycle in living room, oil on carpet."

As we continued our inspection, each and every apartment had it's own unique way of contributing to what was beginning to look more and more like a lump of coal, rather than a diamond in the rough. At one particular unit, the young man living there had to remove his wild-eyed, raving-mad pit bull terrier before we could enter. I didn't have a whole lot of confidence in the leash the man used to take his pit bull out with. That dog looked like he'd take your leg off in one chomp if you got too close to him. Just what I needed, another liability. Another note, "pit bull in # 24."

And so the story goes. With the inspection of each building and each unit, things did not get any better. The more I inspected the less I liked what I saw. My manager worked up cost estimates for all of the repairs the buildings needed; I then reviewed and forwarded them to the broker. Our estimates revealed that a minimum of $128,000 in repairs would be needed to bring the property up to respectable living conditions. Because the seller was unwilling to make any price or repair concessions, I immediately terminated my interests in the property. This story represents a good example of what could have been done to improve the property had we been able to reach a mutual agreement on price and terms.

Part Three

INTERIOR IMPROVEMENTS

7

GENERAL INTERIOR

46: OVERALL CLEANLINESS

About a month ago, I went to a tree farm to purchase several large trees for our yard. Although it was my first visit here, I didn't really expect anything out of the ordinary. The owner of the farm had set up his business in a large barn, situated in a field with grass and mud to park on. Upon arriving there, I discovered, hanging by a door at the rear of the barn, a large cow bell that was used to alert the owner that a customer had arrived. In the downstairs portion of the barn were all kinds of tools and small equipment used on the tree farm.

The owner's office was located upstairs. I was directed to it by a series of worn and tattered signs. I climbed the dimly lit stairway and knocked on the door to the office, at which time the owner shouted a hearty, "Come on in!" Upon opening the door, I couldn't believe what my eyes were seeing! The office, which was fairly large, had stacks of paper and files on every square inch of desk and table space! There was litter, trash, debris, and you name it, scattered everywhere in the office.

After taking a brief moment to recover from my initial shock, I then glanced over at the owner, who was not that much different in appearance than his office. He was an elderly man dressed in old, worn clothes, and he wore a long, white Kris Kringle beard. The owner's unkempt appearance, along with an office that was in complete disarray, was almost enough to scare me away. I relented to stay to look at a few trees, however, I kept a safe distance from him for fear of being overcome by any possible body odor.

A few days later, I took my wife and three sons to another tree farm to compare the variety and price of trees to those at the first tree farm. Upon arriving there, we pulled into a paved parking lot surround by beautifully landscaped grounds. It was evident that the plants and bushes were meticulously cared for because each one appeared as if it had been recently pruned and manicured with great care.

After getting out of our van, we were not greeted by a cow bell but rather by an elderly gentleman who was friendly and personable. My sons took to him right away. Even my little Ben, who is only one-and-a-half years old, warmed up to this jovial old soul. Before I knew it, the two of them were walking hand in hand across the parking lot to the office building, much as a grandfather would take his own grandson, gently and tenderly, taking every precaution to safeguard this little one. I was witnessing salesmanship at its very finest. That kind, old gentleman had won the hearts of my entire family within just a few short minutes.

As we walked into the building together, I immediately noticed a stark contrast to the tree farm I had just been to a few days ago. There were no stacks of paper or files laying around. There was no debris or trash on the floor. The inside of this owner's building was in perfect order with everything neatly arranged and in its place. After spending a few minutes describing what we were interested in, the owner invited us to walk with him outdoors to look at some of the many trees he had available. We gladly followed and spent the next hour or so walking and listening to this gracious gentleman describe the characteristics of each tree.

We spent $3,600 on trees that week. Guess which tree farm we bought them from? If you guessed the latter of these two examples, you are exactly right. My initial impression of the first owner's office building was one of shock and horror. The degree of confidence I had in him and his ability to operate a business properly was very low. My judgment was based primarily on what my eyes told me, that this was an individual who's whole life seemed to be one of chaos and disorder. How could I possibly do business with a man who didn't appear to have a grasp on his business? The answer is I couldn't.

The owner of the second tree farm, on the other hand, made the buying decision easy for us. Not only was he as kind as could be to my wife and children, but it was apparent that this owner was an owner who knew how to run a business. It was evident that his office building was in order, his business was in order, and his life was in order. My degree of confidence in his abilities to conduct business was very high.

By now you may be wondering what any of this has to do with your house or with home improvements. The answer is really very simple. Cleanliness and order can have a significant affect on a prospective buyer's first impression of your house. Ask yourself this question, which for some of you may be tough to answer. Is the inside of your house more like the first business owner's office, or is it more like the second owner's office? Perhaps the answer lies somewhere in between. If your house is not in order, spend a day or two and clean out all of the old junk lying around that you are likely to never use anyway. There really is a lot of truth in the old adage about "first impressions." Be sure yours is a good one by taking time to organize and clean your house.

Impact value: ★★★★★ Strong. The impact value of this home improvement is strong because it costs very little, if anything, to clean and organize your house. A prospective buyer's impression of a house will be much better if it is clean and orderly. If, on the other hand, the house is in total disarray, the buyer will likely have doubts as to the condition of the rest of the house. After all, if a homeowner can't take care of even the simplest daily or weekly tasks of cleaning, how can he possibly have time to address more serious maintenance issues as they arise?

47: FLOORING

Yikes! Is the carpet in your house bright orange or lime green and happen to have a shag appearance? If it does, then it's time to throw it out! If it's been several years since any of the flooring in your home has been replaced, there's a good chance that it may need it now. Because flooring doesn't wear out overnight, you may not have noticed the paths or walkways worn in the carpet in some of the rooms, or maybe you are oblivious to the stains in the family room from spilled juice and milk. I suggest making a close examination of the flooring in your home for some of these telltale signs of wear and tear and replacing the flooring as necessary. Installing new flooring can do absolute wonders for most any home.

If you're getting ready to put your home on the market and the flooring needs to be replaced, but you aren't sure whether to give the buyer a flooring allowance or replace it yourself, my advice is to spend the money now and go ahead and put in the new flooring. My wife and I went the flooring-allowance route a number of years ago on our personal residence, but we soon discovered that most buyers had a difficult time seeing the home's potential with the new flooring, even though they would be the ones making all of the selections. Our home was priced below market and was in good condition other than the flooring. We thought that by offering a flooring allowance, a family could move in and select their own flooring. After all, who wouldn't want to choose their own flooring?

As it turns out, hardly anyone wanted to. Because we had already moved into another home and didn't want to carry both house payments, we ended up selling the house for about $10,000 less that what we believed its true value was. For half that amount we could have replaced all of the flooring and sold the house for it's market value. I am not suggesting that there aren't any buyers who can't see the benefit of having a flooring allowance and selecting it themselves, but as a general rule, people like to buy a house that's ready to move in to. This is especially true in more expensive neighborhoods. These people don't want to fool around with painting and replacing carpet and fixing the house up. In the world of fast food and instant gratification, people just want to buy a house and move in.

Almost all homes have at least one of the four most common types of flooring used in houses today—carpet, vinyl, ceramic tile, and hardwood. Each type offers its own unique set of advantages and disadvantages. They include cost, durability, and the ease with which they can be cleaned. Generally speaking, of the four types of flooring listed here, carpet tends to be the least expensive. Carpet is available in just about any color or pattern you can imagine. It comes in various lengths and weights as well. The shag carpet referred to earlier was popular in the 1960s and 1970s, but it has long since fallen by the wayside. The trend in recent years has been to use carpet of primarily neutral colors, such as earth tones, that are much shorter in length than the old shag carpets were.

Besides cost, one primary advantage of using carpet is that it is soft and easy on the feet, unlike the other types of much harder flooring. Depending on the style and quality of carpet used, as well as how much foot traffic it must endure, carpet will usually last about ten years or so. Of the four types, carpet is the most difficult to clean because any kind of spilled liquid will be almost immediately absorbed by its fibers. Stains are difficult to remove at best, if not downright impossible. Carpet is most often used in areas such as the family room or bedrooms.

Vinyl, sometimes referred to as linoleum, is generally slightly more expensive than carpet, but this will vary by style and quality. Like carpet, vinyl is available in many styles and colors. For resale purposes, it's best to stay with neutral colors that have a slight pattern to them. If the colors are too bold, for example, they may not go with or match a potential buyer's furniture and decor. Vinyl is fairly durable and on average will last 10 years to 15 years.

One disadvantage of vinyl to be aware of, however, is that if a heavy or sharp object is dropped, it can damage the vinyl surface by putting a nick or tear in it. It's difficult to replace a small piece of vinyl because the seams and patterns have to match exactly for it to look right. Of the four floor types referred to in this segment, vinyl is the easiest to clean. It is often used in places like the kitchen because it is so easy to wipe up spills or food.

Ceramic tile is usually slightly more expensive than vinyl, and it, too, can be purchased in most any color desired. Once again, if you're getting your house ready to sell, then you'll want to be sure to stick with the more neutral earth tone colors. Tile can be laid in all sorts of patterns because it comes in individual pieces that are usually anywhere from 4 inches to 12 inches in size.

Ceramic tile is extremely durable and can easily last 20 years to 30 years. Like vinyl, however, if a sharp or heavy object is dropped on it, the damage can potentially result in a crack or break. Unlike vinyl, however, because tile is laid in individual pieces, the damaged piece can easily be replaced without affecting the rest of the floor.

Finally, tile is easy to keep clean because spills and most anything else can be quickly wiped up. As a matter of fact, only five minutes ago, I had the high honor of wiping up a mess made by my little Ben, who as you may recall, is only one-and-a-half years old. I had just finished getting Ben out of the bathtub to dry him off and to get the little guy ready for bed, when no sooner had I done this than he decided to piddle right there on our ceramic tile floor! Oh well. That's what parents are for anyway, right?

Of the four types of flooring, hardwood is typically the most expensive. Price will vary by the type and thickness of the wood. Oak is the most commonly used, in part because it is a less expensive hardwood than other types, but also because of its strength and durability. While cherry and mahogany woods can easily run two times to three times as much in cost as the less expensive oak, they provide a rich and elegant beauty superior to that of any other type of hardwood flooring.

I recently had the flooring in the entryway of my office building, weary and fatigued from its many years of use, replaced with a beautiful new cherry wood. The difference in appearance is remarkable! When clients first enter the building, they are now greeted by the exquisite beauty of cherry wood that helps to exude a sense of quality and the finest craftsmanship in our homes, which is exactly what we want! Finally, just as vinyl and ceramic tile can easily be wiped clean, so can most hardwood floors. In fact, almost all precut hardwood floor planks are treated with a protective polyurethane coating that helps them to resist damage and staining from spills.

Impact value: ★★★★★ Strong. The impact value of installing new flooring is strong because the cost of doing so, although somewhat expensive, can result in a significantly positive impact in the appearance of your home. A word of caution. Be sure not to overspend by too wide of a margin on flooring relative to the rest of the houses in your neighborhood. It's certainly okay to upgrade a little, just don't get carried away.

48: DRYWALL REPAIRS

Drywall problems occur in most all houses irrespective of their age. Brand new houses have them, and century-old houses have them. Because minor problems are often barely visible to the casual observer, they are likely to go unnoticed. Although drywall problems are quite common, they are usually easy to repair. A little spackling paste and some paint to touch the area up is often all that is required.

Drywall problems most often show up as tiny, hairline cracks along seams and in corners that result from minor settling of the house, along with temperature changes that cause constant contracting and expanding of surface areas. Because drywall is a relatively soft substance, whenever movement does occur in a house or wall structure, it shows up in the drywall often before it does anywhere else. These smaller, hairline cracks are easy to repair by simply using a little bit of spackling paste to fill them in. Be careful not to use too much or you'll find yourself having to sand the area once the paste has dried to smooth it out. After filling in the cracks, apply some fresh paint over the area to make it look as good as new again!

More severe cracks in the drywall are a good indicator that there may be a more serious problem with the house, such as a foundation that has settled. If this is the case, it will take a lot more than spackling paste and paint to repair it. Cracks resulting from a cracked slab or foundation that has shifted may start out along the corners or seams, but don't necessarily follow them. This type of crack is a "stress crack" and can happen almost anywhere. If you find a stress crack in your house, you should probably have the foundation inspected. This is one repair you don't want to procrastinate about because it's only going to get worse.

Another common drywall problem is nail pops that occur around the head of a nail, creating a flaw in the surface of the drywall. Nail pops are more common in newly constructed homes, and after six months to a year or so, most of the nails that are going to "pop" have done so. Like surface cracks, nail pops are easy to repair. Light sanding may be required, followed by spackling paste, and finally by a dab of paint to touch the area up.

Although not as common as surface cracks and nail pops, another type of damage that can occur to drywall is an actual hole in the surface. Holes can be large or small, and they can happen any number of ways. If a door stopper is missing, for example, the constant banging of the door knob against the wall will eventually put a hole in it. Holes are also made every time a picture is hung in the house, although they are not visible because a picture is covering it. If, however, you decide to move the picture or take it down, you're left with an unsightly hole in the wall.

If the hole is small, such as a nail hole, you should be able to fill it in with a little paste. For larger holes, spackling paste will not be enough. The area must be patched with drywall tape or mesh to reinforce the damaged area and then filled in with drywall "mud," as it is called, which is somewhat thicker than paste. After the mud dries, a second, and possibly even a third application may be required. Once the area has been properly patched, it can then be sanded and painted to look like new again.

Impact value: ★★★ Moderate. The impact value of repairing damaged drywall areas is moderate. Although the cost of making drywall repairs is very low, the visibility of most surface drywall cracks is also very low.

49: PAINTING

Remember the principle we discussed in Chapter 1 about visibility and its relationship to value? We said that visibility adds value and the more visible an improvement is, the greater its potential is to add value. This principle is especially true of painting the interior of a house because the walls and ceiling are the most visible aspects of it. As soon as people walk into a house, one of the very first things they notice is the color and condition of the paint. If the colors are outdated or the paint is in poor condition from years of normal wear and tear—tiny hand prints, crayon marks, or scratches from Ms. Kitty—other people entering the house will surely notice.

As the homeowner, you may not notice the poor condition of the paint in your own home because the process of deterioration is a gradual one. A mark here and a nick there year after year will eventually result in a house that desperately needs to be painted. A house like this is in need of a makeover. That's right. Painting the interior of a house is like giving it a makeover. I'm sure you've seen on various television programs the before-and-after pictures of women who have been given a complete makeover. In the before pictures, they are often rather frumpy looking with loose-fitting clothing and are sporting a haircut that is ten years out of style.

The women are then whisked backstage to allow the experts to go to work. First the hair stylists work their magic cutting and shaping their hair, then the makeup artist meticulously shapes their eyebrows and applies color to the faces of the women, and finally the fashion designer fits them with the latest style of clothing that complements the different shapes of their bodies.

When the women are finally brought back out on stage, the audience, who applauds and cheers wildly, can't believe the difference in the way these women look. In just a short time, they have been transformed from ugly ducklings into beautiful swans for all to gaze upon and admire! Like the women on the television programs, you, too, can give your house a complete makeover by applying a fresh coat of paint and transforming it from an ugly duckling into a beautiful swan!

There are a few points to keep in mind when painting your house. First is the type of paint to use. For interior walls, latex or lacquer paints are the most commonly used. Latex paint is a water-based paint and is the preferred paint for walls and ceilings, while lacquer paint is an oil-based paint and is often used for the trim around doors and windows. Because latex is water based, it is much easier to clean up than a lacquer paint.

Paints are available in several finishes including flat, satin, semigloss, and gloss. Flat paints are usually the least expensive, but they are not as durable and are more difficult to clean. Wiping the surface of a wall with flat paint, for example, can leave smudge marks behind. Paint that has a satin finish is a little more expensive than flat paint, but it is easier to clean and has a slightly shinier appearance. Semigloss paint is a little more expensive and slightly shinier in appearance than satin. Paint with a gloss finish is the shiniest and is also usually the most expensive of the four types. Unlike walls with a flat finish, walls with a gloss finish can easily be wiped clean without leaving smudge marks. My personal favorite is paint with a satin finish. It provides just enough shine to keep the paint looking new without being too shiny.

I suggest using color to really transform your house. When I say color, I don't mean white either. Lighter earth tone colors such as taupe, for example, can be used in most rooms of the house. Be careful about using darker colors, except perhaps in formal rooms such as a living room or dining room. The house should be made to feel bright and cheery, not dark and dreary. Using lighter colors is the best way to accomplish this.

Using darker colors such as a deep wine or burgundy color are effective in creating an elegant or more dramatic look in formal rooms. The color scheme can be accented by using a high gloss white on any trim in the room, such as around the windows and doors. The baseboard and any crown molding in the room can also be painted white. Using darker and more dramatic colors in the formal rooms accented with high gloss white painted trim sets up a sharp contrast between the two colors creating a rich and elegant feeling fit for a king and queen!

If it's been several years since your house has been painted and you're thinking about selling it, go ahead and dress it up by giving it a much needed makeover. Remember to use paint that has at least a little shine in its finish giving it a finer appearance and making it easier to clean. Finally, stick with lighter colors in the majority of the house, but consider using darker colors in the formal rooms to create beauty and elegance.

Impact value: ★★★★★ Strong. The impact value of this home improvement is strong. In fact, painting the interior of your home will probably provide a greater return on the money invested in paint and labor than almost any other home improvement you can make. Painting can transform most any house from an ugly duckling into a beautiful swan.

50: WALLPAPER

Using wallpaper to decorate and dress up a home can be a great way to improve the way prospective buyers perceive it. Wallpaper can be especially effective at setting certain rooms off, such as a bathroom, kitchen, or formal dining room. I've personally used wallpaper in many of my own homes, as well as in the model homes for our company, Symphony Homes.

With so many choices of wallpaper available today, selecting just the right color or style for your home can seem overwhelming. Many of the home improvement stores have areas set aside where they have shelf after shelf of wallpaper books to look at. They are usually organized by type, such as "Contemporary" or "Traditional," or maybe "Bath and Kitchen." There are a wide range of rich and vibrant colors and patterns available including copper, gold, and bronze colors, as well as turquoise, aqua, and burgundy colors. Each one has the ability to transform a room into something with its own unique character.

In one of our model homes, for example, the theme used throughout the home is very traditional and includes a collection of beautiful artwork featuring the classical musicians such as Bach, Mozart, and Beethoven. The wallpaper selected for the model home in the kitchen and breakfast area, which are semiformal, complements the underlying theme by using musical instruments such as violins, cellos, and harps in it. Using symbols, such as musical instruments, helps convey feelings of quality and excellence among our clients, who have expressed to us on many occasions the high level of craftsmanship present in our homes.

You can either hang the wallpaper yourself or hire an experienced hanger to do it for you. Over the years, I've hung wallpaper myself on several occasions. That was when I had more time than I did money. I don't necessarily have more money than time now, but I do have enough to pay someone to do the work for me. Not that hanging paper is beneath me, it's just that I'd rather be doing other things.

Hanging wallpaper takes an individual who has lots of patience. Every piece must be cut just right and then dipped in water (if the paper already has a self-adhesive backing on it) to moisten the adhesive. Finally, while hanging the paper, you must take special care to line up and match any patterns to the paper that has already been hung. Because it's easy to mess things up when trying to hang wallpaper, you may have to start over with a new piece. At least, that's been my experience when trying to hang paper. It may have been more operator error than anything else. If you have the patience and the time, by all means, I suggest giving it a try. On the other hand, if you're like me with neither the patience or the time, you might want to pass on doing it yourself and call an experienced hanger.

One disadvantage of using wallpaper to decorate a room is that once the paper is hung, it is difficult to remove. If the buyer of your home likes the wallpaper as is, then removing the paper becomes irrelevant. If, however, the new homeowner wants to replace the wallpaper, the process of removing and replacing it can be challenging. There are special solvents designed to facilitate the removal of the paper, but you should be aware that they don't always work as advertised. That's not to say the paper can't be removed. It can, but it's usually accompanied by a degree of aggravation.

Once the old paper has been removed, the surface will need to be prepared to hang the new paper. Sometimes pieces of the old paper will stick and must be pulled off individually. There may also be some rough spots that will have to be smoothed out before hanging the new wall paper.

Impact value: ★★★★ High. The impact value of this home improvement is high because the cost of using wallpaper is low relative to its potential impact. One caveat to using wallpaper, however, is that not everyone has the same preferences when it comes to color and style selections, so you have to exercise caution before committing yourself to hanging it.

51: CABINETS

If your house is more than 15 years to 20 years old, it may be time to replace the cabinets. Based on feedback from the many homebuyers in our Symphony Homes' communities, cabinets are one of the most important features in a house. Consumers are telling us that they like to have as much cabinet space as possible and that the cabinets should be both stylish and functional. Finally, the cabinets must be the right color to match the consumers' decor.

Cabinets are located primarily in the kitchen and bathrooms, but they are also sometimes found in the laundry room. Wherever they happen to be located, it seems as though there can never be too many. If you're thinking about replacing all of the cabinets in your kitchen, I suggest looking at ways to reconfigure the kitchen to maximize the number of available cabinets. For example, if the kitchen area opens up directly into the breakfast room with nothing separating the rooms, you may be able to extend the cabinets to form a bar area where family members can sit on bar stools. This makes a great place to feed the kids without having to get the kitchen table dirty. It also provides a bit of separation between the rooms while at the same time adds more cabinet space. You may also want to consider putting in a center island if there is room to do so. Center islands are very popular features among homebuyers.

Cabinets are available in a variety of sizes and styles. Most upper cabinets today measure 36 inches in height. Upper cabinets 42 inches high are also quite popular, but are not as prevalent as 36-inch high cabinets because they cost more. If you're looking to maximize cabinet space, however, using the taller cabinets is the way to go. One drawback to using the taller cabinets is that by doing so, there may not be much room left in between the top of the cabinet and the ceiling. This will depend on whether or not your house has a standard eight-foot ceiling height, a nine-foot ceiling height, or even a ten-foot ceiling height.

So what's the big deal about having space in between the top of the cabinets and the ceiling? A lot of people like the extra space above the cabinets because it's a great place to decorate. My wife has all kinds of plants (artificial so they don't require watering) as well as uniquely decorated vases and spice jars placed around the tops of our cabinets. They help add more color and life to a dull kitchen.

Another disadvantage of using taller cabinets is that, by definition, they're taller! If you are an average height or shorter person, you won't be able to reach the upper shelves without using a step stool of some sort. One suggestion to take advantage of the additional space the taller cabinets provides is to store items you don't use very much at the upper levels. For example, if you have a large platter used only at Thanksgiving or Christmas, then using a stool to get it down once or twice a year is easy enough to do.

Cabinets are available in many colors, including white, various shades of oak stain, cherry, maple, and even black. While selecting the right color for your cabinets will in part be a function of the overall decor in your home, you should also think about the buyer who will purchase the house when the time comes to sell it. One of the most popular colors we sell to our new home buyers is a medium oak-stained cabinet. White cabinets are also a favorite choice among homeowners, but generally they cost about 25 percent more than oak-stained cabinets.

Although replacing all of the cabinets in your house may seem like a big deal, it really is not that difficult. The whole process can easily be done in one day to two days by an experienced cabinet hanger. The old cabinets are first removed and disposed of, and the new ones are installed immediately after. You will most likely have to replace the countertop and sink at the same time all of the cabinets are being replaced. After all, if your cabinets are outdated, there's a good chance your countertops and sink are as well.

Impact value: ★★★★ High. The impact value of this home improvement is high. Although replacing all of the cabinets in a house can range from about $2,000 to well over $10,000, because they are such an important feature within a home, the cost of doing so is certainly justified when compared to the benefits derived from doing so.

52: COUNTERTOPS

If you are thinking about replacing the cabinets in your kitchen, you may have to consider replacing the countertops at the same time. Updating kitchen countertops is an affordable way to give your kitchen a fresh, new look while at the same time adding value to your home. Like the cabinets, if the countertops are 15 years to 20 years old or older, then it's probably time to replace them. Even if you've take good care of the countertops and they are still in excellent condition, there's a good chance the colors and materials used then are no longer in style now.

For example, I recently had one of our crews replace all of the cabinets and countertops in a house we purchased with that improvement in mind. The material for the old countertops used in the kitchen was a laminate that had a teal green marbled appearance. That color scheme might work okay in a bathroom but not in the kitchen. I do recall a number of years ago when teal green was very popular. The color could be seen almost everywhere. New clothing, new cars, kid's lunch boxes and note-books, and even house exteriors featured the once popular teal green. I personally think it's still a nice color, although it's been a bit overused in recent years. Anyway, by now I think you get the point. If the colors or styles in your kitchen are a decade or two old, it's probably time for a change.

When it comes to countertops, you need a surface that can stand up to the rigors of cooking and cleaning and that will look good for years to come. A wide range of both materials and col-ors are available from which to choose. The ideal selection for your kitchen should be a function of what is most commonly found in homes in your specific price range as well as your bud-get. Some of the more common choices available for countertops today include granite, tile, Silestone, Corian, and laminate.

Granite, an igneous rock composed of feldspar and quartz, is extremely hard and therefore resistant to scratches and heat. Pol-ished granite is lustrous and offers a timeless, elegant beauty and the brilliance of natural stone. The material is known for its unique variation in color, veining, and special characteristics that make its surface as artful as it is useful. Because granite is porous, special care must be taken to apply a sealer periodically so that the surface doesn't absorb any food substances. Compared to other countertop materials, granite is quite expensive and can easily cost between $5,000 and $10,000 to complete a kitchen.

The use of tile for countertops seems to come and go in pop-ularity. I remember a small, three-bedroom house I purchased many years ago that had tile countertops. The tiles used at that time were tiny, one-inch squares laid out very neatly in several rows. I distinctly remember not liking the smaller tiles because the surface was difficult to keep clean. Whenever bread crumbs or other food particles were dropped, they fell in between the many tiny grooves in between the individual tile pieces. Because the tile was old to begin with, the food particles tended to stick in the grout. Furthermore, if grape juice happened to spill on the surface, which it did, that was even worse. The grout absorbed a portion of the juice and took on a rather purplish color.

Tile used on countertops today is typically larger in size, but it can still be as small as two inches per square. The absorption problem can be alleviated by using a grout sealer, which may have been available to me 20 years ago, but I just wasn't aware of it at the time. Tile is both scratchproof and heat resistant and is generally very durable. If a heavy object such as a pot is dropped on it, however, the tile can crack, in which case individual pieces can be replaced as necessary. Tile is usually much more affordable than granite, costing on average about half as much.

Silestone is an engineered stone composed of natural materials, 93 percent of which is the quartz and granite aggregate. Through extensive engineering, a manufacturing process was developed utilizing intense heat and pressure to increase the color consistency, stain resistance, and strength of this natural stone product. Because Silestone isn't porous, it doesn't require the use of sealants, so you won't have to worry about spilling grape juice on it as I did with the tile.

Professionally developed colors are calibrated through the use of computers to maintain consistency allowing designers and customers to make just the right selection from samples. The process is similar to having your local hardware store custom mix a gallon of paint from a color sample you furnished them.

Silestone is a more durable and distinctively attractive alternative to solid plastic surfaces. Its consistent pattern and coloration make this product an attractive, functional, and popular countertop. The manufacturer also offers a ten-year warranty on the product. Finally, the product is easy to install and is more affordable than an alternative such as granite.

Corian, made by Dupont, is made from a blend of natural materials and pure acrylic polymer resulting in a plastic-like material. The company boasts several features of the product, including over 90 different color selections. In addition, Dupont claims the Corian product can be "cut, routed, drilled, sculpted, bent, or worked like a fine wood." Corian is not a veneer overlay, but is solid throughout and can therefore withstand the challenges of daily use. Corian also makes countertops with sinks built right into them providing a smooth and seamless finish.

One disadvantage to using Corian products is that they are not designed to withstand the hotter temperatures that granite and tile can. Dupont states that "Corian remains stable and undamaged in temperatures up to 212 degrees Fahrenheit," meaning you have to take extra care not to place on it a hot baking pan you just pulled from the oven. While Corian is somewhat expensive, it is generally more affordable than granite.

Laminate countertops are one of the most commonly used materials and certainly one of the most affordable. Laminate is a thin, veneer-like material that is glued to a less expensive surface such as particle board to provide strength and support. Laminate countertops come in a variety of contemporary, as well as traditional, colors and styles. It is also very durable, easy to maintain, and can be used in many settings besides kitchens, including bathrooms and laundry rooms. Finally, because laminate is a veneer that is glued down, it's both easy and inexpensive to replace, so if the color becomes outdated or if you just get tired of it, it won't break the bank to have it replaced.

Impact value: ★★★★ High. The impact value of this home improvement is high provided the style and design are kept consistent with that of other houses that are comparable in price and size to yours. Because countertops are highly visible and one of the first things a prospective buyer sees when entering the kitchen, be sure yours are up to date and in style.

53: TRIM AND MOLDING

The office building our company, Symphony Homes, is located in is actually a historic home built in 1903. I still find it amazing that I work out of an office building that is literally over a century old! When I purchased the building, it was still being used as a residence by an older couple who had spent the last 20 plus years there. The building is situated in an ideal location right in the heart of the downtown area where the average daily traffic count exceeds 20,000 cars. When the couple bought the home back in 1980, I'm sure the traffic was not nearly as heavy as it is today. Because it is located on a busy street, it's unlikely that very many families, if any, with small children would want to live there. For me, though, it represented the ideal location for an office and was actually a fraction of the cost that I would have paid for an existing office building.

After purchasing the home, I completely renovated it and converted it into office space at the same time. Most of the house was fully gutted, including the kitchen and bathrooms, the roof, the heating and air-conditioning system, the flooring, and much of the plumbing. What was *not* gutted or removed, however, was all of the beautiful old woodwork throughout the house. The trim and molding used throughout the house is the original woodwork that was installed at the time of construction back in 1903. It has been carefully preserved over the last century and, for the most part, is in very good condition.

The baseboard is solid oak and is a full ten inches wide, unlike the newer trim used in houses today, which is typically only about three inches wide. Moreover, rather than being painted, the natural beauty of the wood has been brought out through the use of stains manifesting an aura rich in tradition. The house, or office building, also features an elegant stairway complete with hand-turned oak spindles and features a small, circular landing at the top. Finally, the doorways are trimmed with stained wood that ranges from four inches to six inches in width, once again unlike the newer much narrower trim used today.

It is the abundance of trim and molding along with its uniqueness that gives this old building charm and character. Without it, it would just be another old house. If your home currently has only the bare minimum trim in it such as around the doors and the baseboard, then a great way to dress it up is by adding more decorative trim throughout the home.

Molding comes in many different styles and varieties. Crown molding, for example, is used in the upper corners of a room where the wall meets the ceiling and is usually about four inches to six inches wide. Dental molding looks like a series of small blocks, or teeth, and can be used to wrap around doors and entryways, or in conjunction with crown molding to provide an additional accent. Chair railing is trim that is attached horizontally to the wall at roughly the same height as the back of a chair, or about 42 inches. Narrower pieces of trim are often used in conjunction with chair railing in a dining room, for example. The molding is attached to the wall below the chair railing to form a decorative pattern such as a rectangle with curved corners.

What really helps molding to set off a room is to paint it a color that creates a sharp contrast between the molding and the wall. For example, molding is often painted a very high gloss white, while a medium to darker color is used on the walls. The effect can be stunning and will most assuredly enhance the appearance of most any room. Although molding can be stained, it is most commonly painted.

I once built a house in which the living room was designed to be very formal. To help create this effect, the room was loaded with trim and molding. Leading from the foyer into the living room were two broad archways supported by majestic columns that were completely wrapped in fluted molding, which is a series of grooves cut into the wood designed to give it depth and dimension. The archways were trimmed with fluted molding as well, while the room was trimmed with crown molding and then accented with dental molding. The molding was all cut by hand and created by master craftspeople with the utmost precision and skill. It was then painted a high-gloss white and was set against rich, mauve colored walls designed to complement furnishings using royal colors such as wine, green, and gold. The end result was absolutely stunning!

Molding is priced by the linear foot and is relatively inexpensive. It ranges anywhere from 50 cents per foot to as much as $10 per foot, depending on the width, style, and type of wood used. As a general rule, the wider the trim the more it costs per foot. In addition, if the trim is plain and flat with no detail, it will cost less than trim that is more detailed and ornate in its design. Finally, softwoods such as pine, which are usually painted, will cost less than hardwoods such as oak, which can be stained.

Let's look at an example. To install crown molding around the top of the walls in a room, simply measure its size. Now, if the cost of the molding is $5 per linear foot, and the room is 10 feet by 12 feet, then the cost of trim for one room in this example would be as follows:

$$((10 + 12) \times 2) \times \$5 = \$220$$

You can then either install the molding yourself or pay a trim carpenter to do the job for you. The most important element to be aware of when installing the trim is that it must be cut with precision, especially the ends that will fit together in the corners of the room. A miter saw is the best tool to use for this job. Once the molding is installed, it must then be painted. If the complete job is hired out, it shouldn't cost more than $500.

Impact value: ★★★★★ **Strong.** The impact value of this home improvement is strong because the cost of adding molding is low relative to its potential impact on value. Molding is highly visible and can be used in various strategic locations throughout your house. Molding is especially effective when used in the more formal rooms such as the living and dining room. When done properly, molding can make a very positive impression on prospective buyers of your home.

54: DOORS AND HARDWARE

Interior doors are one of the most visible components of a home. They lead to practically every room in the house. There are doors to the bathrooms, doors to the bedrooms, doors to the closets, a door to the pantry, a door to the basement, and a door to the utility room. With so many doors, it's no wonder they're so visible. After all, it's the first thing you see before entering into almost any other room in a house.

Interior doors installed in many older homes were often quite boring. They're kind of like the kid in your high school class who never said anything. Remember him? He just sat there and never said anything. He didn't laugh, he didn't smile, he just sat there like a bump on a log. He was really remarkably boring. Compare Mr. Boring to Ms. Congeniality, who really made a statement when she entered the room. Everyone sat up and took notice when she came in. She wore the latest in fashions and was always dressed to the nines. While Mr. Boring had nothing to say, Ms. Congeniality had everything to say.

Believe it or not, while some interior doors can be just like the Borings, others can be just like the Congenialities. The boring doors are those that are completely flat and have no character whatsoever. They're often painted white and are made of a thin fiberboard material that is almost like compressed cardboard. Because the doors have a hollow core, they provide very little in the way of sound proofing. If the kids are too noisy and you want a little privacy, closing one of these doors won't do you much good because the sound travels right through them. Finally, these doors look cheap because they are cheap.

Congeniality doors, on the other hand, are usually made of either four or six separate and distinct panels that give the doors lots of character. Furthermore, the panels on them are set into the door at angles to give depth and dimension, unlike the flat, boring doors. These doors, too, are usually painted white, but they often have a pattern molded into them that is designed to give the doors a wood-grained appearance. Although the newer style doors are also hollow, they are made of a fiberglass composite and are reinforced on the inside, making them much stronger than the older style doors.

Finally, regardless of what type of interior doors you have, it's easy to dress them up by replacing the hardware on them. There are a variety of decorative door handles that can be purchased to replace the older style handles. One such handle that is relatively inexpensive is a lever type that often has a slight curve in it. The newer door handles are usually given a polished brass finish, but nickel and pewter finishes have become more and more preferred in recent years.

Impact value: ★★★★ High. The impact value of this home improvement is high because the cost of replacing interior doors is low relative to its potential impact. Interior doors are highly visible and can be seen in various places throughout a house. Interior doors can be purchased for $100 or less each in most home improvement stores making the overall cost to replace them fairly low.

55: FURNISHINGS AND DECOR

At the age of 22, I had just completed my tour of duty in the United States Air Force and returned home to Texas with all of my worldly possessions packed into a single military duffle bag. Upon returning to civilian life, I got a job and purchased an inexpensive mobile home. I remember having very little in the way of material things, so little, in fact, that my home was devoid of any furnishings, wall hangings, or plants. I also remember going to the house of my friend, Charles. He was a few years older than I was, was married, and he and his wife were expecting their third child. I remember the first time I went to visit them at their house, thinking to myself as I entered the front door, "Wow, Charles must make pretty good money. They sure do have a lot of stuff." Their house was full of furniture; there were pictures and wall decorations hanging on many of the walls; and a variety of plants provided life and color to blend it all in.

In all likelihood, you, too, can probably recall a time when your circumstances were as meager as mine, perhaps when you were a student in college, perhaps even now. I think you will agree with me that a house looks much better, and even more salable, when it is fully furnished rather than when it is empty. Walls that are barren cry out for decor that will bring them to life. Living rooms, family rooms, and kitchens crave for much-needed, and deserved, attention. Room corners and foyers look abandoned with no plants to keep them company.

Although you may be inclined to think that decorating your home with attractive furnishings and wall hangings can't possibly make a difference in its resale value, consider your own thoughts and feelings when entering into an empty home such as the one I lived in once upon a time. Houses with very little in them don't exactly feel very homey, and if a house doesn't feel homey to a prospective buyer, then guess what? The buyer will pass on it and move on to the next house, and to the next one after that, until she finds one that "feels right" to her.

Creating a homey atmosphere does not mean filling it with so much stuff that it becomes cluttered. Recall that earlier in this book we discussed the notion of getting rid of all the junk in your house. Properly furnishing and decorating a house seeks to find just the right balance between an empty house and one filled with clutter. The right mix of furniture, wall hangings, and plants can help provide that balance.

The first place to start is with your existing furniture. If it's been several years since you've purchased a new sofa set, it may be time to throw out the old and bring in the new. Our tendency is to grow more and more comfortable, one day at a time, with the furniture we have now, not realizing that it is wearing out, one day at a time.

We purchased a brand new sofa set, complete with couch, love seat, and chair, a little over 20 years ago. While my family enjoyed the comfort of that old set for all those many years, I really didn't realize just how worn out it had become until recently. Although my wife and I have been shopping on numerous occasions for new furniture, for one reason or another, we never could seem to agree on a set that we could both be happy with. This went on for several years until finally, just a few months ago, we found a set we could both agree on.

The big day came when the furniture movers delivered our new furniture. The old set was taken down to the basement so we could have a place to sit while we are down there with our children, and the new set took the place of the old set in our family room. Wow! I couldn't believe the difference it made, and neither could other family members and friends when they came over. I wouldn't be at all surprised if they were thinking to themselves something like, "It's about time we got rid of *our* old, junky furniture." I can't say that I would blame them if they did, because that's exactly what I think now when I go downstairs into our basement and see that old furniture myself. If your furniture is as old as ours was, take my advice and move it to the basement, give it to charity, or throw it out! Don't stop there either. Select some decorative lamps and end tables to go with the new furniture as well in order to really dress up your home.

Once the new furniture is in place, it's time to complement it with various types of wall hangings. All kinds of beautiful pieces are available including wall sconces, artwork, family pictures, and decorative clocks. Be patient and take your time when shopping for these pieces. Don't settle for the first cheap piece of framed artwork you see. Instead make it your mission to find the piece or pieces that will enhance the beauty of the new furniture you just purchased.

Finally, you can really add color and life to a room by placing potted plants in strategic locations throughout your house. With so many realistic, artificial plants available, you don't have to be a gardener to enjoy plants in your home. Not only do plants add color to a room, but they also help to balance the way it looks and feels. To properly balance a room, plants should be evenly placed in the room where it is devoid of furniture.

For example, an empty space in the corner between the couch and the love seat is a good place for a plant. Part of properly balancing plants in a room includes ensuring that they are the right height. A couch that is only waist high, for example, and that has a six-foot tall armoire beside it should be balanced by placing a plant in between the two that is taller than the couch and shorter than the armoire. Once again, rather than going overboard by using too many plants, be selective in their placement so that your house doesn't end up looking like my neighbor's, who has plants covering, what seems like, practically every square inch of her house.

Impact value: ★★★★★★ Strong. The impact value of updating your furnishings and decor is strong for two reasons. First of all, the proper balance of furnishings, plants, and decor can help freshen up any home and help prospective buyers to feel good about what they are seeing. If the buyers like what they see and are comfortable in your home, they are more inclined to purchase it. The second reason is that because we are talking about the return on your invested dollars, in this particular case, you get the benefit of having your home show better and sell for top dollar, as well as the added benefit of getting to take your beautiful furnishings with you after your home is sold!

56: CEILINGS

Although you may not initially think there is much that can be done to improve the ceilings in your home, there are actually several options available that can enhance their appearance and give rooms a dramatic look. First of all, depending on when your house was built, the ceilings may have had a cellulose material blown on them rather than being taped, floated, and painted. This type of ceiling has been referred to as a "popcorn ceiling," or as an "acoustical ceiling." If you've never seen a popcorn ceiling before, there's a reason they're called popcorn ceilings. It's because after the cellulose material is sprayed on and has had a chance to dry, it takes on a fluffy appearance much like that of popcorn.

Although popcorn ceilings were very popular in the 1960s and even into the 1970s, they are rarely used in new construction today. Because popcorn ceilings are largely obsolete and outdated, if your home has this type of ceiling, I recommend bringing it up to date by having the cellulose material removed.

One potentially serious matter, however, that you should be aware of before removing a popcorn ceiling is that it may in fact contain asbestos, a health-hazardous substance known to possess cancer-causing agents. As long as asbestos material remains undisturbed, it usually does not pose a health threat. So just because a house has an acoustic ceiling does not mean that it is life threatening. Asbestos contains tiny particles that can become airborne when disturbed. When airborne they pose the greatest threat.

Before attempting to remove an acoustic ceiling, you should have it tested to determine whether or not it contains any asbestos material. If it does, I strongly recommend contacting a representative from the Environmental Protection Agency, or EPA, to determine the corrective measures that should be taken to properly remove it.

Once you have successfully removed the cellulose material from the ceilings, or if the ceilings in your home didn't have any to begin with, there are several ways to create what is known as a "textured" ceiling by making patterns on them. For example, drywall mud can be "stomped" on ceilings with a mop or similar device to create a variety of patterns, including swirls, star bursts, and just plain splotches.

Drywall mud can also be applied using a special sprayer to create what's referred to as a "knockdown" ceiling. The mud is initially sprayed on the ceiling, and the excess is then "knocked down" using a wide plastic or metal tool to scrape the excess part of it off. One of the most important aspects of texturing a ceiling is to make sure the mud is applied evenly and consistently. Whether it is stomped or sprayed doesn't really matter. What counts is ensuring that it's applied evenly.

I recall when one of the houses we built had the entire ceiling textured with a spray application. Our crew used the knockdown technique throughout the whole house to give it an upscale, textured look. After the crew had completed their work, it was decided that a portion of the kitchen would be bumped out by another four feet. Unfortunately, when it was time to match up the two ceilings, it was extremely different to do so.

The crew that had sprayed the majority of the house before the bump out was added was not available to come back and match the new section to the original section. We ended up spending quite a bit of time and money finding another crew who could match the patterns across the two ceiling sections so that they blended together properly without any noticeable difference. Ideally, it is best to completely spray an entire room or house all at the same time so that you don't encounter a problem similar to the one we did.

Another great way to dress up a ceiling is by painting it a color that is different from the walls in the room. The most common color for ceilings is white, or ceiling white. Using a white ceiling in a room with walls painted a different color, usually a darker color, sets up a contrast between them that can help the room to show exceptionally well.

Impact value: ★★★ Moderate. The impact value of this home improvement is moderate due to the somewhat higher cost of the improvement relative to the benefit it provides. Having an acoustic ceiling removed, especially if it has asbestos fibers in it, can cost several thousand dollars. Texturing a ceiling is not very expensive during new construction because there is no furniture or flooring to worry about getting dirty. Once you're settled in, however, and have a house full of furniture, the cost goes up significantly primarily as a result of the additional time required to cover and protect everything from the overspray.

57: MIRRORS

We're all familiar with those infamous words uttered by the wicked queen in *Snow White and the Seven Dwarfs* as she looked into the mirror and asked, "Mirror, mirror on the wall, who is the fairest one of all?" The queen's vanity was not to be satisfied, however, because the magic mirror announced that it was Snow White who was the most beautiful. The evil queen then resorted to deceit and treachery in an attempt to snuff out the life of the lovely Snow White, only to see her efforts foiled by the kiss of a handsome prince.

Mirrors have a long history of being used as both household items and as items of decoration, such as for wall hangings. Some of the earliest mirrors were mirrors that were held by hand. Mirrors that were large enough to reflect a person's entire body did not appear until the first century AD. Handheld mirrors were adopted by the Celts from the Romans and, by the end of the Middle Ages, had become common throughout much of Europe. They were typically made of silver, although polished bronze was used as well. Later in the twelfth and thirteenth centuries as fabrication methods improved, mirrors were made from glass that had a metallic backing.

From the late seventeenth century onward, mirrors and mirror frames played an increasingly important part in the decoration of rooms. Early frames were often made of ivory, silver, ebony, and even tortoiseshell! Skilled craftsman often hand-carved elaborate frames that were part of a complete set. The tradition of incorporating a mirror into the wall space above the mantel and fireplace was established about this time.

Just as mirrors were used above fireplaces centuries ago, they often remain the focal point above them now. As I write these very words, it is a cold and wintry day outside with snow on the ground and I am comfortably seated in my favorite chair in our family room enjoying the warmth of the fireplace. Above the fireplace hangs a large mirror trimmed with a beautiful gold frame. The mirror is just as much a focal point as is the fireplace, and the two compliment each other quite well.

It wasn't until later in the nineteenth century that new and more cost effective techniques of mirror production led to the wide increase in their use. Not only were they incorporated into pieces of furniture, such as wardrobes and sideboards, but they were also used extensively in decorative designs for public places. By the end of the twentieth century, rare was the home or public building that could be found without mirrors.

Today mirrors are utilized in a variety of artful and creative ways to enhance the beauty and character of homes. Because they are reflective devices, mirrors can easily help brighten a room by taking the existing light and reflecting it back into the room. If you happen to have a room that is on the shady side of your house and therefore doesn't get much light, you may want to hang a mirror in it to help capture a portion of the little light that is available. Buyers prefer houses, and rooms in them, to be bright and cheery, not dark and dreary.

If you have a particular room in your house that feels small, try hanging a large mirror on one of the walls. Mirrors will help make a room seem larger than it actually is, once again because of their reflective nature. If you want the room to appear even larger, try hanging two mirrors in it at opposite ends. This will cause light to bounce back and forth between the two in an eternal and seemingly endless path providing an illusory effect which will magnify the room and help it to feel large.

Mirrors are available today in practically every shape and size you could possibly hope for. While there are the more traditional rectangular shaped mirrors, there are also mirrors that have rounded tops, or take on various other patterns such as ovals and circles. Whatever your needs are, you're sure to be able to find one to match them, and if for some reason you can't, most glass and mirror companies can custom make one to suit your needs. Keep in mind also that there are all sorts of decorative mirrors with various styles of frames that can be purchased at discount stores, hardware stores, and furniture stores.

Impact value: ★★★★ High. The impact value of this home improvement is high. The use of mirrors to decorate homes has been in practice for centuries. A mirror's ability to brighten a room or a home due to its reflective nature will enable potential buyers to feel good about the cheery atmosphere that prevails there.

58: FIREPLACES

The use of fire for heating purposes has been around for thousands of years. The fireplace was developed as a method of containing fire so that it could be used for the purpose of heating indoor rooms. The first fireplaces were hearths, recessed into the walls of houses and buildings, with short flues that reached up into the air above, enabling them to breathe. Fireplaces with chimneys, rather than flues, that reached high enough above the roof of a house or building to provide sufficient air for the fire were introduced during the twelfth century. The same design is still used today.

The useful heat given off by a fireplace is a function of direct radiation from the burning fuel, as well as from indirect radiation from the hot sidewalls and back wall. Fireplaces are not at all efficient in their use of fuel as it is estimated that fully 85 percent to 90 percent of the heat from a fireplace is lost in the combustion gases that go up the chimney and out into the atmosphere. Fireplaces today are included in modern homes primarily for aesthetic reasons rather than for thermal efficiency and function.

There are several different types of fireplaces available for homeowners to choose from. Two of the most common types are wood-burning fireplaces and direct-vent fireplaces. Wood-burning fireplaces were prevalent for many years and continued to be up until the last decade or so. The primary source of fuel for a wood burning fireplace is, of course, none other than wood. The main benefit of using this type of fireplace is that a homeowner does not have to rely on any outside source of fuel or power to operate it. As long as you have chopped plenty of wood for the season, or have purchased precut logs from a supplier, you can operate the fireplace without having to worry about power or energy failures.

One drawback to using a wood-burning fireplace is that it must continuously be fed logs to keep it going. Furthermore, a convenient area to store the cut wood is needed, preferably an area that can be kept dry. In addition, an occasional stoking is also required to keep the embers burning hot. Another item of concern is the smoke given off and the odor it can create in a house, especially if the fireplace is not ventilated properly. To properly vent this type of fireplace, however, requires that the flue be almost fully opened, reducing in turn its heating efficiency. Finally, the ashes that accumulate in the firebox must be removed periodically.

Wood-burning fireplaces are most commonly made from brick, although fireboxes can also be used. To add this type of fireplace to an existing house can be done, but doing so is somewhat costly. Fireplaces are most often located on an exterior wall, usually in the family room. Although a freestanding fireplace can be erected in the center of a room, for example, it is much more costly to do so, in large part due to the additional brick work required. A concrete pad must first be poured to support the weight of the brick, after which masons are called in to build the fireplace, complete with chimney. Depending on the size of the fireplace and the height of the chimney, a wood-burning fireplace can cost anywhere from $2,500 to $10,000 or more.

Unlike a wood-burning fireplace, a direct-vent fireplace uses natural gas as its primary fuel. Direct-vent fireplaces solve all the problems inherent in wood-burning fireplaces. For example, no logs are needed to feed the fire because it burns natural gas, which means no storage area is needed to keep logs either. There is also no need to clean out the ashes because there aren't any ashes to clean out. Furthermore, because wood is not consumed, there are no unpleasant odors given off from smoke. Natural gas is completely odorless. Direct-vent fireplaces are also much more efficient than wood-burning fireplaces.

Finally, direct-vent fireplaces are more convenient, especially the newer models. Once a direct-vent fireplace is lit, it stays lit and requires no additional attention. It continues to burn until it is turned off. Most of the new models are wired to a wall switch, so turning the fireplace on and off is no more difficult than turning on a light. Some models even come with options such as a fan motor that blows the warm air out into a room, and also a remote control making it easier than ever before to run and maintain a fireplace.

Installing a direct-vent fireplace is much easier and also much less expensive than an all-brick, wood-burning fireplace. The average cost of having a direct-vent fireplace installed ranges from about $1,500 to $2,500 depending on the brand, style, and options chosen. After selecting an exterior wall (interior models are also available), a hole is cut and the firebox is mounted. Because they are lightweight, no concrete pad is required to support them. Also, as the name implies, this type of fireplace vents directly out of the back of the firebox with a fan, so no chimney is necessary, saving potentially thousands of dollars.

Impact value: ★★★★ High. The impact value of this home improvement is high. Fireplaces are not only exceptionally visible, but they are also popular among homeowners. In addition to providing aesthetic value, they provide warmth and comfort as well.

59: WINDOW COVERINGS

Window coverings are essential to presenting your home in its most favorable light. Speaking of light, the function of window coverings is twofold. First, they are designed to control the amount of light that enters into a room, and second, they serve to beautify and enhance the appearance of the room. As such, window coverings provide both a functional purpose as well as an aesthetic one.

Window coverings are available in an almost innumerable variety of types and styles, including drapes, curtains, blinds, and shades. Each type serves to address the issue of controlling light and providing a unique decorative quality. Drapes, for example, are typically found in more formal rooms such as in a living room. They are designed to run the full length of the window, usually extending from the top of the window frame down to just a few inches above the floor.

Although drapes are designed to serve the functional purpose of helping to control light, once they are hung, they are usually left in place, leaving the responsibility to another type of device, such as blinds. There are just as many types and styles of blinds as there are drapes. Miniblinds, for example, made from lightweight metal and typically one inch wide, were especially popular throughout the 1970s and 1980s. However, their popularity began to wane as wider blinds took their place.

While miniblinds are mostly made of lightweight metal, wider blinds are made from either wood or a composite material. The wider style blinds are commonly two inches in width and provide excellent light control. In addition, they are available in almost any color, but white, off-white, or a light bone color tend to be some of the more favored choices because they are neutral colors and will go with almost any furniture. Your safest bet is to stick with the neutral colors, especially if you're preparing your home for resale.

Vertical blinds are often used to cover a larger window area such as a door opening. For example, if your home happens to have a sliding glass door off of the kitchen or breakfast room area, vertical blinds can be used to cover the large area of glass. The blinds can be left drawn across the window or door, but rotated to allow light to enter if desired. If the door is used during the day when the kids are coming in and out, for example, vertical blinds can be drawn fully open to provide easy access. Vertical blinds are normally three inches to four inches wide and come in a variety of colors, some even having decorative patterns on them. This style of window covering, especially for larger areas, is a popular choice among homeowners today.

Curtains are most often used in less formal rooms such as the kitchen, bathrooms, and kids' bedrooms. Like drapes, because they too provide more of a decorative function than a light controlling function, they are usually hung over a set of blinds. Curtains add color and life to a room, especially to the wall they hang on. Without curtains, a wall with lots of windows and nothing but blinds to cover them seems to just blend together. Curtains help break up the appearance of a wall by giving it variety and color, and by so doing, improve the overall appearance of the room they are in.

Window shades are another favored choice among homeowners. Like blinds, shades can also be used with drapes and curtains. Roller shades, which are the most common type of shade, are available in various degrees of thickness so as to allow some light to filter in, or to block it out altogether. Other styles of shades are three dimensional and collapse much like an accordion does. They also have the ability to be raised from the bottom up, or from the top down. This is especially useful in a bathroom where you want to allow light in. If the shade is raised a foot or so from the bottom up, for example, privacy must be sacrificed for light. On the other hand, if the shade is lowered a foot or so from the top down, no privacy is given up and the light is allowed to shine freely in.

Impact value: ★★★★★ Strong. The impact value of this home improvement is strong due to the ability of window coverings to greatly improve the appearance of a home relative to their cost. Depending on the size of a house, the number of windows that need to be covered, and the type of coverings selected, the cost of this home improvement will range from approximately $1,000 to as much as $7,500.

60: ODORS

Just a couple of evenings ago, my wife and I, along with our three sons, drove through the McDonald's drive-through for a snack, just as millions of Americans do each and every year. My sons and I ordered ice cream cones, while my wife opted for a healthier snack, a bowl of chili. I'm not a big chili fan to begin with, but on this particular evening, the aroma given off by the strong spices in the chili were too much for my olfactory glands, or to put it more directly, the odor from the chili made it difficult for me to enjoy my ice cream. Even though it was cooler that evening, I found it necessary to roll down the windows so I could finish my treat.

This simple experience demonstrates just how powerful the sense of smell can be, as well as how powerful odors can be. I suppose it had something to do with the fact that she was eating a salty and spicy snack while I was eating a sweet one. It's kind of like putting the positive end of one magnet up against the negative end of another magnet. The two magnets repel each other.

Odors in a house can have a similar effect on prospective buyers, especially if they are unpleasant. Just as opposite poles of a magnet repel each other, so do bad odors repel buyers who may be interested in your home. The larger issue at hand is how to determine what distinguishes a pleasant odor from an unpleasant one. For example, the aroma given off by hot chili is a pleasant odor to my wife, but a rather unpleasant one to me. You're probably asking yourself at this very moment what could possibly be wrong with me. Imagine, a guy not liking chili. The answer is, I don't know, but my wife thinks I'm predisposed from birth not to like certain foods, chili being one of them.

As a general rule, rather than attempt to ferret out differences between pleasant and unpleasant odors, your best bet is to maintain an odor neutral environment. An odor neutral environment is one where you can't detect any odors at all. One of the main problems with this, however, is that it is often difficult for people to tell when they have an odor in their own home. This is because people become accustomed to certain odors and to them, those odors begin to smell perfectly normal. Over time, they can even become unnoticeable, and therefore odor neutral, to them because they are so normal.

Let's look at an example. An individual who has smoked some form of tobacco everyday for the past 20 years is unlikely to detect the strong odor of smoke and nicotine when they enter into their home because they have become so accustomed to it. It's the way their house smells, and their house smells normal, at least to them. A nonsmoker, on the other hand, entering into that person's house will immediately notice the odor and will quite possibly even find the odor to be repulsive.

If you're a smoker and you're trying to sell your house, you may have a problem, at least selling it to a nonsmoker, unless you take proactive measures to eradicate any and all odors from your home. This includes changing the air filter in the air-conditioning system, keeping the air circulating as much as possible, and allowing fresh air from the outdoors to flow through when the weather permits. Because carpeting and furniture can absorb odors, you'll also want to call a cleaning service that specializes in cleaning carpets and upholstery.

Air fresheners and deodorizers may also be helpful, especially if sprayed shortly before a buyer comes to see your home. Be careful not to overdo it though. It's kind of like the guy you know down the hall at the office who always wears too much cologne. He thinks he smells great, but everyone else is keeping their distance.

Another major type of odor to be aware of is caused by pets. Pet odors include a dirty or musty smell from good old Spot himself, because he hasn't had a bath since the day he was born, as well as from urinating and defecating in any place other than where he is supposed to. It is the latter of these two that can really create problems. If a pet has routinely taken care of business on the family room carpet, for example, the carpet and the pad underneath it may need to be replaced. Once urine soaks into an absorbent material like carpeting, it's difficult at best to remove the odor, especially if it's been in there for a while. These unpleasant odors can potentially diminish the value of a home unless they are removed.

Other problem odors include musty or moldy smells from leaky basements, foul odors from backed up or leaky plumbing, and smoke from a wood-burning fireplace. Water leaks in a basement can generally be repaired without too much trouble, depending of course on the severity of the leak. Plumbing odors are often caused by a wax ring around the base of a toilet that is not sealing as it should be, or perhaps from a sink trap that is not operating properly. Common causes for fireplace odors include not having the flue open far enough while the fire is burning, and the accumulation of ashes in the firebox. These are minor problems and are usually fairly easy to resolve by either making the repairs yourself or by calling the appropriate professional.

Impact value: ★★★ Moderate. The impact value of making this home improvement is moderate. Although removing unpleasant odors if they exist is vital to being able to successfully sell a home, prospective buyers expect a home to be odor neutral. In other words, they expect it to be free from any unpleasant smells. Although buyers will not reward sellers by paying more for a house that doesn't smell bad, they will in fact punish them by paying less for a house that does smell bad. Furthermore, in keeping with the central premise of this book that visibility adds value, odors, or the lack of them, are not visible and therefore do not add value. The opposite is true in this case because the presence of them can actually diminish value.

61: ATTIC AND WALL INSULATION

You may think that having a super-insulated home would be one of the top selling features and would therefore significantly increase its value. Believe it or not, although living in a home that is insulated well will certainly increase its level of comfort, it will not have a great impact on the value of the home. Buyers are more interested in paying for what they can see, as well as what others can see, than they are for what they cannot see. So while there is a direct benefit derived by having a home that is well insulated, it is not one that most buyers are willing to pay extra for. That isn't to say that some buyers will not pay extra for additional insulation, because some certainly will, but our experience in the new home industry shows overwhelmingly that buyers will not pay extra for additional insulation.

When the Symphony Homes company was first formed, our homes were built with virtually every conceivable aspect of energy efficiency taken into consideration. We included additional insulation in both the walls and the attic, used high-efficiency furnaces and water heaters, and used name-brand windows that are well known in the industry for their insulating qualities. We built these items into the cost of our homes, meaning of course that we had to charge more than our competitors did who were selling comparable homes without these features.

We then heavily promoted the cost saving benefits of our homes thinking that because we were the only builder including these items in our houses as standard features, buyers would surely beat a path to our door. As it turns out, they didn't. When our sales agents told buyers about the many cost saving benefits of our energy efficient homes, they all commented about what a great thing that was. We discovered, however, that although they thought it was a great thing, they weren't willing to pay extra for it. Buyers chose instead to save money up front by purchasing lower priced houses from our competitors.

As a builder of fine quality homes, we were faced with a dilemma. We could either continue to offer only the type of product that we believed in and go out of business, or alter our product to adapt to consumer preferences and survive, and possibly even thrive. We made the decision to remove all of the more expensive energy efficient equipment, but to still make it available through options and upgrades that buyers could purchase if they chose to. We then lowered our prices to more effectively compete with other builders. Shortly after making this strategic shift in the marketing mix of our pricing, product, and promotion, sales of our new homes began to increase. The positive change in sales was gradual at first, but sales began to increase as our promotional efforts had more time to take effect.

If you're planning on staying in your home for several years and comfort is your primary concern, then you may very well want to increase the amount of insulation, especially if your home was built prior to 1970 or so when energy prices weren't much of a concern. Adding insulation to an attic and to exterior walls will no doubt reduce your monthly utility bills, as well as increase the level of comfort in your home. In addition, a house that is insulated well will help to maintain a more even temperature throughout it and also decrease the flow of any drafts that may have been present.

In an existing home that already has insulation in the attic, I prefer to blow in any additional insulation as opposed to using insulation batting. Cellulose is a common fiber material used for insulating both attics and walls and is blown in using hoses and a large blower. It is especially effective at filling in any voids or empty spaces, such as in between ceiling rafters in the attic. Moreover, to add insulation to existing walls, blowing it in is the most cost effective way to do it. Cellulose fiber is blown into the wall by cutting one inch holes into the top of the wall in between each and every wall stud and then using a small hose to fill the cavity that exists between the studs. Once all of the exterior walls have been filled with insulation, the holes must then be plugged, patched, and painted. If your house needs painting anyway, this would be the ideal time to insulate the walls.

Impact value: ★★ Low. The impact value of this home improvement is low because any additional resale value derived from insulating a house is also low. Remember the key to adding value is visibility. Because prospective buyers cannot readily see what is behind the walls or in the attic, very little value is attributed to making this home improvement. Furthermore, as seen, Symphony Homes empirical data supports this assessment.

8

INTERIOR ROOMS
AND COMPONENTS

62: FOYER AND ENTRYWAY

Because the foyer, or entryway, is one of the most important places of a home, it should be in showroom condition. When guests come to visit you at your house, the foyer is the first thing they see when entering into your home. It's where you greet them, take their coats, and help them to feel welcome. Because the entry sets the tone for what prospective buyers will see throughout the entire home, it's important to create there a strong and positive first impression.

Flooring is an important element in creating a favorable first impression in the foyer. The most common choices are vinyl, hardwood, or tile, such as ceramic and marble. Carpet, on the other hand, is seldom used in the foyer because when guests first enter into a home, they are coming in from the outside where the ground may be wet from rain or snow. If carpet were used, it would quickly become soiled and either have to be cleaned or replaced periodically.

Vinyl flooring offers an attractive low cost alternative to carpet and is much more durable. In addition, if it gets wet or dirty, it can easily be wiped clean. Hardwood is one of the most preferred choices among homeowners today. In fact, it is so popular that our company includes it in the entryway as a standard feature in every home we build. Hardwood flooring is available in a variety of colors as well, providing homeowners with a diverse selection of beautiful flooring. Finally, tile offers yet another alternative to homeowners with the most common selections being ceramic and marble. Tile is extremely durable, easy to clean, and is available in many colors.

Other suggestions for improving an entryway include placing various decorative pieces in it for color and accent. For example, a small, rich looking throw rug or piece of carpet placed at the door provides color as well as a place for guests to wipe their feet. Hanging decorative art or pictures of the family on the walls are another great way to add color. Finally, placing a plant in the corner by the doorway, perhaps on a stand or pedestal, not only adds color, but breathes life into the room as well.

Impact value: ★★★★★ Strong. The impact value of this home improvement is strong because the entryway is highly visible and is the first thing prospective buyers will see when they enter your home. The costs to make the suggested improvements are low relative to their impact on value.

63: STAIRWAY

A number of years ago, I built a house for my family that had the most magnificent stairway you could imagine. It was a spiral stairway that curved out and up toward the exterior portion of the home. Natural light flowed in through its tall, narrow windows illuminating the stairway by day, and casting a soft, moonlit glow by night. The banister and spindles, which were made of solid oak and had to conform to the spiral shape of the stairway, were meticulously crafted by hand over a period of several days. When the house was finally completed, the spiral stairway, breathtaking and majestic in its appearance, was unquestionably the focal point of the entryway. That house was the only home I ever lived in that had a spiral stairway, but to this day, it remains my favorite.

Whether your house has a spiral stairway or not, you can do several things to improve its beauty and appearance. For example, many houses with stairways in them are built without any spindles or banister. In their place is what is referred to as a "half-wall" or a "short-wall." A half-wall is just like any other wall in your house, except that it is half the size. It is built using 2 × 4 studs for framing and then covered with drywall. There is no banister and no spindles. A handrail is instead attached to the half-wall, which is then painted. Because the drywall is both hung and painted along with the rest of the house, there is very little additional cost, if any.

As a builder, I know that cost is the primary reason for this type of construction. It is much cheaper to build a half-wall, attach some drywall to it, and then paint it, than it is to build a system incorporating railing and spindles. Depending on what type of handrail and spindle system is used and whether or not you try to install it yourself, the price per foot ranges from $50 per running foot to as much as $200 per running foot. Our company installs a high quality oak system that averages about $125 per running foot.

When we tell homeowners the price, their initial reaction is often one of shock. After we explain the process to them, however, they understand why it costs as much as it does. First the oak materials must be purchased. Then the railing and spindles must be properly installed by a skilled trim carpenter. Finally, it must all be stained, and then finished with a lacquer or polyurethane. Although the process is time consuming and expensive, the finished product is far superior in appearance to a half-wall.

A stairway can also be trimmed with end caps. End caps are typically made of oak and go on the outside edge of each step. They are designed to complement a railing and spindle system. So just because the stairs have spindles and railing does not mean they will also have end caps. Often spindles that run down to each step have carpet around them rather than being fastened to an end cap. Carpet looks okay around spindles, but using end caps helps to really set them off.

Impact value: ★★★ Moderate. The impact value of this home improvement is moderate because the stairway and its railing are highly visible relative to the high cost to install it. While a hand-rail made of oak featuring spindles and end caps can really beautify a stairway, the cost to install it is expensive. Depending on the type of materials used, cost can easily range between $100 per linear foot and $200 per linear foot. For example, 30 feet of railing for stairs and an overlook at $150 per running foot would cost $4,500.

64: LIVING ROOM

When I was a young boy, the average house was much smaller then than it is today. Most homes did not have a separate living room as they do today. If you were fortunate enough to grow up in a home that had a living room, that was probably the one room in the house in which you weren't allowed to play. If your parents caught you in there, more than likely they promptly escorted you out. My boys can attest to this, because that's exactly what happens to them!

Living rooms are typically more formal than all the other rooms in the house, with the exception of perhaps the dining room. While the rest of the house may have toys or books or clothes scattered about, the living room remains clean. In many homes, the living room often goes unused except when company comes to visit—adult company, that is. I don't know who first came up with the name "living room," but the name is really a misnomer because we rarely "live" there.

Having established what a living room is, there are several things you can do to improve it's appearance. Let's start with the walls. This is one room where you can get away with a little more dramatic color, often somewhat darker than the rest of the house. An alternative to painting is wallpaper. Many rich and elegant wallpaper patterns are available to choose from. Once the walls have been taken care of, you may want to consider painting the trim around windows and door an accent color, usually a bright white. If your living room does not have crown molding in it, I recommend having it installed and painting it white also.

Next come the window treatments. Drapes are the most common type of window treatment used in living rooms because they have a more formal appearance. There are a variety of ways to hang them to create different effects, and many types of decorative rods are available from which to hang them. You'll then want to begin filling in the room with furnishings such as a couch and wing chairs, coffee tables, and lamps. You may also want to include a larger piece that will serve as the focal point for the room, such as a baby grand piano. An alternative to a piano is a curio cabinet from which collectibles such as small porcelain statues or items made from crystal can be displayed. Of course, your living room has to be large enough to accommodate larger furniture. Be careful not to overfill the room, but instead strive for a balanced look.

Your living room is now ready for several types of accent pieces. Hanging decorative art work such as paintings is a good place to start. Using medium to wide gold frames will create a more formal look. The living room is a good place to hang family photos as well. Various types of small, decorative pieces such as collectible figurines can also be placed sparingly about the room. Be careful not to overdo it so the room doesn't appear cluttered. Finally, plants can be used to add color and life to any room and are a good way of filling in voids, for example, in between a sofa and a wing chair. Be sure to use plants of the appropriate size and height to achieve the proper balance in appearance. If you don't have a green thumb, artificial plants work just as well and don't require the attention live plants do.

Impact value: ★★★★★ Strong. The impact value of this home improvement is strong because the living room is highly visible and the cost to improve it is low relative to its impact on value. After entering into the home, the living room is one of the very first rooms seen because it is usually located at the front of the house. In addition, many of the living room improvements can be taken with you after the house is sold, in particular, all of your furnishings, wall hangings, and plants.

65: DINING ROOM

Like the living room, the dining room is also most often used as a formal room. Home improvements for this room are similar to those of the living room. Starting once again with the walls, they, too, can be painted darker and with more dramatic colors. If you prefer, wallpaper with beautifully designed patterns can also be used. One thing that is often done differently from the living room, however, is the application of a two-tone effect. For example, the upper half of the walls is painted a darker color, or wallpaper is applied to them, while the bottom half of the walls is painted either a satin or semigloss white. The two colors are separated with chair railing, as it is referred to, which is simply molding attached to the wall at a wall height of approximately three feet or slightly less. Molding can also be used in the bottom portion of the wall in the area painted white to create decorative patterns. The results can be quite remarkable, and the best part of all is that it costs very little to do.

Primary furnishings in this room should naturally consist of a dining room table and chairs. Dining room sets are almost always more formal than the breakfast room set used for everyday eating. A decorative centerpiece, such as a vase with a plant in it, makes a nice accent piece for the table. A china cabinet or hutch is also commonly used to complement the formal dining room set in which china and dinnerware can be displayed.

Lighting for dining rooms often consists of a formal chandelier centered above the table. Wall sconces, which is lighting mounted to the wall rather than to the ceiling, can also be used to complement the chandelier. Framed art, such as oil paintings, are another important part of decorating a dining room. Finally, like the living room, use plants that are the appropriate size to fill in the voids and bring color and life into the room.

Impact value: ★★★★★ Strong. The impact value of this home improvement is strong because the dining room is highly visible and the cost to improve it is low relative to its impact on value. After entering into the home, like the living room, the dining room is one of the very first rooms seen because it is usually located at the front of the house. Finally, many of the dining room improvements can be taken with you after the house is sold, in particular, all of the furniture, wall hangings, and plants.

66: KITCHEN

Next to the family room, homeowners spend more time in the kitchen throughout the day than any other room in the house. As families, we gather together in the kitchen to eat, to pray, to visit, and even to play games. We also work together to prepare meals, and then to clean up after we're done eating. As we work together in a concerted and unified effort, we are building relationships and strengthening family ties. The kitchen is without a doubt one of the most important rooms in the home.

Having established the importance of the kitchen, it is also important to recognize the value of making home improvements to it. Whether your kitchen just needs a little sprucing up or a complete makeover will depend largely on how old it is. If your kitchen is more than ten years old, there's a good chance that it will need a complete makeover, or very close to it. Because cabinets, countertops, sinks, and appliances are ever evolving, it can be a real challenge to keep pace with the current trends.

You can do several things to improve your kitchen. Probably the most prominent feature of a kitchen is the cabinets. Kitchen cabinets built 20 years ago tended to be made from darker woods and had few design features. Today's cabinets are much more stylish, offer more features, and are usually made from lighter colored woods such as maple or oak. Some cabinets are even all white in color. In addition, the doors on newer cabinets are usually more decorative with features such as trim around them and inset panels. Some even have crown molding across the top, providing an attractive accent.

According to data compiled in 2002 by the National Association of Home Builders, one of the most popular of all new home features that was considered by homeowners to be a "must have" was a kitchen island. I have lived in houses without a kitchen island before, but after living in one with an island, it would be difficult, if not impossible, to ever go back to a house without one. Islands are the perfect place for storing larger pots and pans, pizza dishes, and utensils as well as for providing additional working space in the kitchen. It also makes a great place to serve from. For example, whenever we have friends and family over for dinner, all of the food is arranged neatly on the island. This gives us more room at the dinner table and also allows guests to take whatever portions of food for themselves they prefer.

Countertop styles and materials, which were more fully discussed in Section 52, are also constantly changing and improving. Even if you decide not to replace the cabinets, updating the countertops will significantly improve the appearance of a kitchen. A fresh coat of paint or new wallpaper can do wonders for your kitchen as well. Finally, don't forget about the lighting. Some older homes may have a simple, small light fixture with a single incandescent bulb in it. I recommend replacing an older fixture like this with perhaps a florescent light fixture that will more fully fill the kitchen with light. You can also use accent lighting above the sink, for example, and also above and below cabinets to help create a soft glow at night.

Impact value: ★★★★ High. The impact value of this home improvement is high because the kitchen is highly visible and one of the most used and lived in rooms in the house. Although the cost to improve a kitchen can vary from as little as a few hundred dollars to as much as $40,000 or even $50,000, its impact on value is strong due to the importance of this room.

67: APPLIANCES

Remember the once popular, but now very dated, coppertone brown, harvest gold, or avocado green colored appliances? If you still own any of these ancient relics, give them to charity or throw them out! I suppose if they are still in good condition, you might also be able to sell them to an antique dealer, but don't get your hopes up. Because appliances are rather large and prominent in appearance, it only seems natural that they would be quite expensive. Quite the opposite is true, however. Replacing the appliances in your kitchen is one of the easiest and least expensive home improvements you can make. Within as a little as a day or two of making your selections, you can outfit your kitchen with new appliances featuring the most current colors, styles, and features.

I remember buying my very first refrigerator over 20 years ago and paying about $1,000 for it. It was an average sized refrigerator with nothing special about it with the exception that it did have a built-in ice maker. At the time, $1,000 was a lot of money and worth about twice what it is now. Today that same refrigerator can be purchased for about $650, even though the dollar isn't worth as much as it was then. This phenomenon is not only true for kitchen appliances, but it is also true for the entire electronics industry. These improvements in pricing are primarily a function of advances in computer technology allowing manufacturers to achieve increases in their level of operating efficiency.

Due to its large size, the refrigerator is the most noticeable of all the kitchen appliances and is the one I recommend replacing first. Before running out to buy a new refrigerator, however, be sure to measure the opening in your kitchen because refrigerators vary widely in both height and width. You also want to be careful about buying an oversized model because it can make the kitchen feel smaller than it really is. I suggest buying a moderately sized unit with double doors, an ice maker, and a water dispenser. Some models provide more advanced features on the control panel, but my experience has been that they are seldom used and only add to its cost. The cost of replacing a refrigerator is modest and generally ranges in price from $500 to $2,500.

The next most prominent kitchen appliance is the stove or range. While most older ranges had electric coils on the top for cooking, these have largely been replaced by sleek looking glass top ranges that hide the coils underneath the surface. This provides the user with more useable working space as well as a safer surface from which to work. Stoves are almost always complemented by either a range hood or a microwave oven built in above it. I personally like using a glass top stove with a microwave above it. Installing the microwave above the stove is a more effective use of space because it replaces the range hood and frees up more space on the countertop. Believe it or not, glass top stoves can be purchased for as little as $350 while a quality over-the-range microwave can be purchased for as little as $200.

Like the other appliances, tremendous advances have also been made in the quality and function of dishwashers. I remember growing up as a young boy when the only dishwasher we had in our home was me and my brothers and sister. The duties were divided equally among us. While one of us washed the dishes, another rinsed them, and then another dried them, while yet another put them away. Although at the time I wasn't particularly fond of doing the dishes, I sometimes miss those times of old because I remember the lessons of responsibility and working together that were ingrained within me and that are now important for us to teach our own children. New dishwashers range in price from as little as $200 to as much as $1,000. For about $400, you can buy a very nice model with everything on it that you really need.

Impact value: ★★★★★ Strong. The impact value of this home improvement is strong because kitchen appliances are highly visible. The cost of making this improvement is low relative to its overall impact on value. For as little as $2,000 you can replace all of the major appliances in your kitchen with the latest and greatest in both style and functionality. Furthermore, you'll recoup about half of that when you move because most people take their refrigerators with them. Before purchasing any appliances, I suggest reading the reviews in *Consumer Reports* magazine to determine which models offer the best, most energy-efficient product for the best price.

68: PANTRY

According to data compiled in 2002 by the National Association of Home Builders, a walk-in pantry was listed as one feature that was considered to be a "must have" for new home buyers. If your home doesn't have a large pantry area, don't despair. You may be able to build one by enclosing a corner or section of your kitchen. This will, of course, depend on how large your kitchen is now and what kind of space you have to work with. Even if you don't have enough room to enclose a corner in your kitchen, you may be able to enclose a section of a room adjoining the kitchen. A door can then be installed in the wall of the kitchen providing access to your new pantry!

Because the primary purpose of a pantry is to store food items, it should be designed to facilitate maximum use of shelf space. Shelving should be installed from the top of the pantry all the way down to the bottom, leaving a foot or so at the floor for the lowest shelf to store larger items. Whether you already have an existing pantry or you are building a new one, be careful not to overfill it to the point of looking cluttered. It's okay to have a well-stocked pantry as long as it is neatly organized and doesn't make the storage space look smaller than it actually is. Over time, a pantry may end up with a little bit of everything in it, much of which has no business in there to begin with. Clean out the junk and neatly organize your pantry!

Lighting is another important element to consider in the pantry. Check to be sure that the bulb you are using there is at least 100 watts. If the light fixture has two bulbs in it, they should be at least 60 watts each, providing a total of 120 watts of light. Don't be penny-wise and pound-foolish by trying to get away with one 40-watt bulb thinking that you are saving money on the electric bill. The pantry should look bright and cheery, not dark and dreary! A 40-watt bulb will not only make it look dark and dreary, but it will also make the room look smaller than it really is. You want the pantry to look as large as possible, especially to prospective buyers.

An alternative to incandescent lighting is florescent lighting. You may have visited a model home before and observed florescent lighting in the pantry. Builders use this type of lighting because it floods the pantry with light causing it to appear bright and clean and, most importantly, larger than it really is. Some florescent lights used in pantries even have a switch in the door so that when it opens, the light turns on automatically. Most buyers react by saying something like, "Wow, that's neat," or "I like that!"

Impact value: ★★★★★ Strong. The impact value of this home improvement is strong due to its low cost relative to its affect on value. Although a pantry is not as visible as other rooms in a house, it is one of the most desired features in new homes today. The cost to improve an existing pantry is minimal, and the cost to add one is not much more.

69: FAMILY ROOM

Out of all the rooms in our home, the family room is my absolute favorite. This is the place where our family gathers together everyday to enjoy each other's company. This is the room that my wife, my children, and I spend many evenings together enjoying the warmth of the fireplace, as well as the warmth of each other's company. We play games, put puzzles together, and read from our favorite books. We laugh together, counsel one with another, and most importantly, strengthen the bonds of love that unify our family, thereby enabling us to enjoy the fruits of peace and happiness in our home.

One of the most important things that can be done to improve the appearance of a family room is to simply make sure the furniture in it is up to date. In Section 55, I shared the story of what an amazing difference replacing the 20-year-old furniture in my home made. Even though at the time all I did was replace the furniture, it gave our family room a whole new look. The best part about buying new furniture is that while it greatly improves the appearance of the room, when you decide to sell your house, you get to take it with you!

One of the things that makes our family room so enjoyable is the fireplace. If your family room doesn't have a fireplace, you can easily have one installed. Direct-vent fireplaces are very affordable and do not require a chimney. The easiest place to install a direct-vent fireplace is to center it on an exterior wall. You also can install one in a corner if centering it on an exterior wall doesn't work. Direct-vent fireplaces are also available in free-standing, two-sided models as well. After installing the fireplace, you'll want to properly finish it by having a mantle and surround mounted, of which there are many beautiful styles to choose from.

Another way to improve your family room is to improve the view of the outdoors by replacing or adding windows. Depending on the age and style of a house, often it is built with only the minimum number of windows in it. If your house happens to back up to the woods or a lake or some other type of scenery, you may want to replace the smaller windows with one larger one, for example, to improve the view from within the home. To ensure that the view is not obstructed, consider having a large picture-type window put in, which is essentially a large sheet of heavy duty plate glass with no cross members.

Years ago, wood paneling was commonly used on the walls in family rooms to create a semiformal look. Unfortunately, much of the paneling that was used was quite dark and made the room feel small and uninviting. There are a couple of ways to brighten the room up, however, with the first being to remove the paneling altogether and then patching and painting the walls behind it as needed. Another way is to sand the paneling down and strip away any clear lacquer finish used on it. You can then use a paint roller on the sanded area along with the rest of the walls to blend it all together.

Impact value: ★★★★ High. The impact value of this improvement is high because the family room is very visible. It is also where homeowners, their families, friends, and guests spend a good portion of their time each and every day.

70: STUDY OR HOME OFFICE

It wasn't that long ago that a study was a room in the house that consisted primarily of a desk and a comfortable chair, one or two bookshelves filled with books, and perhaps a telephone. The quickly changing pace of technology over the last decade, however, has had a profound effect on the way families use their homes, and in particular, as they relate to a study, or *home office* as this room is now commonly referred to. Today's home offices are no longer equipped with just a telephone, but also high-tech devices such as computers, printers, fax machines, copiers, and scanners. In addition, the U.S. Census Bureau reports that four out five of these homes have access to the Internet.

These changes in technology have had a direct impact on the way we use our homes. According to International Data Corporation (IDC), their company is "the premier global market intelligence and advisory firm in the information technology" industry. In a study conducted by IDC, entitled the *U.S. Home Office Forecast, 2002–2007,* senior research analyst Merle Sandler estimates the current number of households with a home office to be 32.5 million. Furthermore, forecasts for the number of home offices indicates a continuation of this rapid growth adding approximately one-half million new home offices per year. In a separate study conducted by the U.S. Census Bureau, an estimated "54 million households, or 51 percent, had one or more computers in the home in August 2002, up from 42 percent in December 1998." Both of these studies reflect the significant changes taking place in the way rooms in a home are used today.

With the demand for home offices on the rise, you should seriously consider converting one of your spare bedrooms into one if you haven't already done so. Whether or not you use it that regularly is not relevant. The important point to remember is that you are trying to add value by making certain improvements to your home. In this case, converting a bedroom or other room into a home office allows prospective buyers to see how they, too, can utilize the room as a study or home office.

Turning a bedroom into a study or home office requires that it first be properly wired to provide for telephone service, a fax machine, and high-speed Internet access where possible. I recommend having an electrician install a dedicated high amperage line to the room as well to provide plenty of power for computers and office equipment. A 20-amp line run to an outlet with four receptacles built into it is usually sufficient to power all of your office equipment.

Once your home office has been properly wired, the next step is to select attractive office furniture to fill the room without overpowering it. If the furniture is too large, it will make the room feel small. So be careful not to overdo it. After the furniture is in place, it's time to begin neatly arranging a computer, telephone, and other office equipment in the room. Office supplies should be stored neatly on shelves or behind cabinet doors. Finally, I recommend hanging some type of appropriate framed pieces on the walls such as high school or college diplomas, awards, and perhaps motivational posters.

Impact value: ★★★★ Strong. The impact value of this home improvement is strong due to the dynamic increase in demand of home offices in recent years relative to the low cost of making the recommended improvements. In addition, the majority of your investment will be recovered when you sell your home because you are able to keep the office furniture and equipment when you move.

71: POWDER ROOM

Most powder rooms are located on the main living level of a house and are often used by family and friends when they come to visit. Powder rooms are seldom designed to be a full bath.

They are considered a half bath, meaning that they do not provide an area such as a shower or tub to bathe in. As such, powder rooms are usually small and often resemble the size and layout of a closet.

If the powder room in your home is relatively small and designed around a tight space, you can do several things to make it feel bigger and give it a new and modern look. First of all, if the sink has a cabinet under it, you can replace it with a pedestal-style sink that will open up the area underneath it leaving more space for leg and foot room. Taking the cabinet out will mean giving up a little bit of storage space, but the result is well worth it. One cautionary note, however, is that before you remove the old sink and cabinet, be sure to look at the flooring around it. If, for example, it is vinyl, there's a good chance the vinyl was cut and laid after the cabinet was installed, meaning there will be an exposed area once the cabinet is removed. Removing the cabinet in this instance would also require that the flooring be replaced, which may not be a bad idea, depending on the condition of the flooring.

Another improvement you can make with smaller bathrooms is to replace the door on it, which may swing to the inside or outside, with a pocket door. A standard door, especially if it opens into the bathroom, can make areas that are already small feel even smaller. A pocket door, on the other hand, is only visible when it's closed. When the bathroom is not in use, the door can remain neatly tucked away in between the walls where it is out of the way. Pocket doors provide easier access into and out of the bathroom, especially in areas where space is limited.

One of the most important improvements you can make to a powder room is adding a window that will provide lots of natural light into the room. If your powder room is located on the interior of the house, it may not be possible to do. Almost any powder room with an exterior wall, however, should be able to accommodate a window. Next, if the light fixture in your powder room is the older style with an elongated glass enclosure, throw it out!

Don't bother to call antique dealers on this one either. Even they won't want it. Bathrooms should be bright and cheery, not dark and dreary, so take a good look at your powder room to ensure that it has adequate light.

Finally, you can use various decorative items, such as small pictures and art work, to brighten up a powder room. Look for something tasteful to hang on the walls rather than trying to be cute or funny. You'll also want to have some type of air freshener working behind the scenes to help mask any odors that might be present. Everything about a powder room should be designed to be inviting. Enlarging its available space, providing ample light, hanging decorative art work, and using a scented fragrance can all work together to make your powder room welcome your guests.

Impact value: ★★★ Moderate. The impact value of this home improvement is moderate because the powder room is a smaller room which is less visible. In addition, very little time is spent in the powder room, unlike other rooms such as the kitchen and family room.

72: UTILITY ROOM

The utility room, or laundry room as it is more commonly known, is the one room in the house we try to spend as little time in as possible. Imagine that. This is a room we actually try to avoid, unless, that is, you are one of the rare individuals who enjoys doing the laundry. If you're like most people, however, you do the laundry out of pure necessity. If you like wearing clean clothes, you either do the laundry or hire someone to do it for you.

Regardless of your preference for wearing clean clothes, you can make several improvements to at least make life somewhat easier for you while you're in the laundry room. Depending on the size of your utility room, you may be limited in what you can do. If the room is a full-sized, walk-in laundry room, your options to improve it are many.

In my home, our family has formed the habit of removing our shoes when we enter into the house from outside. This habit was developed out of a desire not to track snow and ice into our home during the winter. It became so natural for us after removing our shoes all winter long that before we knew it, we were taking them off in the spring, then in the summer, and finally in the fall. Because the laundry room is located right by the door leading in from the garage where we usually enter, the natural thing to do is to leave our shoes on the floor by the door. That worked okay for a while, until we each began leaving more than one pair of shoes by the door. Before we knew it, there were so many shoes on the floor it made it difficult to walk without tripping over someone's shoes. The problem was solved easily enough by hanging two inexpensive shoe racks behind the door in the laundry room. That's all there was to it.

Another place in the laundry room that often gets overlooked for storage space is the area above the washer and dryer. Cabinets can be purchased at your local hardware store that can then be mounted on the wall over the washer and dryer. Shelves can also be hung in place of cabinets, but while shelves leave all of your items exposed, cabinets help conceal them. If your utility room is large enough, there may be space elsewhere on the walls where additional cabinets or shelving can be hung.

Installing a separate washtub in the laundry can also be quite handy. A washtub is similar to a sink, only it is much larger. Washtubs are typically made out of a white plastic material and can be purchased for as little as $100. If you want something a little nicer than a washtub, a standard sized sink bowl mounted in a countertop can be installed on top of a cabinet, similar to what you would find in a bathroom. Like the other cabinets in the laundry room, this will provide more storage space for detergents and other types of cleaners.

If you haven't noticed by now, a common theme runs among these home improvement ideas for your laundry room: organization. Keep the clutter off the floor and stored neatly behind cabinet doors or on shelves. Don't spend a lot of money decorating a utility room. Yes, its okay to hang a few small pictures if you like, but only if there's enough room left on the walls after you're done hanging the shoe racks, cabinets, and shelves.

Impact value: ★★★ Moderate. The impact value of this home improvement is moderate because people spend as little time in the laundry room as possible. Although the laundry room serves a very important purpose by providing a place to wash and dry clothes, it should not be the focus of your home improvement efforts.

73: BEDROOMS

There's a good chance that when you purchased your home, however long ago it may have been, the walls in all or most of the bedrooms were painted white or off-white. After a while, all white walls begin to look pretty boring. One of the easiest and least expensive ways to improve a bedroom is to decorate it using a theme, which usually means adding color to the walls.

Adding color to the walls doesn't mean they have to be painted. For example, you can use wallpaper on the lower half of the walls with a border in the middle used to separate the upper half of the walls from the lower half. The kids' room in one of our model homes was designed around a Tonka trucks theme with exactly that type of design. The bedroom walls were first painted a light sky blue, then the lower half was covered with wallpaper with Tonka trucks emblazoned across it, and finally the two were separated by a border featuring big yellow Tonka trucks.

Decorating the walls in this particular bedroom was only the starting point. Because the room was designed as a place for children to play while their parents visited with a member of our sales team, we provided a toy box full of Tonka trucks for them! In addition, Tonka books, Tonka toys, and Tonka pictures were sprinkled throughout the room. Finally, we used a children's bunk bed set and covered the beds with none other than matching bedspreads.

For the master bedroom, while a theme can be used, the method should be centered more around the furnishings than decorating the walls with wallpaper and border. That's not to say that you shouldn't add color to them, but rather to say you should focus more on the furniture in the room. I recommend purchasing a bedroom set with all matching pieces that will complement the furnishings in the rest of your home. Whatever you do, don't mix and match the bedroom furniture. For example, you may have bought a bed ten years ago, and then added a night stand five years later that your Aunt Sally gave you, and still later, added a dresser from the nineteenth century you picked up at an antique auction. I know, I know. You really love all those pieces and you can't bear to part with them. I suggest placing them somewhere else and spending the money on a complete set that not only matches, but will also tie in with the rest of the furniture in your home.

Impact value: ★★★★ High. The impact value of this home improvement is high because the cost to make the improvements is low relative to their impact on value. Furthermore, any money invested in bedroom furnishings will be recouped because it will be taken with you when you sell the house.

74: BATHROOMS

Although people don't spend a very high percentage of the day in the bathroom, it nevertheless ranks among one of the top improvements made by homeowners. Unlike the laundry room, which we try to avoid, the bathroom represents a place of refuge from the outside world, or even from family members, when an occasional break is needed. We can relax in a hot bath or take a cold shower.

In many new homes, the master bathroom in particular is designed to look and feel very luxurious. Depending on the size and layout of your bathroom, you may be able to make some of the following improvements. As a builder for Symphony Homes, we differentiate ourselves from our competitors by including several items as standard features in every home we build that would be considered upgrades in our market. This is true in our collection of smaller homes as well. For example, every home gets a double sink in the vanity rather than just a single sink. If you've ever had to share a single sink bowl with another family member, you know how nice it is to have your own. Two sink bowls allow one spouse, for example, to shave while the other spouse brushes her teeth.

Another standard feature we include in the master bathroom of our homes is a separate shower stall and garden tub. An oversized garden tub is provided for that rest and relaxation we all look forward to at the end of a long day. If you're in a hurry or just don't feel like taking a bath, having a large and spacious shower stall is the perfect alternative. If your home has a shower-tub combination unit installed in it, consider installing a separate shower and garden tub instead.

For a few hundred dollars more, you can also upgrade your new garden tub by adding jets and a pump. In addition, lavish faucets are readily available to further beautify your new tub. Matching sets for the sink and shower faucets are usually available, too. Oftentimes, a complete line of bathroom accessories such as towel and cup holders can be purchased to match the decor in the bathroom as well.

Another improvement you can make in the bathroom is to replace the lighting. Often the original lighting installed when a house is built is inexpensive strip lighting that looks inexpensive, or cheap. Most of the larger home improvement stores today carry a wide variety of decorative bathroom lighting that looks much nicer than the strip lighting found in many homes. If your bathroom happens to have a vaulted or raised ceiling, you might also consider hanging a ceiling fan with a light kit attached to it. Another option would be to hang a light fixture from the ceiling, possibly even a chandelier, designed to complement the rest of the decor in your bathroom.

Another popular feature in new bathrooms is ceramic tile flooring. While ceramic tile has been around for many years, its look and style have come a long way. The older style ceramic flooring was typically available in just a few of the basic primary colors such as white or green. It was also smaller in size such as either a one-inch tile or a four-inch tile. Today's ceramic flooring is available in many beautiful colors, many of which have decorative patterns. In addition, many of the newer styles are larger in size with eight-inch tiles and twelve-inch tiles being quite common.

Impact value: ★★★★ High. The impact value of this home improvement is high. Although the cost of improving a bathroom can add up quickly, bathrooms continue to remain near the top of the list among homeowners as one of the most preferred home improvements.

75: CLOSETS

Have you ever invited guests over to your home for a get-together only to find yourself scrambling at the last minute to clean up? If you're like most people, one of the first places that you think to store things in is the closet. It doesn't take long for a closet to get filled up and to start looking cluttered, especially if it is small to begin with.

You may not think having cluttered closets could possibly make that much difference when selling your home, but buyers coming through will want to know where their stuff is going to go. If they see a closet that is bursting at the seams, they may reconsider their buying decision, thinking the house does not have adequate storage space.

Rather than create the impression that the closets in your home are too small, you can create just the opposite impression with just a few simple and inexpensive steps. You'll want to start by removing everything from the closets. Don't try to improve the closets all at once because then your house will look like it's in a shambles as well. Instead, you'll want to start with one of the main closets that buyers are most interested in, such as the one in your master bedroom.

After emptying the closet, take a close look at the condition of the paint in it. Is it bright and cheery or dark and dreary? If it's been a while since the closet has been painted, it may be due for a fresh coat. Be sure to use a light color of paint such as white, even if the bedroom is painted a different color. Brighter and lighter paint colors will help the closet to look bigger, newer, and cleaner.

If there is a light in the closet, it is most likely an ordinary light fixture giving off only minimal lighting. If you're trying to conserve energy, this isn't the place to do it. I suggest either replacing the low wattage bulb with a brighter one or replacing it with a new fixture such as a florescent one. A two-foot to four-foot florescent light fixture will flood the closet with light and help it to look larger as well.

After painting the closet and upgrading the lighting in it, I recommend installing some type of closet organizing system. There are a several types available that vary in price. In the new homes we build, our company installs shelving made of wire or metal racks painted white. We include as a standard feature lots of extra shelving that provides homeowners the ability to organize clothing, shoes, and whatever else they may keep in their closets. You can also purchase inexpensive, prepainted wood shelving that is easy to install, along with different types of drawer organizers to go with it. Finally, there are a number of companies that will install more expensive custom shelving and organizers designed specifically to fit your closet needs.

Now that the shelving and organizers have been installed, it's time to put everything back into your closet. The most important thing here is not to put as much back into the closet as you took out of it. I know that may be a hard concept for some readers to grasp, but there's no point in emptying the closet to begin with if you're going to jam it full of stuff again. Okay, so now what do you do with all of the extra stuff? I suggest taking all of the clothing that has hung in your closet for several years and hasn't been worn for one reason or another and donating it to a local charity. After all, if you're not going to wear the clothing, why not give it to someone who will? Furthermore, your donation may even be tax deductible. On a final note, after you've decided which clothes you're going to keep, be sure to take your time when putting them back into the closet. There's no point in cleaning it out and organizing it if you're only going to clutter the closet up again by carelessly tossing things into it.

Impact value: ★★★★ High. The impact value of this home improvement is high because the cost of making it is low relative to its visibility. Although prospective buyers will not see the inside of your closets unless they look in them, you can bet that anyone who is seriously interested in buying your home will open every closet door in it at one time or another. If buyers see a dark and dreary closet cluttered with stuff, they may feel like the closet is too small. However, if your closet is bright and cheery with newly installed organizers and shelves, they will most certainly appreciate having what appears to be plenty of room.

76: BASEMENT

If you've ever lived in a house that has a basement, you probably already know that converting it into livable space is a cost effective way of adding value to your home. Because a basement already has a floor, walls, and a roof or ceiling, finishing it off costs much less than other types of home improvements, such as building a room addition on to it. Building a room addition is much like building a house, with most of the same steps required. With a basement, however, because the basic structure is already in place, the basement can be finished at a fraction of the cost of a separate room addition.

I know from personal experience that there are many ways to finish a basement, some of which are superior to others. Before spending any money, I recommend that you clearly identify your purpose for improving it. If you're hoping to earn a return on your invested dollars, or at least to break even, then don't try to cut corners by doing everything yourself unless you really know what you're doing.

An acquaintance of mine decided he could tackle the job of finishing a basement on his own and set out determined to do so. The only problem was, however, is that my friend didn't even own any tools, nor had he ever. Thinking that wasn't a big deal, he promptly set out to buy his very first toolbox, complete with tools. Okay, now that he had some tools, it was time to learn how to use them. If this story sounds like an exaggeration to you, trust me, it isn't. You can probably imagine what his so-called "finished basement" looked like when he was all done. While I have to give my friend credit for taking on this job himself, I really can't give him any credit for using his home improvement dollars wisely.

The one bit of advice I can offer to you is this: Don't be like my friend. If you truly have the skills to frame walls, run electrical and plumbing lines, hang and finish drywall, install drop ceilings and light fixtures, paint walls, and finally, install flooring, then by all means, you may want to save yourself some money by doing the work yourself. While many people may have some of these skills, most people do not have all of them. One suggestion is to do the work you are comfortable with and hire the rest out. Finishing a basement is not an overnight process and can even take several weeks or months to complete. The bottom line is to not get in a hurry and don't try to cut corners. Instead, do the job right the first time around.

Impact value: ★★★★ High. The impact value of this home improvement is high as a direct result of adding living space in one of the most cost effective ways possible. One word of caution, however, is not to expect to get an equivalent dollar per square foot for your basement as you do for the rest of the house. It's a common mistake for homeowners to think they can spend $20,000, for example, on finishing a 1,000-square-foot basement, and thereby enabling them to automatically add $100,000 in value to the home. Most appraisal firms will include additional value for a finished basement, but once again, it typically will not be as much as the above-ground living space in the rest of the house.

77: ROOM ADDITIONS

Adding an addition to your home can be a very expensive endeavor. The cost of adding an addition can actually exceed the costs of building a house on a per-square-foot basis. This is due to the additional costs of tying in the new structure to the existing one. Throughout almost every phase of the construction process, each new system of the structure must be tied into the existing system. For example, both the interior and exterior walls, the plumbing and electrical lines, the roof, and the heating and air-conditioning systems must all be connected.

Because investing in a room addition is such a costly undertaking, you'll want to carefully examine the potential resale value of your home before doing so. The most important factor to consider in your analysis is the relevant size of your house compared to the other houses in your neighborhood. If your house is one of the smallest houses compared to those around you, then it may make sense to expand the size of yours by adding another room.

On the other hand, if your house is already one of the largest houses in the neighborhood, investing your hard-earned money to make it even larger would most likely yield negative returns.

Expanding the size of a house by adding on a room can actually cost more than the house's current resale value due to the difference between construction costs of 20 years ago and those of today. This holds true even after compensating for the cost savings in land. For example, if you purchased a 1,000-square-foot home 20 years ago for $30,000, the average cost per square foot at that time was $30 per square foot. Using an assumed annual growth rate of, let's say, 4 percent, the house would be worth a little over $65,000 today, or $65 per square foot. Depending on where you live, the cost of adding a room addition onto a house can easily exceed $100 per square foot. In this example, a 10′ × 10′ room addition (100 square feet) would cost $10,000, but may only be worth $6,500 at the time of resale. This illustration is not intended to serve as a hard and fast rule, but rather as an example of what you need to be aware of before taking on a major home improvement project such as this.

A less expensive alternative to an addition that is tied into the existing house is a sunroom or an all-seasons room. The cost of this type of structure is generally much less than that of adding on an actual addition that is designed to match your house. A sunroom, for instance, typically has exterior walls made of mostly glass reinforced with metal framing, unlike a full room addition that will have exterior walls made of vinyl or brick with insulation and drywall on the inside of them. Furthermore, the roof on a sunroom is usually a lightweight design and does not offer the protection or longevity that a roof with composition shingles on it.

While sun rooms are most often unheated and designed for milder climates, all-seasons rooms incorporate heating and air conditioning into their design. As its name implies, an all-seasons room can be used year round. It's construction is similar to that of a sunroom using less expensive materials, but it includes additional design elements for insulating the room. Both types of rooms, however, offer affordable alternatives to the more expensive room addition.

Impact value: ★★★ Moderate. The impact value of this home improvement is moderate due to the high cost of construction required for a room addition relative to its potential impact on resale value.

Part Four

STRUCTURAL AND MECHANICAL IMPROVEMENTS

C h a p t e r

9

STRUCTURAL

78: SLAB FOUNDATIONS

When it comes to foundations, and in particular, slab foundations, not much can be done in the way of what is typically referred to as a home improvement. Most improvements to foundations are not improvements at all but are instead repairs that result from cracks and settling. Although there is little you can do to actually improve an existing foundation, there are some things you should know before attempting to repair it.

Houses built in southern regions where the climate is not as cold are often built with a slab foundation. A slab foundation is essentially poured concrete that rests on one of three types of support systems. They include a traditional rebar system, a post-tensioned cable system, and a pier-and-beam system.

One common system is a cement slab reinforced with rebar, or steel rods. The traditional rebar system is considered to be a passive reinforcement system because it only provides necessary reinforcement as a slab is forced into tension, or, in other words, as it begins to shift or settle. The rebar acts to strengthen and support the concrete to keep it from shifting or separating, eventually resulting in what is commonly referred to as a "cracked slab." The rebar is not full proof, however, as separation and cracks can still occur over time, especially in areas where clay is present.

When I lived in the Houston, Texas area a number of years ago, it was not at all unusual to see a house with a cracked slab. It was so common, in fact, that many companies were built around the foundation repair business. I knew personally of several close friends and family members who had to hire their services due to foundation problems. I also owned a rental house once that had a foundation that needed to be repaired. A few years after that, I had a duplex under contract that developed foundation problems just before I purchased it. The seller was obligated to hire a company to repair it before we were able to close.

Another type of foundation system uses what is known as "post-tensioned cables." A post-tensioned cable system uses a series of cables made from strands of high strength steel, also known as "tendons," that support the concrete. Post-tensioned tendons are referred to as an "active reinforcement" system because the cables are effective as reinforcements even though the concrete may not be sagging due to a heavy load placed on it. The systems can be designed to have minimal deflection and cracking, even under a heavy load. When properly installed, post-tensioned systems can provide important advantages over a traditional slab foundation reinforced with rebar.

A third type of foundation system is known as a pier-and-beam foundation. A special auger is used to drill a series of holes into the ground approximately 12 inches to 16 inches in diameter and 8 feet to 10 feet in depth at key load-bearing points. A bell-shaped footing is then cut out at the bottom of each hole, providing additional stability. Afterwards, the holes are filled with cement and reinforced with rebar. After the piers dry, a slab foundation reinforced with rebar is then poured on top of the footings. The slab is said to "float" on top of the bell bottom piers.

Although pouring the required number of piers adds to the cost of a traditional slab foundation system, it can be well worth it because it significantly strengthens the foundation and will virtually eliminate any problems that stem from settling or shifting soil conditions. In fact, the foundation repair businesses I referred to previously use similar methods to level houses, with one major exception, that is. The yard must be dug up around the perimeter of the house where the holes are to be dug. Furthermore, if piers are required toward the interior portion of the foundation, the flooring in the house must be removed, and then holes must be bored through the existing slab. This repair process is very expensive and can easily cost several thousand dollars. It's best to spend a little extra and have the piers poured at the initial time of construction. In one particular home I built in Texas several years ago, I used a pier-and-beam system to support a large home that had a total of 52 piers. To my knowledge, that home has never had any foundation problems whatsoever.

Regardless of the type of foundation system a house has, a foundation that has settled or shifted is one problem that can be very costly to repair. In addition, houses with foundation problems are likely to have other structural damage caused by the settling. A close inspection of the interior walls will almost always show evidence of settling as the drywall will crack and separate. It's common to see small, hairline cracks in walls, especially around the seams, so don't be alarmed if you see small cracks such as these. If, on the other hand, you see large cracks running down the wall, you can almost bet the house has a foundation problem.

Impact value: ★ Weak. The impact value of this home improvement is weak because of the high cost to repair a foundation relative to its visibility. A slab foundation is not visible at all because it is covered with flooring. No one really cares what the foundation looks like underneath the carpet or linoleum. They do care that the foundation is in good condition, but this is a basic expectation. While a homeowner will not pay anything extra for a foundation that is in good condition, they will penalize the seller for a foundation that is in disrepair.

79: BASEMENT FOUNDATIONS

A basement foundation is in a sense very much like a pier-and-beam system with the piers poured so close together that they touch, resulting in a continuous wall, a basement wall. Just as piers are poured 8 feet to 10 feet in depth, so are basement walls. Unlike piers, however, basement walls are designed to rest on cement footings. Once the basement has been excavated, the foundation crew comes in and builds forms that are used to pour cement in for the footings. The footings are what support the basement walls.

Basement walls are typically of the poured type, meaning that a series of forms are built on top of the footings and then filled with concrete and reinforced with rebar. Most basement walls are poured to be eight inches thick. Our company, however, uses a ten-inch thick wall for an added measure of strength.

One of the chief concerns of properly constructing a basement is dryness. There are several preventive steps that can be taken when a basement is first built to help keep it dry. First, drain tile must be used around the perimeter of the footings to help channel water away. If you're not familiar with the term, drain tile is a perforated, corrugated plastic pipe laid at the bottom of the foundation wall and used to drain excess water away from the foundation. It prevents ground water from seeping through the foundation wall.

It is also recommended that a vapor barrier be installed between the ground and the basement floor to help keep moisture from penetrating up through the floor. A sump pump must also be installed to keep water from building up underneath the floor. Finally, the exterior of the basement walls should be water-proofed. Most building codes require only that they be damp proofed which is not as effective as waterproofing. The damp-proofing process uses a black tar-like substance that is mopped on the exterior walls, while the waterproofing process uses a synthetic rubber-like substance that is sprayed on and then dries forming a rubberized coating.

In preparation for selling your house, you should take time to thoroughly inspect the basement. Moisture-related problems are fairly common, especially in older homes. Look for cracks in the basement walls that may have evidence of leaking around them, such as staining or mildew. Leaks in the walls can also create a buildup of mold in the basement area, an issue which is becoming a major liability for some homeowners. These smaller cracks are easy to repair and usually just need to be sealed. Using a waterproofing membrane on the exterior of the walls when a house is built is the best way to eliminate this type of problem.

It is not at all unusual to observe hairline cracks in the basement floor or even in the walls. In fact, I don't believe I've ever seen one without some kind of small cracks. The basement floor in my own home is no exception. You don't need to be overly concerned about these types of cracks, because they are usually just surface cracks that do not go all the way through the floor or the wall. If the cracks are more severe, however, it's possible that some major repair work may be required. Just as houses built on slabs with foundation problems can be very costly to repair, so can houses built on basements with similar problems be costly to repair.

Impact value: ★★ Low. The impact value of this home improvement is low because of the high cost to repair a foundation relative to its visibility. This improvement is rated two stars rather than one star due to the fact that its visibility is greater than that of a slab, which is practically invisible. Nevertheless, just like a house having a slab foundation, a homeowner will not pay anything additional for a foundation that is in good condition, but will most certainly penalize the seller for a foundation that is in poor condition.

10

HEATING AND PLUMBING

80: FURNACES

Heating, ventilating, and air-conditioning systems, or HVAC systems, are related processes designed to regulate temperature conditions within a house for comfort. *Heating* an area raises temperature in a given space to a more comfortable level than that of the existing air. *Ventilating,* either separately or together with the heating or air-conditioning system, controls both the supply and exhaust of air within given areas. This helps to provide sufficient air to a home's residents and also helps to eliminate odors. Finally, *air-conditioning* designates control of the indoor environment, especially during warmer periods, to create and maintain a desirable temperature, as well as a comfortable level of humidity.

The heating process may be direct, as from a fireplace or stove in an individual room, or indirect, as in a central system in which steam, heated water, or heated air passing through pipes or other ducts transfers warm air to all the rooms in a house. The earliest heating system was simply an open fireplace used thousands of years ago. Various types of stoves were later developed by the ancient Romans, and stoves are still used in some parts of the world today. Central heating systems, which were developed in the 1800s, provide for one centrally located heating unit to warm an entire house. A type of centralized heating, using hot water, was used to a limited extent in Britain in the early 1800s, but the first successful central system, introduced in 1835, used warm air. This system subsequently came into extensive use in the United States.

The majority of homes in the United States today use some type of central, forced-air heating system that is powered primarily by a furnace. Most use either natural gas or heating oil. In a forced-air circulation system, a fan or blower is placed in the furnace casing which ensures the circulation of high volumes of air even under the most unfavorable conditions. Although the majority of houses utilize central heating systems, there are some older homes that still rely solely on space heaters. I remember one house I lived in as a young boy that had only one space heater in it to warm the entire house. I also recall how I used to stand with my back to it after coming in from the cold to warm my hands and body.

If your home does not have a central heating system with a furnace in it, I strongly recommend having one installed. There are several advantages furnaces offer over old-style space heaters and stoves. First of all, furnaces are much more efficient than gas or electric space heaters and will save you money on your heating bill. In addition, a central heating system provides a much more stable and even temperature throughout the house. Furthermore, the temperature can even be regulated on a room-by-room basis as needed by adjusting its vent control registers. Air filters are also built into each system to help ensure the cleanliness of the air. When combined with cooling, humidifying, and dehumidifying units, forced circulation systems may be used effectively for both heating and cooling. Finally, forced-circulation warm-air systems are very popular for residential installations, in part because the same equipment can be used to provide air-conditioning as well, which is yet another way these systems can save you money.

If your home already has a central heating system in it, but the furnace is more than 15 years old, you may want to replace it. To begin with, older furnaces are not nearly as energy efficient as newer systems. Many older furnaces were rated at only a 60 percent to 70 percent efficiency rating, meaning that as much as 30 percent to 40 percent of the energy generated is lost. Most newer systems today have a minimum energy efficiency rating of 80 percent, which is far superior to those systems built a decade or two ago. For an extra $1,500 or so, you can buy a furnace with a 90 percent to 95 percent energy efficient rating.

Another common problem older furnaces may develop are leaks within the system itself that can result in dangerous carbon monoxide gases being emitted into a home. Having your furnace checked annually by a licensed professional is the best way to stay informed as to its condition. As an additional safety precaution, carbon monoxide detectors are available at most home improvement stores. These detectors are easy to operate. They are simply plugged into an outlet, such as in a bedroom, and are left there to continuously monitor the quality of the air present. If carbon monoxide rises to an unacceptable level, an audible alarm sounds to warn you.

Impact value: ★★★★ High. The impact value of this home improvement is high due to its high level of desirability among homeowners. Although a central forced-air furnace system does not rank high on our visibility test, it's an important enough feature that prospective buyers will certainly inquire about it. My experience has been that most homeowners are satisfied with a system in good working condition that is not older than ten years of age. Be careful about investing additional money, however, on a 90-percent efficient or higher rated system because you may not be able to recoup the additional premium paid for it.

81: AIR-CONDITIONING SYSTEMS

At last! Winter is finally over, spring has arrived, and summer is just around the corner! It seems as if we can hardly wait for it to begin warming up. Why is it then, that when the temperature starts to rise, most people seek the comfort of indoor air-conditioning? We spend several months enduring the cold all the while hoping, waiting, and praying that the winter months will soon pass. It seems as though when summer finally does arrive, we can't wait to get cool again. It's an interesting phenomenon that after all these years I still haven't been able to figure out.

Whatever the reason, the fact remains that people want to be comfortable in the warmer months, meaning they want to be cool. Air conditioners provide them with the means to do so. As strange as it may seem to some people, however, not everyone has or needs an air conditioner. For example, most people living in the southern states such as Arizona and Texas could not imagine living in a home that doesn't have air-conditioning. For many families living in the northern states, however, an air conditioner is not always considered to be a necessity.

Having lived in both climates, I know from experience just how true this is. I spent the better part of my life living in the southern regions of Texas along the Gulf Coast where the humidity was exceptionally high. When high humidity is combined with high temperatures, it makes for an uncomfortable and sticky climate that causes even the bravest of souls to seek the cool indoors. Practically everyone I knew had central air-conditioning in their home, and depending on the size of their home, some even had what is known as "zoned air." A zoned air-conditioning system uses two or more separate air conditioners to cool the same house. For example, one unit is used to control the temperature downstairs while the other unit is used to control the temperature upstairs. All new houses in this region featured a central air conditioner as standard equipment.

When my wife and I flew up to Michigan to search for a new home, I was in for a real surprise. After locating a house that was still under construction, the sales agent representing the builder asked us if we wanted to add central air as an upgrade. "What do you mean by adding it as an upgrade," I asked him. "Don't all houses come with central air?" His reply was direct and to the point. "Not in Michigan they don't," he said. I couldn't believe what I was hearing. I was about to purchase a new home valued at over a half million dollars and the salesman had just told me I would have to pay extra for air-conditioning! That was the most ridiculous thing I had ever heard in my life. As it turns out, my wife and I made an offer on the house at full price but asked the builder to throw in the central-air unit at no additional charge, to which he agreed.

So there you have it. Two different regions, two different climates, and two completely different sets of needs. If your home does not currently have an air-conditioning system and you are thinking about installing one to add value to it, you must first consider the immediate market you are in. If, for example, you reside in one of the southern states such as Florida and almost everyone in your area has a central-air system and you are one of the few who do not, then I highly recommend investing in having one installed. Without this vitally necessary piece of equipment, you may otherwise have a difficult time selling your house. If, however, you live in one of the northern states such as Maine where the climate is much cooler and central-air systems are not common, then it may be better to hold off on installing a central-air system and perhaps to invest in an alternative home improvement such as new flooring or lighting.

Impact value: ★★★ Moderate. The impact value of this home improvement is moderate due to the wide range of needs among homeowners. The impact value of central air-conditioning units is higher in southern states where central-air systems are the norm and lower in northern states where they are not as common.

82: THERMOSTATS

If the thermostat in your home is more than a few years old, there's a good chance that it is the older style with the traditional dial on it. The temperature is set by adjusting the dial to the desired level. The temperature only changes when the dial is manually adjusted. If you want to turn the heat down at night to save money, you must make a mental note to do so before going to bed. Otherwise the temperature will stay set at the higher level. Once adjusting the heat downward, it stays at that level until adjusted again.

If you want to turn the heat up again the next morning when you wake up, you have to get out of bed while it's still cold to do so. Meanwhile, you still have to shave, shower, and dress while the house is warming up. Finally, by the time you have finished eating breakfast, the house has warmed up. Guess what? Now it's time to take off for work, so that means adjusting the thermostat back down while you are away all day to conserve energy and save on the heating bill. I think you get the idea.

Thermostats that have to be manually adjusted are soon to be relics of the past because they are quickly being replaced by newer programmable thermostats. A programmable thermostat allows the user to preset a series of temperatures by programming it in advance. The more common thermostats of this type typically provide a user with the option of programming four preset temperatures for the five weekdays, Monday through Friday, and then another four preset temperatures for the weekend, Saturday and Sunday.

So unlike the old-style thermostats that must be manually turned down before going to bed, programmable thermostats can be preset to automatically lower the temperature each night at a predetermined time. If you usually go to bed at 10:00 PM each night, for example, the thermostat can be preprogrammed to lower the temperature by several degrees starting at 9:30 PM, or whatever time you want it to. Then when it's time to get up in the morning, instead of having to shave and shower in a cold house, the thermostat can be preset to increase the temperature and turn the furnace on so it's nice and warm when you wake up. Running late for work and forgot to adjust the thermostat? No problem. Because you've already preprogrammed it, the temperature will adjust to the predetermined level and maintain it there until just before you return home from work!

Impact value: ★★★★★ Strong. The impact value of this home improvement is strong due to its low cost relative to its impact on comfort and energy efficiency. Although a thermostat is not as visible as many of the other features in a house, it is usually mounted on a wall in the family room, hallway, or a central point within the house where it will be seen at some point during the showing of your house to a buyer. A modern-looking, programmable thermostat mounted neatly on the wall will create a positive impression of the central heating and air system in your house, regardless of its age. Programmable thermostats can be purchased for less than $100 and can easily pay for themselves in a few short months by reducing energy costs in your home.

83: HOT WATER HEATERS

For the most part, hot water heaters sit in a basement or attic or utility closet and go largely unnoticed, until they go out, that is. When a water heater fails, it can do so gradually or all at once. If, for instance, the water heater is old and the tank inside it has rusted through, the water heater can fail instantly. When that happens, the entire family routine is disrupted because there is no hot water for shaving, no hot water for showers, and no hot water for the dishwasher.

If a hot water heater fails suddenly, you'll be hard pressed to find time to shop around for just the right kind or to compare prices. More than likely, you'll accept the recommendation your plumber makes, which will be the type he or she happens to carry. It's not so much that the plumber's recommendation will be a poor one, but it does help to know what your options are.

Water heaters are designed to use one of three types of energy—natural gas, electric, and liquid propane. Natural gas water heaters have under the storage tank a gas burner used to heat the water, unlike electric water heaters that use stainless steel heating elements inside the tank. Water heaters heated with liquid propane use the same burner system natural gas heaters use. Natural gas water heaters are by far the most fuel efficient and cost the least to operate. To save even more money, high-efficiency hot water heaters are also available. Although they cost a little more initially, a high-efficiency water heater can save homeowners money in the long run.

Water heaters range in storage capacity from as little as 30 gallons to as much as 80 gallons. The most common sizes are 40 gallons and 50 gallons. We generally install 50-gallon water heaters in the new homes we build because they are just slightly more in cost than a comparable 40-gallon water heater, yet they provide homeowners with an additional 10 gallons of hot water. The proper size of water heater to choose depends on the number of people living in the house, whether or not the house has a dishwasher or a washing machine, and on the number of bathtubs and showers present in the house.

Other water heater models are designed to make what is referred to as a "fast recovery." Their ability to reheat the water in the tank as it is being used is quicker than a conventional water heater. Fast-recovery models are ideal for those periods of time when several showers or baths are being taken at the same time, or one right after the other. For example, when a family wakes up in the morning and everyone wants to shower and get ready for school or work at the same time, a fast-recovery model will replenish the hot water quicker so that everyone gets to enjoy a hot shower.

Some models also have a self-cleaning system built into them that helps keep the water heater operating properly. Self-cleaning systems work by channeling water through a special inlet tube that keeps sediment from settling at the bottom of the tank. They are also effective at preventing the build up of lime. The primary benefit of a self-cleaning system is that it can extend the life of the water heater while at the same time ensuring that it operates at maximum efficiency.

Impact value: ★★★ Moderate. The impact value of this home improvement is moderate due to its low level of visibility. If you're getting your house ready for sale and the water heater needs replacing, I recommend purchasing a standard heater without all of the optional features, as that can increase the price significantly. A standard 40-gallon water heater, for example, can be purchased for as little as $250, while a high-efficiency heater can easily run $500 or more. If you're not planning on staying, save your money because prospective buyers will be happy just to see a new hot water heater, regardless of whether or not it is the most energy efficient model.

84: WATER AND SEWER LINES

Water and sewer lines are low on the list of home improvements because there isn't a whole lot that can be done to improve them, unless, however, they are not functioning properly. The most important thing you can do is to check them for proper operation. The plumbing can be checked by flushing toilets, inspecting underneath sink cabinets, and looking for leaky faucets.

With homes more than 20 years old, you'll want to make a special note to determine if the roots from mature plants and trees are causing any blockage. Recurring problems in the same line are usually symptomatic of root damage. Some older sewage lines are made of a clay-like material and when trees are planted nearby, the roots can actually grow right through the sewer lines, creating a blockage within them and causing the sewer system to back up.

I bought a house many years ago that was 40 years old or so, which I had purchased for rental purposes at the time. The house had one sewage line in particular that kept getting backed up. It cost me $75 every time the plumber came out to clear the line. As it turned out, the line had become obstructed with roots that had grown through it. I finally had the plumber dig up the line, which was made of clay, in the backyard and had him replace it with a new PVC line.

Another type of problem that can occur has to do with sewer lines running through a concrete slab type of foundation or through concrete driveways. The lines can get backed up if any settling or shifting of the concrete occurs. As the concrete settles, the sewer lines will crack and break. The separation in the line does not allow the sewage to drain properly and can also cause the line to back up.

In another house I purchased many years later, the driveway had a large crack in it due to settling. When I bought the house, I wasn't really too concerned about the crack because I thought I would have the driveway patched with cement. The repair turned out to be much more costly because the driveway had to be broken up with a jackhammer to replace what ended up being a collapsed sewage line running through it. Once the line was repaired, a new driveway then had to be poured. Because broken sewer lines can be difficult to detect and are much more expensive to repair, be sure to keep an eye out for any evidence of problems that can occur.

One of the most common improvements to water lines is the installation of filtration systems. Water filtration systems can be installed to filter water for the entire house or at individual faucets. Rural area homes that rely on wells for their source of water are especially dependent upon filtration systems. Well water often has in it an excess of minerals, such as lime and iron, that need to be removed. Filters must be maintained by checking them periodically and cleaning them as needed.

Impact value: ★ Weak. The impact value of this home improvement is weak due to in part to the low visibility of water and sewer lines. Most homeowners don't care what's behind the walls of a house just as long as everything works. Rest assured though that although homeowners are unwilling to pay more for improvements made to water and sewer lines, they will certainly penalize you for any lines that are not working properly.

85: KITCHEN AND BATHROOM FAUCETS

It was just this last Saturday that I spent the better part of an hour lying on my back underneath our kitchen sink to replace the faucet. The faucet, which was a designer white style, was only about four years old. The sprayer hose attached to it had developed a leak about a year ago and yours truly finally just got around to fixing it. Like most leaks, this one started out very slow with an occasional drip or two. Also, like most leaks, it got progressively worse until I finally did something about it. Nancy, my wife, had placed a small tray under the sink to catch the dripping water. At first the tray had to be emptied once a month or so. By the time I got around to fixing the faucet, however, she was emptying the tray every other day!

If your house is more than ten years old and still has the original, inexpensive, builder-grade faucets in it, they're probably due for a change, especially if you're thinking about selling soon. Using attractive kitchen and bathroom faucets throughout your house is an excellent way to dress it up. The selection of faucets used should be coordinated with the decor in the kitchen and respective bathrooms. Select faucets that complement and accent a room rather than detract from it. Faucets make a statement about your house. It's up to you to decide what they say.

There are a wide variety of faucets for both kitchens and bathrooms available to suit most anyone's needs. The old faucet I replaced on our kitchen sink was white and matched the white porcelain sink it was affixed to. The new one, however, is a much different style and is made primarily of chrome, but it is trimmed with white porcelain handles. Faucets are available with many different finishes including chrome, polished and antique brass, nickel, as well as a wide variety of colors. Most kitchen faucets also come with a sprayer hose to rinse dishes. Faucets vary widely in price ranging from as little as $20 to as much as several hundred dollars. If you're trying to get your house ready for sale, I suggest passing on the cheaper models and buying those that are a little nicer.

Impact value: ★★★★★ Strong. The impact value of this home improvement is strong due to its low cost relative to its impact on visibility. Kitchen and bathroom faucets become the focal point several times each day as dishes are rinsed and hands are washed. Be sure that focal point is an appealing one.

86: WHIRLPOOL TUBS

My family and I are members of a local fitness center that has a myriad of activities and equipment to suit most anyone's needs. The center has all of the traditional free weights and modern exercise machines, such as treadmills, basketball courts, rock climbing walls, and two, large year-round indoor pools. I personally enjoy an intense workout with the weights, along with participating in various martial arts activities. I'm not the kind of guy who is interested in getting "bulked up," but I prefer instead to strive for "muscle toning." The most enjoyable part of my workout, however, is not lifting weights. It's when I get home and relax in a nice, hot bath in our whirlpool tub. As I lay in the tub with a good book, the pulsating jets do wonders for my body, massaging every muscle and helping me to completely relax for a good night's sleep. Whirlpool tubs are unquestionably a terrific way to relax and soothe aching muscles and joints for anyone wanting to unwind at the end of a long day.

As a new homes builder, I can attest to the fact that whirlpool tubs are a popular feature among homeowners and are one of the most frequently requested upgrades. On average, approximately one out of two new homebuyers in our communities orders a tub with a whirlpool option. Many of those who do not order a jetted tub are on fairly tight budgets and are purchasing less expensive homes.

Whirlpool tubs come in a variety of shapes, styles, and sizes, each offering the same basic jetted action with minor differences. The water is circulated by a pump through lines, mixed with air, and returned to the tub to create the jetted action. Pumps range in size from ½ to 2 horsepower with some models offering variable speed options. The jets are typically designed using what is referred to as "specific point jets" or "fish hook jets." Tubs using the specific point jet system typically have more jets that are smaller in size and are designed to massage a specific point of the body. Tubs using the fish hook jet system typically have fewer jets that are larger in size and are designed to provide a gentler massage.

Finally, if you decide to add a whirlpool tub as a home improvement, be sure your existing hot water heater is large enough to accommodate it. Whirlpool tubs are usually deeper than standard tubs and therefore hold more water. As a general rule, a hot water heater should hold approximately two-thirds the amount of water that the tub will hold. For example, if the hot water heater you currently have has a 40-gallon capacity and you don't want to have to buy a new one, you'll want to limit the selection of your new tub to no more than 60 gallons in capacity.

Impact value: ★★★★ High. The impact value of this home improvement is high due to its high level of desirability among homeowners. As a new homes builder, our direct experience ranks jetted bathtubs high on the list of desired upgrades. Whirlpool tubs are attractive in design and styling and are the focal point of a master bathroom, which is where they are most commonly located. In addition to having aesthetic value, they also provide personal value by helping to relax the various muscles of one's body.

87: SINKS

Choosing the right sink, whether for a kitchen or a bathroom, can be a daunting task because there are so many different types and styles to choose from. For example, you can get an oval sink, or a round one, or even one that is shaped like a seashell. As a general rule, bigger is better. The more room you have in your kitchen or bathroom for a larger sink, the better off you'll be. Larger sinks, especially in the kitchen, provide more room to work with, or more room to stack dishes in, depending on how often you get around to loading the dishwasher.

Sinks are available in many different finishes as well. Stainless steel is one of the least expensive types available. Although they are easy to clean and very durable, scratches and dents are more visible in thinner stainless steel models. Furthermore, unless you really like the look of the silver colored stainless steel, for a little more money, there are much nicer looking sinks to choose from. Stainless steel is so common that it's a pleasant surprise to see a kitchen sink that isn't made of stainless. I suggest upgrading to something, anything, with a nicer finish and more color in it.

Cast iron sinks are also very popular and come in a variety of colors. They, too, are easy to clean and also resist scratches better than the stainless steel models. Furthermore, because they are made of cast iron, you don't have to worry about getting dents in them either. Cast iron sinks are slightly more expensive than stainless steel sinks, but they look much nicer and have better finishes. Although white is the most common color, there are many other colors to choose from.

Another popular choice used primarily for bathrooms is the sink made from cultured marble in precast molds. Cultured marble is a synthetic material that is poured into molds of various shapes and sizes, one of them being the seashell shape previously referred to. When new, the cultured marble is quite beautiful and does much to enhance the appearance of a bathroom. One primary drawback to it, however, is that because the material is soft and porous, it scratches easily and does not hold up to abuse very well.

In one particular home I used to live in, I hired a cleaning service to come in and clean the entire house, bathrooms and sinks included. The bathroom featured a double vanity with cultured marble countertops and sinks. As it turned out, the lady who cleaned them was unaware that special care must be taken when doing so. She used a cleaning product with a mild abrasive in it that completely ruined the countertops and sinks! Although she got them nice and clean, the countertops and sinks were covered with fine scratches that resulted in damage beyond repair.

There are almost as many styles and designs of sinks as there are colors to choose from. One popular choice is a pedestal sink. They are great for small spaces such as a small bathroom or powder room. However, they don't provide any counter space on top or storage space below. A vanity style sink, on the other hand, offers more counter space as well as storage space below. While they are perfect for larger bathrooms, such as a master bathroom, they do require more floor space and are therefore limited in use due to their larger size.

Impact value: ★★★★ High. The impact value of this home improvement is high due to its high level of visibility throughout the home. I recommend upgrading to a more colorful and stylish design to set your home apart from all those with the more common sinks, such as stainless steel.

11

ELECTRICAL

88: LIGHTING

The overriding philosophy of our company, Symphony Homes, is to provide customers with a quality built home backed by superb customer service at a great value. One of the ways we do this is by *not* skimping on the lighting packages that come with our homes. I've seen all too often brand new homes offered by other builders with the most basic of lighting packages installed in them. What many other builders fail to realize is that for just a little more money, they can actually purchase a very nice upscale lighting package for the entire home. Cheap light fixtures make the whole house look cheap. By simply increasing their lighting budget by another $300 to $500, these builders could greatly improve the way their homes show. Yes, you can spend a lot more money than $500, even for one light fixture, but you can also purchase very attractive lights for much less.

Lighting plays a vital role in the way prospective buyers literally see a house. If there isn't enough lighting, a house can feel dark and cold. If there is too much lighting, it may create a harsh effect and even make the house feel hot, especially in warmer climates or during the summertime. To create what I refer to as the Goldilocks effect, the lighting in a house should be just right. Remember the story of Goldilocks and the three bears? Goldilocks happened upon the three bears' house one day while they were away, only to discover three bowls of porridge on the kitchen table. After sitting down at the table, she first took a bite of Papa Bear's porridge, only to discover that it was too hot. Next she took a bite of Mama Bear's porridge, only to discover that it was too cold. Finally, Goldilocks took a bite of Baby Bear's porridge and was delighted to learn that it was just right, and she ate it all up.

To create an atmosphere in your home that is not too hot, and not too cold, but is just right, you need to adopt the Goldilocks method. This means selecting the proper mix of light fixtures to create an atmosphere that is warm and inviting, rather than cold and harsh. I suggest starting with the entryway, or foyer, in your home. If your home is a single story with a standard eight foot ceiling, then you don't have a whole lot of room to work with. On the other hand, if you live in a two-story home with a two-story entry, then you should have ample room to hang a light fixture that will really make a statement to your guests. In fact, if a prospective buyer comes to see your home in the evening after it is already dark, one of the first things they'll notice is the beautiful chandelier hanging in the entryway. Lighting such as this will help create a positive mindset for buyers even before they enter your home.

There are numerous chandeliers available that come in all shapes and sizes. I suggest asking the salesperson which light fixtures are the most popular and which ones they sell the most of, and then taking care to ensure that their recommendation matches the style and decor of your home. When selecting a chandelier for the foyer, you'll also want to be sure that its size fits appropriately with the size of your foyer. For example, if the entryway in your home is large and spacious, don't hang a tiny light fixture in it. The light fixture will get lost, and because it is so small, it will look cheap. On the other hand, don't try to hang a light fixture that is too large in a smaller foyer. The fixture will overpower the space and will detract from the way it should feel. Not too hot and not too cold, but just right!

If your home has a formal dining room, examine the lighting in it to determine whether or not it complements the style of furnishings in the room. If there's a formal dining room table complete with an armoire or china cabinet in it, the lighting should be formal as well. Chandeliers are probably the most commonly used light fixtures in dining rooms for two reasons. First, they are dressier and more formal than an ordinary light fixture, and second, they hang down from the ceiling at the appropriate height above the dining room table to provide light while eating.

To further enhance the look of a dining room, wall sconces can also be used. If you're not familiar with wall sconces, they are light fixtures designed to mount on the surface of a wall rather than hang from the ceiling. If your dining room is not already wired for sconces, you may have to hire an electrician to run the wires and mount the receptacles. Chandeliers and matching wall sconces often can be purchased as a set. So when you get ready to replace the lighting in your dining room, be sure to look for matching sets.

One often overlooked place that accent lighting can be used in a house is the kitchen. Most kitchens have plenty of overhead lighting in them, but they rarely have under-cabinet lighting. Under-cabinet lighting can easily be installed, provided there is an outlet or wiring nearby, by mounting florescent light fixtures under the cabinets. The best way to wire the lights, however, is by routing all of them to one or two switches. This allows you to turn on all of the lights from a central location rather than having to do so individually.

Finally, the same type of florescent lighting can also be mounted on top of the cabinets, providing soft accent lighting behind plants and other decor that may be on top of the cabinets. The kitchen in my house has both under-cabinet and over-cabinet lighting. In the evenings after we are through with dinner and are enjoying time together in the family room, we prefer to have the softer accent lighting rather than the harsher overhead lighting.

Impact value: ★★★★★ Strong. The impact value of this home improvement is strong because the cost of replacing light fixtures is low relative to their impact on value. Not only are the light fixtures themselves highly visible, but the effect they create, especially at night, is also very visible. When properly done, this effect can be exceptionally powerful and dramatic.

89: WIRING AND BREAKERS

Earlier in this book, I mentioned the house I bought that was built in 1903. Because the house was 100 years old, I was concerned about the electrical wiring in it. I decided to hire an inspector to have the wiring checked—as well as the rest of the house—to ensure that the wiring was up to current code. Because replacing all the wiring in a house can be expensive, it was important to know its condition before purchasing the house. As it turned out, the electrical wiring did in fact meet current code requirements, so the $335 I spent on the home inspection was well worth it to me.

Before putting your house on the market for sale, you'll want to be sure that the electrical wiring is in proper working condition. A simple check of outlets and light switches can tell you a great deal about a house's electrical condition. If they are working properly, chances are the system is okay. If you see any kind of flickering, however, I recommend having a licensed electrician check it for you.

Homes older than 30 years or 40 years tend to have more problems because breakers and switches do wear out. In some homes, the wiring may be so old that it will have to be completely replaced. Installing an entirely new electrical system can cost several thousand dollars, due in part to the fact that much of the wiring is run behind the walls of a house. The new wiring will either have to be "fished" or pulled through openings from the attic or basement if there are any, or cuts will have to be made in the plaster or drywall that will afterward have to be repaired and repainted.

Improvements to wiring primarily consist of updating old wiring as we have just discussed, as well as adding more capacity to existing electrical systems. Most houses are equipped with the minimum amperage circuit breaker box allowed by the electrical building code at the time of installation, usually 150 amps or less. In most homes a 150 amp circuit breaker box is adequate. However, improvements, such as building a room addition, adding a swimming pool, or installing a hot tub, may require more power than your breaker box is capable of. It may be necessary to install a larger breaker box, such as a 200 amp box, along with additional breakers and circuits.

Impact value: ★ Weak. The impact value of this home improvement is weak due to in part to the low visibility of the wiring system. Prospective home buyers expect that all of a house's basic mechanical and electrical components function properly. This includes its electrical wiring and circuit breakers.

90: SWITCHES AND OUTLETS

Depending on the age of your home, it might be time to update its light switches and electrical outlets. Older homes, for example, used an old style plug that has more of a rounded appearance while new plugs tend to have more of a square appearance. The old style plugs will definitely date a home. Furthermore, these wall outlets have often yellowed over the years and no longer have the clean ivory or white appearance they once had.

If the wall switches and electrical outlets in your home don't need to be replaced, you may still want to dress them up a bit with decorative covers. Less expensive covers include the type that are available at most hardware stores and come in various colors such as white, ivory, and brown. When using this type of cover to replace the existing ones, you'll want to make sure that they match the color of the switch or receptacle. In other words, don't use a dark brown cover with a white light switch.

The more decorative type covers can sometimes be found in discount stores in the hardware department, in hardware stores in the lighting or electrical department, or in specialty lighting stores. Designer covers are available to match most any type of decor. For example, there are antique gold covers made of brass to complement a traditional setting and bolder colors such as burgundy to complement a contemporary setting. Furthermore, there are all kinds of decorative covers for children's bedrooms including those in the shape of a race car, or a honey pot, or even a favorite action hero or cartoon character.

Finally, there are different types of switches other than the traditional off and on switch. For example, there are rotating switches that are used as dimmer switches or fan control switches. In addition, there are switches used for similar purposes that slide up and down. There are even switches equipped with a remote control device, allowing you to turn a fan or lights on from the comfort of a chair. Finally, you've probably seen at one time or another the commercials featuring a little old lady who claps her hands together to turn a light on or off with a "clap on, clap off" type of switch.

Impact value: ★★★★ High. The impact value of this home improvement is high because the cost of replacing covers and receptacles is low relative to their visibility. Modern or decorative switch and receptacle covers are very visible because they are on almost every wall in a house. Furthermore, covers for light switches are even more visible because they are just below eye level.

PUTTING IT ALL TOGETHER

12

CASE STUDY ANALYSIS

91: PRIMARY PRINCIPLES OF VALUATION

In Part Five, we explore the culminating effects of combining multiple improvements to a home to determine their potential impact on value. Before we can do this, however, we need to understand more about value and the methods used to determine it. In *The Complete Guide to Investing in Rental Properties* (New York; McGraw-Hill; 2004), I discussed at length the subject of property valuation methods and, in particular, how they can be applied to investment property. I refer to these precepts as the "primary principles of valuation" and discussed them in part as follows.

Let me begin this chapter by emphatically stating that I thoroughly enjoy the subject of finance, and in particular as it applies to real estate. Finance and real estate are the two greatest passions of my professional life. For as long as I can remember, I have always been fascinated with money. This fascination eventually helped shape my course in life as I later majored in finance in both my undergraduate and graduate studies. After graduating, I had the opportunity to work as a financial analyst at one of the largest banks in Texas. As part of the mergers and acquisitions group, my work there centered around analyzing potential acquisition targets for the bank.

One way companies grow is by acquiring smaller companies that do the same thing they do. This is especially true of banks. Big banks merge with other big banks, and they buy, or acquire, other banks that are usually, but not always, smaller than they are. I believe our bank was at the time about $11 billion strong in total assets. It was my job to analyze banks that typically ranged in size from about $25 million up to as much as about $2 billion. I used a fairly complex and sophisticated model to properly assess the value of the banks. This experience provided me with a comprehensive understanding of cash flow analysis which I later applied to real estate.

I might point out that to the best of my knowledge, you won't find a chapter like the one here in any other real estate book by another author. What you will find, however, and what I have the good fortune of writing, is an entire book devoted to the subject of finance as it applies to all types of real estate investing including single-family rental houses, multifamily apartment complexes, rehab properties, condominium projects, and commercial buildings. The book, due out in late 2004, will be entitled *The Complete Guide to Real Estate Finance for Investment Properties: How to Analyze Any Single Family, Multifamily, or Commercial Property.*

As is stated above, my background in analyzing banks has allowed me to gain greater insight into the subject of cash flows and their affect on value. The output from the thorough analysis of cash flows can be extrapolated to derive value, whether it be from rental properties, home improvements, or any other asset. I continued my discussion in the rental properties book with the following.

The smart investor knows that perhaps more important than any other part of the investment process is having a thorough understanding of the concept of real estate values. I like to compare the process of purchasing rental houses to that of shopping for a new car. If you're anything at all like most people, before you buy a new car you're likely to look at all of the newspaper ads related to the type of car you want. Then you'll probably call several of the local dealers to gather some general information and determine which models they have in stock. After that, you'll begin comparison shopping by going around to several dealerships to see which one is offering the best deal. Somewhere along the way, you will have narrowed your selection of cars down to one or two models. Finally, you'll begin the arduous task of negotiating price and terms with the salesperson. Since you've shopped around quite a bit already, you are already familiar with the car's price and what represents a good value. A good value in this case means that the price is equal to or less than fair market value relative to all other cars that are similar in design and features. If you can't reach an agreement with the salesperson, then it's on to the next dealer to try again until finally, you've found just the right car at just the right price.

Since purchasing a rental house for investment purposes costs anywhere from five to ten times more than a new car, don't you think it would be in your best interests to spend at least as much time shopping for a house as you do a car? Yes, of course it would. The more houses you look at in a particular market, the greater you understand their relative values. The fact that a 1,200 square-foot house with three bedrooms, two baths, and a two car garage is priced at $125,000 in a particular neighborhood means absolutely nothing by itself. It is only when you compare the price of that house to the price of all other similar houses in the same area that its price becomes meaningful.

92: SECONDARY PRINCIPLES OF VALUATION

In Section #91, we established that the primary principles of valuation are based on the premise of relative values, that is, how the value of one property compares to the value of another similar property. It doesn't matter if you're comparing houses, diamond rings, or automobiles. Value is relative. The second principle of valuation as it relates to income property is a function of cash flow. Following is another excerpt taken from *The Complete Guide to Investing in Rental Properties* that summarizes both principles.

To properly analyze rental property for investment purposes requires that each and every property that goes into your real estate portfolio meet two vitally important criteria. First, the house should be purchased only at or below fair market value. Fair market value is determined by examining comparable properties that have sold at some point in the past and applying those values to the house you are considering. Although this is what appraisers are paid to do, you should have a keen sense of value based on your research for the area. The appraisal process is not an exact science and is fairly subjective in nature. This means that appraisers can select certain comparable sales to help them derive a value that is close to the contract price. Although this is an unintended consequence of the appraisal process, it nevertheless happens all the time.

The second criterion is equally as important as the first. Your investment must cash flow properly, which means that you must be able to charge high enough rents to pay all the expenses, service the debt, and still have some left over. After all, what good does it do you if you are able to buy a house for let's say, $40,000 below fair market value, if you can't charge enough rent to cover all of the related expenses? The answer is absolutely none, unless you are buying the house for a quick flip or resell. Every house you buy for rental income purposes should cash flow positively. Cash is the vehicle that provides businesses with life-sustaining nutrients. I've seen many beginning investors ultimately fail because they thought they could buy a house without properly analyzing its market value and its ability to generate income. Promise me that as a smart investor, you'll do your homework, exercise patience, and not make the same mistake!

93: APPRAISAL METHODS

An appraisal is an opinion of value as it applies to real estate based on one or more valuation methods. An appraisal helps to establish a property's market value. *Market value* is the most likely sales price the property would bring if it were offered in an open and competitive real estate market. An appraisal can be ordered for any number of reasons. For example, if you refinance your home or sell it, the new lender will want to ensure that the property has value sufficient to satisfy loan-to-value ratios because the property will be held as collateral for the loan. Other reasons to obtain an appraisal include lowering your tax liability if the assessed value is in dispute, or perhaps to dispose of a property held in an estate.

An appraiser should be an objective third party who has no financial interest whatsoever in the subject property being appraised. An appraiser is required by state law to procure a license

FIGURE 12.1 *The Three Leading Appraisal Methods*

1. Replacement cost method
2. Income capitalization method
3. Sales comparison method

within the individual state for which he or she will be providing appraisal services.

An appraisal of real estate is the valuation of the rights of ownership as they relate to that property. The appraiser does not create value, but rather interprets the market to arrive at an estimated value. As the appraiser compiles data relevant to the report, consideration must be given to the site and amenities as well as the physical condition of the property. Although an appraiser may spend just a short time inspecting the actual property, that's only the beginning of his job. A good deal of research and the collection of general and specific data must be completed before the appraiser can arrive at a final opinion of value.

An appraisal, which we have defined as an opinion of value, is derived by using one or more of the three most commonly accepted valuation approaches. They are the *cost approach,* the *income approach,* and the *comparable sales approach.* (See Figure 12.1.) Each valuation, or appraisal, method has its place and serves a unique function in determining value. Income-producing buildings and apartment buildings, for example, rely primarily on the income approach. Single family houses, on the other hand, rely primarily on the comparison approach. Both types of properties rely on the cost approach largely for the purpose of ensuring that the level of insurance is adequate.

94: APPRAISAL METHOD #1

The first leading appraisal method is known as the *replacement cost method,* or cost approach. It is most commonly used for estimating the replacement value of a house or building for insurance purposes. An insurance company would want to know what the actual cost to replace a house is, for example, that was destroyed by a natural disaster such as a flood or fire. Because the insurance company is only interested in replacing the actual physical structure, the income method and the sales comparison method are irrelevant as neither approach reflects replacement costs. The insurance on your own personal residence most likely includes a replacement cost policy with built-in premium adjustments that automatically increase each year due to rises in labor and material costs.

When using the replacement cost method, an appraiser will separate the various components of the subject property. First of all the cost of the land is estimated separately from the dwelling because the land or earth will remain in tact in most cases. An exception might be in coastal areas along the shore line where hurricanes can quickly destroy beach front property and even wash away the ground it is on.

Next, the appraiser estimates the cost to replace any improvements that were on the property, such as a dwelling or house. In addition, the appraiser may very well estimate a deduction for depreciation. For example, if a house was 30 years old and had only the minimum of repairs and maintenance performed on it, the appraiser would take the wear and tear of the house into consideration and most likely make a deduction for it. This kind of depreciation is referred to as *physical depreciation*.

Another kind of depreciation is known as *functional obsolescence*. This type of depreciation refers to elements that make a property less desirable or marketable because they are outdated. In addition to functional obsolescence is *external obsolescence*. These are factors that make a property less desirable due not so much to the house itself, but rather due to changes in the community around it, such as a deteriorating neighborhood. As new communities are built in outlying suburban areas, for example, older communities may gradually decline in property value due to neglect, high crime rates, and changes in employment conditions.

95: APPRAISAL METHOD #2

The second leading appraisal method is known as the *income capitalization method,* or income approach. This method is used primarily to value those properties that are income producing and are considered to be used for investment purposes. The income method is most often used to value income producing assets such as retail strip centers, office buildings, industrial buildings, and multifamily apartment buildings. The value from income-producing real estate is a direct function of the net cash flow of income generated by an asset. In other words, it is the asset's *yield.* The yield, which is also referred to as the *capitalization rate,* should not be confused with an asset's *return on investment,* or ROI. The ROI refers to an investor's return on the actual investment made.

Investors compare the rates of return produced from various types of assets balanced against their perceived risks and deploy their capital accordingly. Assuming that risk is held constant, an investor's return on his capital is the same regardless of whether it is derived from real estate, stocks, or bonds. Each of these asset classes has varying degrees of risk and reward attributes that make them unique to investors.

96: APPRAISAL METHOD #3

The third leading appraisal method is the *sales comparison method,* or comparable sales approach, and is the approach that is deemed most appropriate to use for the proper determination of value for single-family houses. The sales comparison method is the one that most people are familiar with, because it is used thousands of times a day all across America to determine property values. Virtually all mortgage companies and lenders require this type of appraisal to be completed before financing a home to ensure that their funds will be adequately collateralized.

The sales comparison method is based upon the premise of *substitution* and maintains that a buyer would not pay any more for real property than the cost of purchasing an equally desirable substitute in that property's respective market. The sales comparison method examines two or more like properties and adjusts their value based upon similarities and differences among them. An appraiser estimates the subject property's market value by comparing it to similar properties that have sold in the same area. The properties used are referred to as *comparable sales,* or *comps.*

Because no two properties are exactly alike, the appraiser studies the differences in the properties and makes various compensating adjustments to bring their features more in line with the subject property. The process results in a figure that shows what each comparable sale would have sold for if it had the same qualities as the subject. An appraiser's report typically shows side-by-side comparisons of three comparables so that their differences can more easily be compared. Furthermore, an appraiser typically includes a report describing the overall real estate market in the area as well.

97: CASE STUDY ANALYSIS—ASSUMPTIONS

In Section #96, we examined the sales comparison method of appraising real estate, which is the most commonly used approach for assessing property values for houses. Now we'll look at an example of how the sales comparison method can be used to help you determine the potential resale value of your home after having made various improvements to it.

Throughout this book, we've examined over 90 ways to make improvements to a house. We've also discussed which of those improvements are likely to have the most impact on value based upon the premise that visibility adds value. Figure 12.2 shows a hypothetical example of a homeowner who has made several improvements to his house. In this example, the buyer, who we'll call

Mr. Fixit, purchased the house with the understanding that extensive repairs would be required in order to bring it up to a standard similar to that of homes in the surrounding community.

Now take a moment to study Figure 12.2, the Property Analysis Worksheet. The worksheet you see is a proprietary model I developed that I use to quickly and easily analyze potential value play investment opportunities. I call it "The Value Play Rehab Analyzer." Once I have gathered the necessary data, I can input the information into the model and in less than five minutes, know within a reasonable degree of accuracy whether or not a rehab opportunity makes sense based upon my investment criteria. All I have to do is key in the information and the model automatically makes all of the calculations. Although the model was designed specifically for flipping and rehab opportunities, its application is suitable here because the process of a homeowner making improvements to her own house is really no different than an investor who purchases a property to flip.

Under the Purchase Assumptions section, the basic property information is listed, including a project name, address, and pricing information. The value of the land does not really matter as long as the price of the land plus the price of the house is equal to the total purchase price. There are two sections for Financing Assumptions—one for primary financing and another one for secondary financing. The primary financing section is used for the primary source of financing; it can be in the form of a loan from a mortgage company, bank, or private individual as this example illustrates.

This example assumes that the total purchase price was $150,000 and that Mr. Fixit will put down 5 percent, or $7,500, of his own money to purchase the house. This leaves a loan balance of $142,500 that he must borrow to purchase the house. The loan is financed over a 30-year period at an annual interest rate of 6.40 percent, making the amount of the monthly payment $891 for the primary financing. If Mr. Fixit arranged to make interest-only payments, the amount of his monthly payment would be $760.

FIGURE 12.2 *The Value Play Rehab Analyzer Property Analysis Worksheet*

Purchase Assumptions		Financing Assumptions–Primary			Financing Assumptions–Secondary		
Project Name:	TLC	Primary Mortgage or Loan:			Secondary Financing/Line of Credit:		
Address:	123 South State St.	Total Purchase	100.00%	150,000	Total Imprvmnts	100.00%	59,300
City, State, Zip:	Anywhere, TX 77520	Down Payment	5.00%	7,500	Down Payment	0.00%	0
Contact:	Mr. Fixit	Balance to Finc	95.00%	142,500	Balance to Finc	100.00%	59,300
Telephone:	(800) 555-1234						

			Annual	Monthly		Annual	Monthly
Land	25,000						
Building/House	122,500	Interest Rate	6.400%	0.533%	Interest Rate	7.250%	0.604%
Closing Costs	2,500	Amort Period	30	360	Amort Period	20	240
Other Related Costs	0	Payment	10696	891	Payment	5,624	469
Total Purchase Price	150,000	Interest Only	9,120	760	Interest Only	4,299	358

Estimate for Improvements

Appliances		Flooring		Lighting	3,600
Dishwasher	425	Carpet	2,200	Masonry	0
Disposal	85	Ceramic Tile	800	Other	500
Microwave	0	Hardwood	1,800	Other	0
Range	600	Vinyl	1,400	Other	0
Refrigerator	0	Subtotal	6,200	Painting: Exterior	1,225
Subtotal	1,110			Painting: Interior	2,200
		Foundation	0	Permits	275
Architectural Drawing	0	Framing	0	Subtotal	7,800
Cabinets	4,325	Garage	0		
Caulking	250	Gas & Electric Hookup	0	Plumbing	
Subtotal	4,600	Glass: Mirrors, showers	0	Commodes	0
		Gutters	1,400	Drain Lines	0
Cement Work		Subtotal	1,400	Faucets	500
Basement Floor	0			Fixtures	500
Driveway	0	HVAC		Hot Water Heater	400
Garage Floor	0	Air Conditioner	1,800	Showers	1,275
Porches	0	Duct Work	0	Tubs	0
Sidewalks	1,200	Filters	45	Water Lines	0
Subtotal	1,200	Furnace	3,00	Subtotal	2,675
		Subtotal	4,845		
Cleaning	500			Roofing	3,400
Counter Tops	1,450	Insulation	1,900	Siding	0
Decorating	3,400	Insurance Premiums	875	Site Planning & Engineering	0
Doors	2,245	Subtotal	2,775	Steel	0
Drywall	675			Trim	0
Electrical	500	Landscaping		Utility: Gas & Electric	250
Engineering	0	Irrigation System	2,400	Utility: Water & Sewer	130
Equipment Rental	345	Lot Clearing	0	Warranty	0
Excavation Work	0	Mowing Services	100	Windows	4,000
Fences	600	Sod	300	Subtotal	7,780
Fireplace	1,400	Trees, Plants, & Shrubs	5,000		
Subtotal	11,115	Subtotal	7,800	Total Cost of Improvements	59,300

Comp #1		Comp #2		Comp #3	
Address:		Address:		Address	
Sales Price	237,000.00	Sales Price	244,500.00	Sales Price	254,000.00
Adjustments to Price	1,400	Adjustments to Price	(1,650.00)	Adjustments to Price	0.00
Adjusted Price	238,400.00	Adjusted Price	242,850.00	Adjusted Price	254,000.00
Square Feet	1,950.00	Square Feet	2,000	Square Feet	2,050.00
Price Per Square Foot	122.26	Price Per Square Foot	121.43	Price Per Square Foot	123.90

Comp Averages		Subject Property 123 South State St.		Description	Adjustment to Comps Best Case	Most Likely	5.00 Worst Case
Sales Price	245,166.67	Square Feet	2,000.00	Est Sales Price	255,083	245,083	235,083
Adjustments to Price	(83.33)	Price/Sq Ft	75.00	Purchase Price	150,000	150,000	150,000
Adjusted Price	245,083.33	Imprvmnts/Sq Ft	29.65	Improvements	59,300	59,300	59,300
Square Feet	2,000.00	Total Price/Sq Ft	104.65	Interest Charges	4,473	4,473	4,473
Price Per Square Foot	122.54			Taxes	850	850	850
				Closing Costs	0	0	0
Turn Comps Off/On	ON	Estimated Time To		Total Costs	214,623	214,623	214,623
Est Price/Sq Ft If Turned OFF	120.00	Complete Project	4.00	Profit Margin	40,460	30,460	20,460
				Return On Inv	539.47%	406.14%	272.80%

WWW.THEVALUEPLAY.COM–COPYRIGHT PROTECTED 1998

The secondary financing section is used for any additional loans secured, such as a home equity line of credit, or HELOC. Home equity loans are generally easy to obtain, especially if your credit is decent. For lower cost improvements, you may want to use all cash. On the other hand, if the costs of the improvements are greater than the amount of capital you want to use, then this is the appropriate section to use. Rates and terms are typically different for a line of credit, such as a home equity line or a credit card, than they are for a regular mortgage. So having two sections for financing allows you to more accurately determine the carrying costs, or interest charges.

The total cost of home improvements made in this example is $59,300. Mr. Fixit elected not to use any of his own money to make the repairs and instead financed the entire amount using a home equity loan. The loan is amortized over a 20-year period at an annual interest rate of 7.25 percent, making the amount of the monthly payment $469 for the secondary financing. If Mr. Fixit arranged to make interest only payments, the amount of his monthly payment would be $358.

98: CASE STUDY ANALYSIS—ESTIMATES

Under the Estimate For Improvements section of the worksheet, there is quite a bit of detail that allows you to estimate the costs for virtually everything in a house. The Estimates for Improvements section is organized alphabetically by category with related subcategories as needed. Estimating these costs accurately is especially important for the proper analysis of making home improvements on a larger scale such as is illustrated in this example. The more experience a homeowner has, the easier estimating costs will become.

At first, you may need to obtain bids or estimates from contractors to help determine how much the required improvements will cost. As you gain experience, however, you'll be able to estimate many of the costs on your own. In this example, Mr. Fixit is making extensive home improvements to his house to bring it to tip-top condition. The total cost of the improvements based on Mr. Fixit's estimates is $59,300.

99: CASE STUDY ANALYSIS—COMPARABLE SALES

The next section of the model allows an individual to enter information for comparable home sales. This information is needed to help make accurate projections of the estimated resale value of your home. Any sales agent can provide you with comparable sales data for your area. You can also check the Internet for Web listings in your area that will give you a good idea of what houses are selling for.

There is also provision in this model section for making adjustments to the sales price of the comps. This provision permits you to compare "apples to apples." For example, if the home you are buying has a two-car garage and the comparable home sale has a three-car garage, you will need to revise the price downward in the Adjustments to Price section. This is exactly how real estate agents and appraisers derive the market value of a house. They start with an average price per square foot of several similar houses and make compensating adjustments to estimate value.

In this example, three hypothetical comparable sales were used. Comp #1 had a sales price of $237,000 with an adjustment upward of $1,400 resulting in an adjusted sales price of $238,400. Because the house had 1,950 square feet, the average price per square foot after adjustments is $122.26. Comp #2 had a sales price of $244,500 with an adjustment downward of $1,650 resulting in an adjusted sales price of $242,850. Because the house had 2,000 square feet, the average price per square foot after adjustments is $121.43. Comp #3 had a sales price of $254,000 with no adjustments. Because the house had 2,050 square feet, the average price per square foot after adjustments is $123.90.

The Comp Averages section simply takes an average of the three comps sales prices to come up with an average sales price, which in this example is $245,166. The adjustments to the sales price are minimal resulting in a downward adjustment of only $83.33, which gives us an adjusted average sales price of $245,083. Because the average square footage of the three homes is 2,000 square feet, the average price per square foot after adjustments is $122.54. The result is a weighted average price per square foot of the three homes.

The Comp Averages section also has a provision that allows you to turn the comps section off or on. If you're already familiar with home values in your neighborhood, you most likely know what the average sales price per square foot is, so you really don't need to key in sales comp data. Instead, the comps section can be turned off and your own estimate can then be entered.

100: CASE STUDY ANALYSIS—OUTPUT ANALYSIS

The average sales price per square foot from the Comp Averages section is then fed into the Subject Property section. All of the information keyed into the rest of the model is summarized in this section. You must know the square footage of the house you are buying so that you can make an accurate comparison. The purchase price per square foot is automatically calculated, as is the total cost of the proposed improvements per square foot. The two numbers are then added together to give you the total cost of the project. In this example, the Total Cost of Improvements of $59,300 was added to the Total Purchase Price of $150,000. The resulting sum was then divided by 2,000 square feet for a Total Price Per Square Foot of $104.65. This number is the cost basis and represents the total cost of the house after all improvements have been made.

Below the Total Price Per Square Foot section is a provision that allows you to estimate the total time for completion and resell in months. In other words, it calculates the carrying costs for interest, a factor that many less-experienced investors do not consider. If the home is your own, however, the number should be set to zero because you are receiving the benefit of living there while the improvements are being made. In the example here, the number of months is set to four because Mr. Fixit is an investor and is therefore receiving no benefit from the house while the repairs are being made.

The Adjustment to Comps cell is used to create the Estimated Sales Price for three different sales scenarios—Best Case, Most Likely, and Worst Case. In this example, $5.00 per square foot is used. For the Best Case Sales Price, the model adds $5.00 to the Price Per Square Foot cell in the Comp Averages section, and then multiplies the sum of the two by the square feet of the subject property. Here's how it works:

(Average Price per Square Foot + Adjustment to Comps)
× Subject Property Square Feet = Best Case Sales Price
($122.54 + $5.00) × 2,000 = $255,083

The Most Likely Sales Price calculation in the model neither adds nor subtracts the value of $5.00 to the Price Per Square Foot cell in the Comp Averages section. It is simply the product of the Average Price Per Square Foot and the Square Feet. Take a moment to study Figure 12.2.

Average Price per Square Foot × Subject Property Square Feet
= Most Likely Sales Price $122.54 × 2,000 = $245,083

For the Worst Case Sales Price, the model subtracts $5.00 from the Price Per Square Foot cell in the Comp Averages section, and then multiplies the difference of the two by the square feet of the subject property.

(Average Price per Square Foot – Adjustment to Comps)
× Subject Property Square Feet = Worst Case Sales Price
($122.54 – $5.00) × 2,000 = $235,083

The purpose of creating three different scenarios in the model is to provide a range for the estimated sales price. This allows you to evaluate the very minimum you might expect on the low end of the price range, and the very most you might expect on the high end of the price range. Take a moment to refer back to Figure 12.2. The Purchase Price, Improvements, Interest Charges, Taxes, and Closing Costs remain constant across all three scenarios because these values are not affected by the Adjustment to Comps variable of $5.00. The Profit Margin is the dollar amount that can be expected from the sale after all costs have been accounted for. The Return on Investment is calculated as the ratio of the Profit Margin divided by the total cash invested in the property. It is calculated for the Most Likely scenario as follows:

$$\frac{\text{Profit Margin}}{\text{Primary Down Payment} + \text{Secondary Down Payment}} = \text{ROI}$$

$$\$30,460 \div (\$7,500 + \$0) = 406.133 \text{ or } 406.14\%$$

In this simple example, Mr. Fixit would earn a very respectable return of 406.14 percent on his investment if the property were sold under the most likely scenario. Considering the project took only four months to complete, Mr. Fixit earned a return of a little more than 100 percent per month, representing potentially an annualized return of over 1,200 percent. My guess is you won't find returns like that in the stock market anytime soon, or anywhere else for that matter.

I'm sure you'll agree with me that there is great value in having a dynamic model such as the one illustrated here. By keying in the basic assumptions, you can very easily change a few variables that allow you to quickly identify any upside potential. For additional information regarding the availability of the model used in this example, see the Resources.

101: SUMMARY AND CONCLUSION

In Part One of this book, we discussed the importance of making improvements to your home and how to go about getting started, including obtaining the requisite approvals and the issuance of permits, as well as suggestions for working with subcontractors. While Part Two focused on the many types of exterior improvements that can be made to add value to a home, Part Three focused on the various types of interior improvements. Later, in Part Four, we examined several of the different mechanical components of a house and the effect of improvements made to them as it relates to value. Finally, in Part Five, we explored the culminating effects of combining multiple improvements to a home to determine their potential impact on value.

A ranking system was established from the outset to help quantify the effect of making certain home improvements on value based on the premise that visibility is the key to adding value. It was also determined that there are numerous external forces that can affect value including interest rates, local and national market conditions, and supply and demand forces. Because each of these forces working in conjunction with each other will affect the market value of a home, regardless of any improvements that may have been made to it, they must be taken into consideration before committing investment resources to a home improvement project.

SAMPLE
SUBCONTRACTOR
AGREEMENT

This Agreement, Made as of (Current Date), In the Year of (Current Year),

Between the Contractor: **Contractor's Name**
License Number
Address
Phone Number

And the Sub-Contractor: **Sub-Contractor's Name**
License Number
Address
Phone Number

For the Project: **Project Name**
Address

Article 1.   Scope of Work

1.1   Sub-Contractor has heretofore entered into a contract with said Contractor to furnish all labor, materials and equipment to perform all work described below according to the construction documents.

Article 2.   Payment Terms

2.1   The Contractor agrees to pay the Sub-Contractor within (number of days) after the completion of the work and payment by the owner for such work.

2.2   Sub-Contractor understands and agrees that progress payment requests shall be written and given to the contractor/job superintendent before Wednesday for payment on the following Friday. All work for the portion requested must be completed prior to the request for payment. The Contractor will request a draw and payment will be made to the Sub-Contractor after the draw is received. Please note that a certificate of Workman's Compensation Insurance must be received before the first payment is made or the contractor will hold a percentage needed to cover the labor portion of the job.

2.3   The Total Contract Amount shall be $_____.

Article 3.   Time of Completion

3.1   Sub-Contractor shall keep both an adequate size and properly trained crew on the job site so as to complete the project within (number of days) and work within the project schedule.

Article 4.   Change Orders

4.1   Sub-Contractor understands and agrees that no change orders or contract additions will be made unless agreed to in writing by Contractor. If any additional work is performed and not covered in this contract, the Sub-Contractor proceeds at his own risk and expense. No alterations, additions, or small changes can be made in the work or method of the performance, without the written change order signed by the Contractor and Sub-Contractor.

Article 5.   Clean-up

5.1   Sub-Contractor will be responsible for cleaning up the job on a daily basis, including all generated construction debris, drink cans, food wrappers, and/or other trash. If it becomes necessary, the Sub-Contractor will be back charged for appropriate clean up by deducting clean up costs from payments.

Article 6.   Taxes and Permits

6.1   The Sub-Contractor understands and agrees that he shall be responsible for all taxes, fees and expenses imposed directly or indirectly for its work, labor, material and services required to fulfill this contract. The Sub-Contractor is responsible for all permits pertaining to the law, ordinances and regulations where the work is performed.

Article 7.   Insurance

7.1   The Sub-Contractor shall maintain, at his own expense, full and complete insurance on its work until final approval of the work described in the contract. The Sub-Contractor shall not hold the Contractor liable from any and all costs, damages, fees and expenses from any claims arising on the project. Failure of the Sub-Contractor to maintain appropriate insurance coverage may deem a material breach allowing the Contractor to terminate this contract or to provide insurance at the Sub-Contractor's expense.

Article 8.   Liquidated Damages

8.1   If the project is not substantially completed on the stated completion date, the Sub-Contractor shall pay to the Contractor the sum of ($ cost per day) for each calendar day of inexcusable delay until the work is substantially completed, as liquidated damages.

Article 9.   Warranty

9.1   Sub-Contractor shall warranty all labor, materials and equipment furnished on the project for (number of years) against defects in workmanship or materials utilized. The manufacturers warranty will prevail. No legal action of any kind relating to the project, project performance or this contract shall be initiated by either party against the other party after (number of years) beyond the completion of the project or cessation of work.

Article 10.   Hazardous Materials, Waste and Asbestos

10.1   Both parties agree that dealing with hazardous materials, waste or asbestos requires specialized training, processes, precautions and licenses. Therefore, unless the scope of this agreement includes the specific handling, disturbance, removal or transportation of hazardous materials, waste or asbestos, upon discovery of such hazardous materials the Sub-Contractor shall notify the Contractor immediately and allow the Contractor to contract with a properly licensed and qualified hazardous material contractor.

Article 11. Arbitration of Disputes

11.1 Any controversy or claim arising out of or relating to this contract, or the breach thereof, shall be settled by arbitration administered by the American Arbitration Association under its Construction Industry Arbitration Rules, and judgment on the award rendered by the arbitrator(s) may be entered in any court having jurisdiction thereof.

Article 12. Attorney Fees

12.1 In the event of any arbitration or litigation relating to the project, project performance or this contract, the prevailing party shall be entitled to reasonable attorney fees, costs and expenses.

Article 13. Acceptance

Witness our hand and seal on this _____ day of _____ , 20____ .

Signed in the presence of:

_____   _____
Contractor's Name   Date

_____   _____
Sub-Contractor's Name   Date

Initialed by: Owner_____ Sub-Contractor_____

Homeowners will find the Glossary helpful for understanding words and terms used both in real estate transactions and in construction. There are, however, some factors that may affect these definitions. Terms are defined as they are commonly understood in the mortgage and real estate industry. The same terms may have different meanings in another context. The definitions are intentionally general, nontechnical, and short. They do not encompass all possible meanings or nuances that a term may acquire in legal use. State laws, as well as custom and use in various states or regions of the country, may in fact modify or completely change the meanings of certain terms defined. Before signing any documents or depositing any money preparatory to entering into a real estate contract, the purchaser should consult with an attorney of his or her choice to ensure that his or her rights are properly protected.

abstract of title A summary of the public records relating to the title to a particular piece of land. An attorney or title insurance company reviews an abstract of title to determine whether there are any title defects that must be cleared before a buyer can purchase clear, marketable, and insurable title.

agreement of sale Known by various names, such as contract of purchase, purchase agreement, or sales agreement according to location or jurisdiction. A contract in which a seller agrees to sell and a buyer agrees to buy, under certain specific terms and conditions spelled out in writing and signed by both parties.

amortization A payment plan that enables the borrower to reduce a debt gradually through monthly payments of principal thereby liquidating or extinguishing the obligation through a series of installments.

appraisal An expert judgment or estimate of the quality or value of real estate as of a given date. The process through which conclusions of property value are obtained. It also refers to the formalized report that sets forth the estimate and conclusion of value.

appurtenance That which belongs to something else. In real estate law, an appurtenance is a right, privilege, or improvement that passes as an incident to the land, such as a right of way.

attic ventilators Screened openings provided to ventilate an attic space.

back charge Billings for work performed or costs incurred by one party that, in accordance with the agreement, should have been performed or incurred by the party to whom billed. Owner's bill back charges to general contractors, and general contractor's bill back charges to subcontractors. An example of a back charge includes charges for cleanup work that should have been done by a subcontractor, but was left for the owner or general contractor to do.

base or baseboard A trim board placed against the wall around the room next to the floor.

bay window Any window space projecting outward from the walls of a building, either square or polygonal in plan.

beam A structural member transversely supporting a load. A structural member carrying building loads (weight) from one support to another. Sometimes referred to as a "girder."

bid A formal offer by a contractor, in accordance with specifications for a project, to do all or a phase of the work at a certain price in accordance with the terms and conditions stated in the offer.

bill of sale A written document or instrument that provides evidence of the transfer of right, title, and interest in personal property from one person to another.

blown insulation Fiber insulation, frequently cellulose, in loose form and used to insulate attics and existing walls where framing members are not exposed.

blueprint A type of copying method often used for architectural drawings. Usually used to describe the drawing of a structure that is prepared by an architect or designer for the purpose of design and planning, estimating, securing permits, and actual construction.

bona fide Made in good faith; good, valid, without fraud; such as a *bona fide* offer.

bond (1) Any obligation under seal. A real estate bond is a written obligation, usually issued on security of a mortgage or deed of trust.

bond or bonding (2) An amount of money (usually $5,000 to $10,000) that must be on deposit with a governmental agency in order to secure a contractor's license. The bond may be used to pay for the unpaid bills or disputed work of the contractor. Not to be confused with *performance bonds,* that are rarely used in residential construction; a performance bond is an insurance policy that guarantees proper completion of a project.

breach The breaking of law, or failure of a duty, either by omission or commission; the failure to perform, without legal excuse, any promise that forms a part or the whole of a contract.

breaker panel The electrical box that distributes electric power entering the home to each branch circuit (each plug and switch) and composed of circuit breakers.

brick ledge Part of the foundation wall where brick (veneer) will rest.

brick lintel The metal angle iron that brick rests on, especially above a window, door, or other opening.

brick mold Trim used around an exterior door jamb that siding butts to.

brick tie A small, corrugated metal strip about 1″ × 6″ × 8″ nailed to wall sheeting or studs. They are inserted into the grout mortar joint of the veneer brick and hold the veneer wall to the sheeted wall behind it.

brick veneer A vertical facing of brick laid against and fastened to sheathing of a framed wall or tile wall construction.

bridging Small wood or metal members that are inserted in a diagonal position between the floor joists or rafters at midspan for the purpose of bracing the joists/rafters and spreading the load.

building code Regulations established by local governments setting forth the structural requirements for building.

building line or setback Distances from the ends and/or sides of the lot beyond which construction may not extend. The building line may be established by a filed plat of subdivision, by restrictive covenants in deeds or leases, by building codes, or by zoning ordinances.

cantilever An overhang. Where one floor extends beyond and over a foundation wall. For example, at a fireplace location or bay window cantilever. Normally, not extending over two feet.

caveat emptor The phrase literally means "let the buyer beware." Under this doctrine the buyer is duty bound to examine the property being purchased and assumes conditions that are readily ascertainable upon view.

casement Frames of wood or metal enclosing part (or all) of a window sash. May be opened by means of hinges affixed to the vertical edges.

casement window A window with hinges on one of the vertical sides and swings open like a normal door

casing Wood trim molding installed around a door or window opening.

caulking (1) A flexible material used to seal a gap between two surfaces, e.g., between pieces of siding or the corners in tub walls. (2) To fill a joint with mastic or asphalt plastic cement to prevent leaks.

celotex Black fibrous board that is used as exterior sheathing.

ceiling joist One of a series of parallel framing members used to support ceiling loads and supported in turn by larger beams, girders, or bearing walls. Also called "roof joists."

cement The gray powder that is the "glue" in concrete. Portland cement. Also, any adhesive.

ceramic tile A human-made or machine-made clay tile used to finish a floor or wall. Generally used in bathtub and shower enclosures and on counter tops.

certificate of title A certificate issued by a title company or a written opinion rendered by an attorney that the seller has good, marketable, and insurable title to the property that he or she is offering for sale. A certificate of title offers no protection against any hidden defects in the title that an examination of the records could not reveal. The issuer of a certificate of title is liable only for damages due to negligence. The protection offered a homeowner under a certificate of title is not as great as that offered in a title insurance policy.

chain of title A history of conveyances and encumbrances affecting the title to a particular real property.

chair rail Interior trim material installed about 3 feet or 4 feet up the wall, horizontally.

chalk line A line made by snapping a taut string or cord dusted with chalk. Used for alignment purposes.

change order A written document that modifies the plans and specifications and/or the price of the construction contract.

chase A framed enclosed space around a flue pipe or a channel in a wall, or through a ceiling for something to lie in or pass through.

CO An abbreviation for *certificate of occupancy*. This certificate is issued by the local municipality and is required before anyone can occupy and live within the home. It is issued only after the local municipality has made all inspections and all monies and fees have been paid.

condemnation The taking of private property for public use by a government unit, against the will of the owner, but with payment of just compensation under the government's power of eminent domain. Condemnation may also be a determination by a governmental agency that a particular building is unsafe or unfit for use.

condominium Individual ownership of a dwelling unit and an individual interest in the common areas and facilities that serve the multiunit project.

consideration Something of value, usually money, that is the inducement of a contract. Any right, interest, property, or benefit accruing to one party; any forbearance, detriment, loss, or responsibility given, suffered, or undertaken, may constitute a consideration that will sustain a contract.

contractor In the construction industry, a contractor is one who contracts to erect houses, buildings, or portions of them. There are also contractors for each phase of construction, such as heating, electrical, plumbing, air conditioning, road building, bridge and dam erection, and others.

covenant An agreement between two or more persons entered into by deed whereby one of the parties promises the performance of certain acts, or that a given state does or shall, or does not or shall not, exist.

crown molding A molding used on cornice or wherever an interior angle is to be covered, especially at the roof and wall corner.

culvert Round, corrugated drain pipe (normally 15 inches or 18 inches in diameter) that is installed beneath a driveway and parallel to and near the street.

damper A metal "door" placed within the fireplace chimney. Normally closed when the fireplace is not in use.

damp proofing The black, tar-like waterproofing material applied to the exterior of a foundation wall to prevent moisture from penetrating it.

deed A formal written instrument by which title to real property is transferred from one owner to another. The deed should contain an accurate description of the property being conveyed, should be signed and witnessed according to the laws of the state where the property is located, and should be delivered to the purchaser on the day of closing. There are two parties to a deed—the grantor and the grantee. (*See also* deed of trust, general warranty deed, quitclaim deed, and special warranty deed.)

deed of trust Like a mortgage, a security instrument whereby real property is given as security for a debt; however, in a deed of trust there are three parties to the instrument—the borrower, the trustee, and the lender (or beneficiary). In such a transaction, the borrower transfers the legal title for the property to the trustee who holds the property in trust as security for the payment of the debt to the lender or beneficiary. If the borrower pays the debt as agreed, the deed of trust becomes void. If, however, he or she defaults in the payment of the debt, the trustee may sell the property at a public sale, under the terms of the deed of trust. In most jurisdictions where the deed of trust is in force, the borrower is subject to having the property sold without benefit of legal proceedings. A few states have begun in recent years to treat the deed of trust like a mortgage.

default Failure to make mortgage payments as agreed to in a commitment based on the terms and at the designated time set forth in the mortgage or deed of trust. It is the mortgagor's responsibility to remember the due date and send the payment prior to the due date, not after. Generally, 30 days after the due date if payment is not received, the mortgage is in default. In the event of default, the mortgage may give the lender the right to accelerate payments, take possession and receive rents, and start foreclosure. Defaults may also come about by the failure to observe other conditions in the mortgage or deed of trust.

Department of Veterans Affairs (VA) A federal agency that insures mortgage loans with very liberal down payment requirements for honorably discharged veterans and their surviving spouses.

depreciation Decline in value of a house due to wear and tear, adverse changes in the neighborhood, or any other reason. The term is most often applied for tax purposes.

documentary stamps A state tax, in the forms of stamps, required on deeds and mortgages when real estate title passes from one owner to another. The amount of stamps required varies with each state.

dormer An opening in a sloping roof, the framing of which projects out to form a vertical wall suitable for windows or other openings.

double glaze Window or door in which two panes of glass are used with a sealed air space between. Also known as "insulating glass."

down spout A pipe, usually of metal, for carrying rainwater down from the roof's horizontal gutters.

drain tile A perforated, corrugated plastic pipe laid at the bottom of the foundation wall and used to drain excess water away from the foundation. It prevents ground water from seeping through the foundation wall. Sometimes called perimeter drain.

draw The amount of progress billings on a contract that is currently available to a contractor under a contract with a fixed payment schedule.

drywall (or gypsum wallboard (GWB), sheet rock, or plasterboard) Wallboard or gypsum—a manufactured panel made out of gypsum plaster and encased in a thin cardboard. Usually ½″ thick and 4′ × 8′ or 4′ × 12′ in size. The panels are nailed or screwed onto the framing and the joints are taped and covered with a "joint compound." The "green board" drywall resists moisture better than regular (white) plasterboard and is used in bathrooms and other "wet areas."

ducts Part of the heating system. Usually round or rectangular metal pipes installed for distributing warm (or cold) air from the furnace to rooms in the home. Also a tunnel made of galvanized metal or rigid fiberglass that carries air from the heater or ventilation opening to the rooms in a building.

due-on-sale A clause in a mortgage contract requiring the borrower to pay the entire outstanding balance upon sale or transfer of the property.

duress Unlawful constraint exercised upon a person, whereby the person is forced to perform some act, or to sign an instrument or document against his or her will.

earnest money A sum paid to the seller to show that a potential purchaser is serious about buying.

earthquake strap A metal strap used to secure gas hot water heaters to the framing or foundation of a house. Intended to reduce the chances of having the water heater fall over in an earthquake and causing a gas leak.

easement A formal contract that allows a party to use another party's property for a specific purpose, e.g., a sewer easement might allow one party to run a sewer line through a neighboring property.

eaves The horizontal exterior roof overhang.

egress A means of exiting the home. An egress window is required in every bedroom and basement. Normally a 4' × 4' window is the minimum size required.

elbow A plumbing or electrical fitting that lets you change directions in runs of pipe or conduit.

economic life The period over which a property may be profitably utilized or the period over which a property will yield a return on the investment, over and above the economic or ground rent due to its land.

economic obsolescence Impairment of desirability or useful life arising from economic forces, such as changes in optimum land use, legislative enactments that restrict or impair property rights, and changes in supply and demand relationships.

electrical rough Work performed by the electrical contractor after the plumber and heating contractor have completed their phases of work. Normally all electrical wires, and outlet, switch, and fixture boxes are installed (before insulation).

electrical trim Work performed by the electrical contractor when the house is nearing completion. The electrician installs all plugs, switches, light fixtures, smoke detectors, appliance "pig tails," bath ventilation fans, wires the furnace, and "makes up" the electric house panel. The electrician does all work necessary to get the home ready for and to pass the municipal electrical final inspection.

eminent domain The superior right of property subsisting in every sovereign state to take private property for public use upon the payment of just compensation. This power is often conferred upon public service corporations that perform quasi-public functions, such as providing public utilities. In every case, the owner whose property is taken must be justly compensated according to fair market values in the prevailing area.

encroachment An obstruction, building, or part of a building that intrudes beyond a legal boundary onto neighboring private or public land, or a building extending beyond the building line.

encumbrance A legal right or interest in land that affects a good or clear title and diminishes the land's value. It can take numerous forms, such as zoning ordinances, easement rights, claims, mortgages, liens, charges, a pending legal action, unpaid taxes, or restrictive covenants. An encumbrance does not legally prevent transfer of the property to another. A title search is all that is usually done to reveal the existence of such encumbrances, and it is up to the buyer to determine whether he or she wants to purchase with the encumbrance, or determine what can be done to remove it.

equity The value of a homeowner's unencumbered interest in real estate. Equity is computed by subtracting from the property's fair market value the total of the unpaid mortgage balance plus any outstanding liens or other debts against the property. A homeowner's equity increases as he or she pays off their mortgage or as the property appreciates in value. When the mortgage and all other debts against the property are paid in full the homeowner has 100 percent equity in his or her property.

escheat The reverting of property to the state by reason of failure of persons legally entitled to hold, or when heirs capable of inheriting are lacking the ability to do so.

escrow The handling of funds or documents by a third party on behalf of the buyer and/or seller.

estimate The amount of labor, materials, and other costs that a contractor anticipates for a project as summarized in the contractor's bid proposal for the project.

execute To perform what is required to give validity to a legal document. To execute a document, for example, means to sign it so that it becomes fully enforceable by law.

faced concrete To finish the front and all vertical sides of a concrete porch, step(s), or patio. Normally the "face" is broom finished.

facing brick The brick used and exposed on the outside of a wall. Usually these bricks have a finished texture.

fascia Horizontal boards attached to rafter/truss ends at the eaves and along gables. Roof drain gutters are attached to the fascia.

felt paper Tar paper that is installed under the roof shingles. Normally rated at 15 lb. or 30 lb.

fee simple The largest estate a person can have in real estate. Denotes totality of ownership, unlimited in point of time, as in perpetual.

fiduciary A person to whom property is entrusted; a trustee who holds, controls, or manages for another. A real estate agent is said to have a fiduciary responsibility and relationship with a client.

fixed rate loan A loan where the initial payments are based on a certain interest rate for a stated period. The rate payable will not change during this period regardless of changes in the lender's standard variable rate.

fixed rate mortgage A mortgage with an interest rate that remains the same, or "fixed," over the years.

flashing Sheet metal or other material used in roof and wall construction to protect a building from water seepage.

flat mold Thin wood strips installed over the butt seam of cabinet skins.

flat paint An interior paint that contains a high proportion of pigment and dries to a flat or lusterless finish.

flatwork Common word for concrete floors, driveways, basements, and sidewalks.

fluorescent lighting A fluorescent lamp is a gas-filled glass tube with a phosphor coating on the inside. Gas inside the tube is ionized by electricity that causes the phosphor coating to glow. Normally with two pins that extend from each end.

flue Large pipe through which fumes escape from a gas water heater, furnace, or fireplace. Normally these flue pipes are double walled, galvanized sheet metal pipe and are sometimes referred to as a "B Vent." Fireplace flue pipes are normally triple walled. In addition, nothing combustible shall be within one inch from the flue pipe.

footer or footing Continuous 8" or 10" thick concrete pad installed before and supports the foundation wall or monopost.

forced-air heating A common form of heating with natural gas, propane, oil, or electricity as a fuel. Air is heated in the furnace and distributed through a set of metal ducts to various areas of the house.

foreclosure A legal term applied to any of the various methods of enforcing payment of the debt secured by a mortgage, or deed of trust, by taking and selling the mortgaged property, and depriving the mortgagor of possession.

form Temporary structure erected to contain concrete during placing and initial hardening.

foundation The supporting portion of a structure below the first floor construction, or below grade, including the footings.

foundation ties Metal wires that hold the foundation wall panels and rebar in place during the concrete pour.

foundation waterproofing High-quality, below-grade moisture protection. Used for below-grade exterior concrete and masonry for wall waterproofing to seal out moisture and to prevent corrosion. Normally looks like black tar, but it forms a rubberized coating and is applied much thicker than the tar used for damp proofing.

frame inspection The act of inspecting the home's structural integrity and it's compliance to local municipal codes.

framer The carpenter contractor who installs the lumber and erects the frame, flooring system, interior walls, backing, trusses, rafters, decking; installs all beams, stairs, soffits, and all work related to the wood structure of the home. The framer builds the home according to the blueprints and must comply with local building codes and regulations.

framing Lumber used for the structural members of a building, such as studs, joists, and rafters.

functional obsolescence An impairment of desirability of a property arising from its being out of date with respect to design and style, capacity and utility in relation to site, lack of modern facilities, and the like.

GFCI or GFI Ground fault circuit interrupter; an ultra-sensitive plug designed to shut off all electric current. Used in bathrooms, kitchens, exterior waterproof outlets, garage outlets, and wet areas. Has a small reset button on the plug.

gable The end, upper, triangular area of a home, beneath the roof.

general contractor A contractor who enters into a contract with the owner of a project for the construction of the project and who takes full responsibility for its completion, although the contractor may enter into subcontracts with others for the performance of specific parts or phases of the project.

general warranty deed A deed that conveys not only all the grantor's interests in and title to the property to the grantee, but also warrants that if the title is defective or has a "cloud" on it, such as mortgage claims, tax liens, title claims, judgments, or mechanics' liens against it, the grantee may hold the grantor liable.

girder A large or principal beam of wood or steel used to support concentrated loads at isolated points along its length.

glazing The process of installing glass that commonly uses glazier's points and glazing compound.

gloss enamel A finishing paint material. Forms a hard coating with maximum smoothness of surface and dries to a sheen or luster (gloss).

grade beam A foundation wall that is poured about level with or just below the grade of the earth. An example is the area where the 8' or 16' overhead garage door "block out" is located, or a lower (walk out basement) foundation wall is poured.

graduated payment mortgage (GPM) A fixed-rate, fixed-schedule loan. A GPM starts with lower payments than a level payment loan; payments rise annually, with the entire increase being used to reduce the outstanding balance. The increase in payments may enable the borrower to pay off a 30-year loan in 15 years to 20 years, or less.

grantee That party in the deed who is the buyer or recipient; the person to whom the real estate is conveyed.

grantor That party in the deed who is the seller or giver; the person who conveys the real estate.

ground Refers to electricity's habit of seeking the shortest route to earth. Neutral wires carry it there in all circuits. An additional grounding wire or the sheathing of the metal-clad cable or conduit. Protects against shock if the neutral leg is interrupted.

grout A wet mixture of cement, sand, and water that flows into masonry or ceramic crevices to seal the cracks between the different pieces. Mortar made of such consistency (by adding water) that it will flow into the joints and cavities of the masonry work and fill them solid.

gusset A flat wood, plywood, or similar type member used to provide a connection at the intersection of wood members. Most commonly used at joints of wood trusses. They are fastened by nails, screws, bolts, or adhesives.

gutter A shallow channel or conduit of metal or wood set below and along the (fascia) eaves of a house to catch and carry off rainwater from the roof.

hazard insurance Protects against damages caused to property by fire, windstorms, and other common hazards.

header (1) A beam placed perpendicular to joists and to which joists are nailed in framing for a chimney, stairway, or other opening. (2) A wood lintel. (3) The horizontal structural member over an opening (for example over a door or window).

hearth The fireproof area directly in front of a fireplace. The inner or outer floor of a fireplace, usually made of brick, tile, or stone.

heat rough Work performed by a heating contractor after the stairs and interior walls are built. This includes installing all duct work and flue pipes. Sometimes, the furnace and fireplaces are installed at this stage of construction.

heat trim Work done by a heating contractor to get the home ready for the municipal final heat inspection. This includes venting the hot water heater, installing all vent grills, registers, air-conditioning services, turning on the furnace, installing thermostats, venting ranges and hoods, and all other HVAC-related work.

hip A roof with four sloping sides. The external angle formed by the meeting of two sloping sides of a roof.

hip roof A roof that rises by inclined planes from all four sides of a building.

HVAC An abbreviation for **H**eating, **V**entilation, and **A**ir **C**onditioning.

I-beam A steel beam with a cross section resembling the letter "I." It is used for long spans as basement beams or over wide wall openings, such as a double garage door, when wall and roof loads bear down on the opening.

I-joist Manufactured structural building component resembling the letter "I." Used as floor joists and rafters. I-joists include two primary parts: *flanges* and *webs*. The flange of the I joist may be made of laminated veneer lumber or dimensional lumber, usually formed into a 1½″ width. The web or center of the I-joist is commonly made of plywood or oriented strand board (OSB). Large holes can be cut in the web to accommodate duct work and plumbing waste lines. I-joists are available in lengths up to 60 feet long.

implied warranty or covenant A guaranty of assurance the law supplies in an agreement, even though the agreement itself does not express the guaranty or assurance.

injunction A writ or order of the court to restrain one or more parties to a suit from committing an inequitable or unjust act in regard to the rights of some other party in the suit or proceeding.

insulating glass Window or door in which two panes of glass are used with a sealed air space between.

insulation board, rigid A structural building board made of coarse wood or cane fiber in ½-inch and $^{25}/_{32}$-inch thickness. It can be obtained in various size sheets and densities.

insulation Any material high in resistance to heat transmission that, when placed in the walls, ceiling, or floors of a structure, will reduce the rate of heat flow.

J channel Metal edging used on drywall to give the edge a better finished appearance when a wall is not "wrapped." Generally, basement stairway walls have drywall only on the stair side. J channel is used on the vertical edge of the last drywall sheet.

jamb The side and head lining of a doorway, window, or other opening. Includes studs as well as the frame and trim.

joint The location between the touching surfaces of two members or components joined and held together by nails, glue, cement, mortar, or other means.

joint compound A powder that is usually mixed with water and used for joint treatment in gypsum or wallboard finish. Often referred to as spackling or drywall mud.

joist Wooden 2 × 8s, 2 × 10s, or 2 × 12s that run parallel to one another and support a floor or ceiling, and supported in turn by larger beams, girders, or bearing walls.

joist hanger A metal "U" shaped item used to support the end of a floor joist and attached with hardened nails to another bearing joist or beam.

judgment The decision or sentence of a court of law as the result of proceedings instituted therein for the redress of an injury. A judgment declaring that one individual is indebted to another individual when properly docketed creates a lien on the real property of the judgment debtor.

lien A claim by one person on the property of another as security for money owed. Such claims may include obligations not met or satisfied, judgments, unpaid taxes, materials, or labor. *See also* special lien.

lineal foot A unit of measure for lumber equal to 1 inch thick by 12 inches wide by 12 inches long. Examples: $1'' \times 12'' \times 16' = 16$ board feet, $2'' \times 12'' \times 16' = 32$ board feet.

lintel A horizontal structural member that supports the load over an opening such as a door or window.

load bearing wall Includes all exterior walls and any interior wall that is aligned above a support beam or girder. Normally, any wall that has a double horizontal top plate.

marketable title A title that is free and clear of objectionable liens, clouds, or other title defects. A title that enables an owner to sell his or her property freely to others and that others will accept without objection.

market value The amount for which a property would sell if put upon the open market and sold in the manner that property is ordinarily sold in the community where the property is situated. The highest price estimated in terms of money that a buyer would be warranted in paying and a seller would be justified in accepting, provided both parties were fully informed, acted intelligently and voluntarily, and furthermore that all the rights and benefits inherent in or attributable to the property were included in the transfer.

masonry Stone, brick, concrete, hollow-tile, concrete block, or other similar building units or materials. Normally bonded together with mortar to form a wall.

mastic A pasty material used as a cement for setting tile, or a protective coating for thermal insulation or waterproofing.

mechanic's lien A lien on real property, created by statue in many areas, in favor of persons supplying labor or materials for a building or structure, for the value of labor or materials supplied by them. In some jurisdictions, a mechanic's lien also exists for the value of professional services. Clear title to the property cannot be obtained until the claim for the labor, materials, or professional services is settled. Timely filing is essential to support the encumbrance, and prescribed filing dates vary by jurisdiction.

metal lath Sheets of metal that are slit to form openings within the lath. Used as a plaster base for walls and ceilings and as reinforcing over other forms of plaster base.

metes and bounds A term that comes from the old English word "metes" meaning measurements, and "bounds" meaning boundaries. It is generally applied to any description of real estate; describes the boundaries by distance and angles.

microlam A manufactured structural wood beam. It is constructed of pressure-and-adhesive-bonded strands of wood. These beams have a higher strength rating than solid sawn lumber. The beam normally comes in a 1½″ thickness and 9½″, 11½″, and 14″ widths.

milar (mylar) Plastic, transparent copies of a blueprint.

miter joint The joint of two pieces at an angle that bisects the joining angle. For example, the miter joint at the side and head casing at a door opening is made at a 45° angle.

molding A wood strip having an engraved, decorative surface used as trim for interior walls in a house or building.

monopost An adjustable metal column used to support a beam or bearing point.

mortar A mixture of cement or lime with sand and water used in masonry work to hold bricks together.

mortgage A lien or claim against real property given by the buyer to the lender as security for money borrowed. Under government-insured or loan-guarantee provisions, the payments may include escrow amounts covering taxes, hazard insurance, water charges, and special assessments. Mortgages generally run from 10 years to 30 years, during which the loan is to be paid off.

mortgage note A written agreement to repay a loan. The agreement is secured by a mortgage, serves as proof of indebtedness, and states the manner in which it shall be paid. The note states the actual amount of the debt that the mortgage secures and renders the mortgagor personally responsible for repayment.

mortgage (open end) A mortgage with a provision that permits borrowing additional money in the future without refinancing the loan or paying additional financing charges. Open-end provisions often limit such borrowing to no more than would raise the balance to the original loan figure.

mortgagee The lender in a mortgage agreement.

mortgagor The borrower in a mortgage agreement.

oriented strand board (OSB) A manufactured 4′ × 8′ wood panel made out of 1″ to 2″ wood chips and glue. Often used as a substitute for plywood.

outrigger An extension of a rafter beyond the wall line. Usually a smaller member nailed to a larger rafter to form a cornice or roof overhang.

outside corner The point at which two walls form an external angle, one you usually can walk around.

overhang Outward projecting eaves or soffit area of a roof; the part of the roof that hangs out or over the outside wall.

padding A material installed under carpet to add foot comfort, isolate sound, and to prolong carpet life.

percolation test A test that a soil engineer performs on soil to determine the feasibility of installing a leech field type sewer system on a lot. A test to determine if the soil on a proposed building lot is capable of absorbing the liquid affluent from a septic system.

performance bond An amount of money (usually 10 percent of the total price of a job) that a contractor must put on deposit with a governmental agency as an insurance policy that guarantees the contractors' proper and timely completion of a project or job.

perimeter drain A 3″ or 4″ perforated plastic pipe that goes around the perimeter either inside or outside of a foundation wall, prior to being back-filled, that collects and diverts ground water away from the foundation. Generally, it is routed into a sump pit inside the home, and a sump pump is sometimes inserted into the pit to discharge any accumulation of water.

permeability A measure of the ease with which water penetrates a material.

permit A governmental municipal authorization to perform a specified building process, such as a building permit, a plumbing permit, or an electrical permit.

personal property Moveable property that is not by definition real property and includes tangible property, such as moneys, goods, chattels, as well as debts and claims.

pier A column of masonry, usually rectangular in horizontal cross section, used to support other structural members.

plat A map or chart of a lot, subdivision, or community drawn by a surveyor showing boundary lines, buildings, improvements on the land, and easements.

plate Normally a 2 × 4″ or 2 × 6″ board that lays horizontally within a framed structure, such as in a *sill plate*—a horizontal member anchored to a concrete or masonry wall; *sole plate*—bottom horizontal member of a frame wall; or *top plate*—top horizontal member of a frame wall supporting ceiling joists, rafters, or other members.

plan view Drawing of a structure with the view from overhead, looking down.

plenum The main hot-air supply duct leading from a furnace.

plot plan An overhead view plan that shows the location of the home on the lot. Includes all easements, property lines, set backs, and legal descriptions of the home. Provided by the surveyor.

plumbing rough Work performed by the plumbing contractor after the rough heat is installed. This work includes installing all plastic ABS drain and waste lines, copper water lines, bath tubs, shower pans, and gas piping to furnaces and fireplaces. Lead solder should not be used on copper piping.

plumbing stack A plumbing vent pipe that penetrates the roof.

plumbing trim Work performed by the plumbing contractor to get the home ready for a final plumbing inspection. Includes installing all toilets, hot water heaters, sinks, disposal, dishwasher, all plumbing items, and connecting all gas pipes to appliances.

plumbing waste line Plastic pipe used to collect and drain sewage waste.

ply A term to denote the number of layers of roofing felt, veneer in plywood, or layers in built-up materials, in any finished piece of such material.

plywood A panel (normally 4′ × 8′) of wood made of three or more layers of veneer, compressed and joined with glue, and usually laid with the grain of adjoining plies at right angles to give the sheet strength.

point load A point where a bearing or structural weight is concentrated and transferred to the foundation.

prepayment Payment of mortgage loan, or part of it, before the due date. Mortgage agreements often restrict the right of prepayment either by limiting the amount that can be prepaid in any one year or charging a penalty for prepayment. The Federal Housing Administration does not permit such restrictions in FHA insured mortgages.

principal The basic element of the loan as distinguished from interest and mortgage insurance premium. In other words, principal is the amount upon which interest is paid. The word also means one who appoints an agent to act for and in behalf of; the person bound by an agent's authorized contract.

property The term used to describe the rights and interests a person has in lands, chattels, and other determinate things.

purchase agreement An offer to purchase that has been accepted by the seller and has become a binding contract.

quitclaim deed A deed that transfers whatever interest the maker of the deed may have in the particular parcel of land. A quitclaim deed is often given to clear the title when the grantor's interest in a property is questionable. By accepting such a deed the buyer assumes all the risks. Such a deed makes no warranties as to the title but simply transfers to the buyer whatever interest the grantor has. *See* deed.

rafter Lumber used to support the roof sheeting and roof loads. Generally, 2×10s and 2×12s are used. The rafters of a flat roof are sometimes called *roof joists*.

rafter, hip A rafter that forms the intersection of an external roof angle.

rafter, valley A rafter that forms the intersection of an internal roof angle. The valley rafter is normally made of double 2-inch-thick members.

rail Cross members of panel doors or of a sash. Also, a wall or open balustrade placed at the edge of a staircase, walkway bridge, or elevated surface to prevent people from falling off. Any relatively lightweight horizontal element, especially those found in fences (split rail).

railroad tie Black, tar, and preservative impregnated, $6'' \times 8''$ and $6'$ to $8'$ long wooden timber that was used to hold railroad track in place. Normally used as a member of a retaining wall.

real property Land and buildings and anything that may be permanently attached to them.

rebar, reinforcing bar Ribbed steel bars installed in foundation concrete walls, footers, and poured in place concrete structures designed to strengthen concrete. Comes in various thicknesses and strength grade.

receptacle An electrical outlet. A typical household will have many 120-volt receptacles for plugging in lamps and appliances and 240-volt receptacles for the range, clothes dryer, air conditioners, etc.

recording The placing of a copy of a document in the proper books in the office of the Register of Deeds so that a public record will be made of it.

redemption The right that an owner-mortgagor, or one claiming under her or him, has after execution of the mortgage to recover back her or his title to the mortgaged property by paying the mortgage debt, plus interest and any other costs or penalties imposed, prior to a the occurrence of a valid foreclosure. The payment discharges the mortgage and places the title back as it was at the time the mortgage was executed.

reformation The correction of a deed or other instrument by reason of a mutual mistake of the parties involved or because of the mistake of one party caused by the fraud or inequitable conduct of the other party.

release The giving up or abandoning of a claim or right to the person against whom the claim exists or against whom the right is to be exercised or enforced.

release of lien The discharge of certain property from the lien of a judgment, mortgage, or claim.

rescission of contract The abrogating or annulling of a contract; the revocation or repealing of contract by mutual consent of the parties to the contract, or for other causes as recognized by law.

restrictive covenants Private restrictions limiting the use of real property. Restrictive covenants are created by deed and may run with the land, thereby binding all subsequent purchasers of the land, or may be deemed personal and binding only between the original seller and buyer. The determination whether a covenant runs with the land or is personal is governed by the language of the covenant, the intent of the parties, and the law in the state where the land is situated.

Restrictive covenants that run with the land are encumbrances and may affect the value and marketability of title. Restrictive covenants may limit the density of buildings per acre, regulate size, style or price range of buildings to be erected, or prevent particular businesses from operating or minority groups from owning or occupying homes in a given area. This latter discriminatory covenant is unconstitutional and has been declared unenforceable by the U.S. Supreme Court.

revocation The recall of a power or authority conferred, or the vacating of an instrument previously made.

r value A measure of a material's resistance to the passage of heat. New home walls are usually insulated with 4 inches of batting insulation with an R value of R-13, and a ceiling insulation of R-30.

right of survivorship Granted to two joint owners who purchase property using that particular buying method. Stipulates that one gets full rights and becomes the sole owner of the property upon the death of the other. Right of survivorship is the fundamental difference between acquiring property as joint owners and as tenants in common.

roof joist The rafters of a flat roof. Lumber used to support the roof sheeting and roof loads. Generally 2×10s and 2×12s are used.

roof sheathing or sheeting The wood panels or sheet material fastened to the roof rafters or trusses on which the shingle or other roof covering is laid.

roof valley The "V" created where two sloping roofs meet.

rough opening The horizontal and vertical measurement of a window or door opening before drywall or siding is installed.

rough sill The framing member at the bottom of a rough opening for a window that is attached to the cripple studs below the rough opening.

roughing in The initial stage of a plumbing, electrical, heating, carpentry, and/or other project, when all components that won't be seen after the second finishing phase are assembled. *See also* heat rough, plumbing rough, and electrical rough.

sand float finish Lime that is mixed with sand, resulting in a textured finish on a wall.

sanitary sewer A sewer system designed for the collection of waste water from the bathroom, kitchen, and laundry drains, and is usually not designed to handle storm water.

sash A single light frame containing one or more lights of glass. The frame that holds the glass in a window, often the movable part of the window.

semi-gloss paint or enamel A paint or enamel made so that its coating, when dry, has some luster but is not very glossy. Bathrooms and kitchens are normally painted with semi-gloss paint.

septic system An on-site waste water treatment system. It usually has a septic tank that promotes the biological digestion of the waste and a drain field that is designed to let the leftover liquid soak into the ground. Septic systems and permits are usually sized by the number of bedrooms in a house.

setback The distance from a curb or other established line within which no buildings or structures may be erected. A "setback ordinance" prohibits the construction of buildings or structures within the defined setback areas.

sheet metal duct work Usually round or rectangular metal pipes and sheet metal designed for the return air system and installed for distributing warm or cold air from the furnace to rooms in the home.

sheet rock, drywall, wall board, or gypsum A manufactured panel made out of gypsum plaster and encased in a thin cardboard. Usually ½″ thick and 4′ × 8′ or 4′ × 12′ in size. "Green board" drywall has a greater resistance to moisture than regular plasterboard and is used in bathrooms and other wet areas.

shim A small piece of scrap lumber or shingle, usually wedge shaped, that when forced behind a furring strip or framing member forces it into position. Also used when installing doors and placed between the door jamb legs and 2 × 4 door trimmers. Metal shims are $1\frac{1}{2}'' \times 2''$ sheet metal wafers of various thickness used to fill gaps in wood framing members, especially at bearing point locations.

shingles Roof covering of asphalt, asbestos, wood, tile, slate, or other material cut to stock lengths, widths, and thickness.

shutter Usually lightweight, louvered, decorative frames in the form of doors located on the sides of a window. Some shutters are made to close over the window for protection.

side sewer The portion of the sanitary sewer that connects the interior waste water lines to the main sewer lines. The side sewer is usually buried in several feet of soil and runs from the house to the sewer line. It is usually owned by the sewer utility, must be maintained by the owner, and may only be serviced by utility approved contractors. Sometimes called *sewer lateral*.

siding The finished exterior covering of the outside walls of a frame building.

siding, lap siding Slightly wedge-shaped boards used as horizontal siding in a lapped pattern over the exterior sheathing. Varies in butt thickness from ½ inch to ¾ inch and in widths up to 12 inches.

sill (1) The 2×4 or 2×6 wood plate framing member that lays flat against and bolted to the foundation wall with anchor bolts and upon which the floor joists are installed. Normally the sill plate is treated lumber. (2) The member forming the lower side of an opening, as a door sill or window sill.

sill cock An exterior water faucet or hose bib.

sill plate Bottom horizontal member of an exterior wall frame that rests on top of a foundation, sometimes called a *mud sill*. Also *sole plate*, bottom member of an interior wall frame.

sill seal Fiberglass or foam insulation installed between the foundation wall and sill (wood) plate. Designed to seal any cracks or gaps.

slab on grade A type of foundation with a concrete floor that is placed directly on the soil. The edge of the slab is usually thicker and acts as the footing for the walls.

soffit The area below the eaves and overhangs. The underside where the roof overhangs the walls. Usually the underside of an overhanging cornice.

soil pipe A large pipe that carries liquid and solid wastes to a sewer or septic tank.

soil stack A plumbing vent pipe that penetrates the roof.

sole plate The bottom, horizontal framing member of a wall that is attached to the floor sheeting and vertical wall studs.

special assessment A legal charge against real estate by a public authority to pay the cost of public improvements, such as for the opening, grading, and guttering of streets, the construction of sidewalks and sewers, or the installation of street lights or other such items to be used for public purposes.

special lien A lien that binds a specified piece of property, unlike a general lien, which is levied against all one's assets. It creates a right to retain something of value belonging to another person as compensation for labor, material, or money expended in that person's behalf. In some localities it is called "particular" lien or "specific" lien. *See* lien.

special warranty deed A deed in which the grantor conveys title to the grantee and agrees to protect the grantee against title defects or claims asserted by the grantor and those persons whose right to assert a claim against the title arose during the period the grantor held title to the property. In a special warranty deed the grantor guarantees to the grantee that he has done nothing during the time he held title to the property which has, or which might in the future, impair the grantee's title.

specific performance A remedy in court of equity whereby the defendant may be compelled to do whatever he or she has agreed to do in a contract executed by him or her.

statute A law established by the act of the legislative powers; an act of the legislature; the written will of the legislature solemnly expressed according to the forms necessary to constitute it as the law provides.

subdivision A tract of land divided into smaller parcels of land, or lots, usually for the purpose of constructing new houses.

subfloor The framing components of a floor to include the sill plate, floor joists, and deck sheeting over which a finish floor is to be laid.

subordination clause A clause in a mortgage or lease stating that one who has a prior claim or interest agrees that his or her interest or claim shall be secondary or subordinate to a subsequent claim, encumbrance, or interest.

sump Pit or large plastic barrel placed in the basement that is designed to collect ground water from a perimeter drain system.

sump pump A submersible pump in a sump pit that pumps any excess ground water to the outside of the home.

suspended ceiling A ceiling system supported by hanging it from the overhead structural framing.

survey A map or plat made by a licensed surveyor showing the results of measuring the land with its elevations, improvements, boundaries, and its relationship to surrounding tracts of land. A survey is often required by the lender as assurance that a building is actually sited on the land according to its legal description.

survivorship The distinguishing feature of a tenancy by the entirety, by which on the death of one spouse, the surviving spouse acquires full ownership.

tax As applied to real estate, an enforced charge imposed on persons, property, or income, to be used to support the state. The governing body in turn utilizes the funds in the best interest of the general public.

tax deed A deed given where property has been purchased at public sale because of the owner's nonpayment of taxes.

tax sale A sale of property for nonpayment of taxes assessed against it.

time is of the essence A phrase meaning that time is of crucial value and vital importance and that failure to fulfill time deadlines will be considered to be a failure to perform the contract.

title As generally used, the rights of ownership and possession of particular property. In real estate usage, title may refer to the instruments or documents by which a right of ownership is established (title documents), or it may refer to the ownership interest one has in the real estate.

title insurance Protects lenders or homeowners against loss of their interest in property due to legal defects in title. Title insurance may be issued to a mortgagee's title policy. Insurance benefits will be paid only to the "named insured" in the title policy, so it is important that an owner purchase an "owner's title policy" if he desires the protection of title insurance.

title search or examination A check of the title records, generally at the local courthouse, to make sure the buyer is purchasing a house from the legal owner and there are no liens, overdue special assessments, or other claims or outstanding restrictive covenants filed in the record that would adversely affect the marketability or value of title.

tread The walking surface board in a stairway on which the foot is placed.

treated lumber A wood product that has been impregnated with chemical pesticides such as CCA (chromated copper arsenate) to reduce damage from wood rot or insects. Often used for the portions of a structure that are likely to be in contact with soil and water. Wood may also be treated with a fire retardant.

truss An engineered and manufactured roof support member with zig-zag framing members. Does the same job as a rafter but is designed to have a longer span than a rafter.

trust A relationship under which one person, the trustee, holds legal title to property for the benefit of another person, the trust beneficiary.

trustee A party who is given legal responsibility to hold property in the best interest of or "for the benefit of" another.

The trustee is one placed in a position of responsibility for another, a responsibility enforceable in a court of law. *See* deed of trust.

unimproved As relating to land, vacant or lacking in essential appurtenant improvements required to serve a useful purpose.

useful life The period of time over which a commercial property can be depreciated for tax purposes. A property's useful life is also referred to as its *economic life*.

usury Charging a higher rate of interest on a loan than is allowed by law.

valid Having force, or binding forces; legally sufficient and authorized by law.

value Ability to command goods, including money, in exchange; the quantity of goods, including money, that should be commanded or received in exchange for the item valued. As applied to real estate, value is the present worth of all the rights to future benefits arising from ownership.

vapor barrier A building product installed on exterior walls and ceilings under the drywall and on the warm side of the insulation. It is used to retard the movement of water vapor into walls and prevent condensation within them. Normally, polyethylene plastic sheeting is used.

variance An exception to a zoning ordinance granted to meet certain specific needs, usually given on an individual case by case basis.

veneer Extremely thin sheets of wood. Also a thin slice of wood or brick or stone covering a framed wall.

vent A pipe or duct which allows the flow of air and gasses to the outside. Also, another word for the moving glass part of a window sash, such as a window vent.

vermiculite A mineral used as bulk insulation and also as aggregate in insulating and acoustical plaster and in insulating concrete floors.

visqueen A 4 mil or 6 mil plastic sheeting often used as a vapor barrier.

void That which is unenforceable; having no legal force or effect.

waiver Renunciation, disclaiming, or surrender of some claim, right, or prerogative.

warranty deed A deed that transfers ownership of real property and in which the grantor guarantees that the title is free and clear of any and all encumbrances.

wrapped drywall Areas that get complete drywall covering, as in the doorway openings of bi-fold and bi-pass closet doors.

Y "Y" shaped plumbing fitting.

yard of concrete One cubic yard of concrete is $3' \times 3' \times 3'$ in volume, or 27 cubic feet. One cubic yard of concrete will pour 80 square feet of $3\frac{1}{2}''$ sidewalk or basement/garage floor.

z bar flashing Bent, galvanized-metal flashing that's installed above a horizontal trim board of an exterior window, door, or brick run. It prevents water from getting behind the trim or brick and into a house.

zone The section of a building that is served by one heating or cooling loop because it has noticeably distinct heating or cooling needs. Also, the section of property that will be watered from a lawn sprinkler system. *See also* zoning.

zone valve A device usually placed near the heater or cooler which controls the flow of water or steam to parts of the building. It is controlled by a zone thermostat.

zoning A governmental process and specification that limits the use of a property such as single-family use, high-rise residential use, industrial use, etc. Zoning laws may limit where you can locate a structure.

zoning ordinances The acts of an authorized local government establishing building codes and setting forth regulations for property land usage.

THEVALUEPLAY.COM

Current ordering information for The Value Play Rental House Analyzer and other real estate products can be found at http://www.thevalueplay.com.

SYMPHONY-HOMES.COM

For information regarding Symphony Homes, one of Michigan's premier builders, please log on to http://www.symphony-homes.com.

A

Accent pieces (decor), 175
Acoustical ceiling, 156
Additions (room), 197–99
Air-conditioning systems, 210, 211–12
    air filters, 167
    zoned air, 211
Alcoves (gazebos), 78–79
All-seasons room, 198–99
Appliances, 179–81
Appraisers/appraisal methods, 9, 235–39
    income approach, 238
    replacement cost approach, 236
    sales comparison method, 238–39
Approvals, required, 19–33
    building permit application, 25–30
    deed restrictions/home-owner associations, 32–33
    inspections, 23–25
    meeting with building inspector, 19–21
    permits/fees, 21–23
    revisions and, 26
Arbitration of disputes, 46
Art, 175
Asbestos, 46, 156
Asphalt driveways, 118, 122
Asset, 3–18, 238
    consumer preferences, 12–18
    impact value rating system, 11–12
    relativity of value, 9–11
    visibility, and added value, 7–9
Associations, of homeowners, 32–33
Atmosphere, and lighting, 224
Attic insulation, 168–70
Attorney fees, 46

B

Backyard, structures in. *See* Exterior structures
Bacon, Francis, 78
Baker, Kermit, 5
    Basement foundations, 206–7
Basements, 36–37, 195–97
Bathroom(s), 191–93
    countertops, 147
    faucets, 218–19
    master, 192
    powder room, 186–88
    sinks, 221–22
Bedrooms, 190–91
Bicycles, 58
Blinds, 163–64
Boats, 122–23
Bonding requirements (subcontractors), 42–43
Breakers, 226–27. *See also* Electrical
Brick, 102–5
    brick ledge, 103
    driveways, 118, 119
    fireplaces and, 161–63
    pavers, 77
Brown patch, 59
Building codes, 115
Building inspector, meeting with, 19–21
Building line, 115
Building permit(s)
    application, 25–30
    porches and, 117
Bylaws, 32–33

C

Cabinets, 142–44
    kitchen, 178
    utility/laundry room, 189
Capitalization rate, 238
Carbon monoxide leaks, 210
Carpeting, 132–34
Cars, 122–23
Case study analysis, 231–47
    appraisal methods, 235–39
    assumptions, 239–42
    comparable sales, 243–44
    estimates, 242–43
    output analysis, 244–46
    valuation, primary, 231–34
    valuation, secondary, 234–35
Cash flow, 235
Cedar fences, 111, 112
Ceilings, 156–58
    paint for, 138
Cellulose, 170
Cement board, 95–96
Cement/concrete driveways, 118, 120
Ceramic tile, 134–35, 193
Chain-link fences, 111
Chair railing, 149
Chandeliers, 225
Change orders, 44

Cleaning/cleanliness
    hot tubs/spas, 83
    odors, 71, 165–68
    overall, 129–32
    pets and, 70–71
    power washing, 76, 105,
        111, 122
    property and grounds,
        55–58, 122–23
    by subcontractors, 45
Closets, 193–95
Clutter, 122–23, 193–94
Color, 139
Community amenities, 13, 15
Comparable sales, 9, 238–39,
    243–44
*Complete Guide to Buying and
    Selling Apartment Buildings,
    The* (Berges), 6, 123
*Complete Guide to Flipping
    Properties, The* (Berges), 6, 35,
    73
*Complete Guide to Investing in
    Rental Properties, The* (Berges),
    6, 8, 84, 98–99, 112, 231, 234
*Complete Guide to Real Estate
    Finance for Investment
    Properties, The* (Berges), 232
Composition shingles, 97–98.
    See also Roof
Computers, 14, 185
Consumer preferences, 12–18
    community amenities, 15
    features, 13–16
    for future homes, 17–18
Cooling. *See* Heating,
    ventilating, and air
    conditioning systems (HVAC)
Corian countertops, 146–47
"Cost Versus Value Report"
    (*Remodeling* magazine), 10
Countertops, 144–47, 178–79
Cracked slab, 204
Crown molding, 149, 150
Cultured marble, 222
Curtains, 164

D
Damp proofing, 206–7
Decks, 10–11, 15, 22–23, 75–77
Decor, 152–55
Deed restrictions, 32–33
Dental molding, 149
Depreciation, 237
Dining room, 14, 176–77
    lighting, 225
Direct-vent fireplaces, 161,
    162–63, 183–84
Dishwasher, 180–81
Dogs. *See* Pet(s)
Dollar patch, 59
Doors
    exterior, 105–7
    hardware, 152
    insulated, 106
    interior, 151–52
    pocket door, 187
Double glazed windows, 108–9
Drain tile, 206
Drapes, 163, 175
Draw schedule, 50–51
Driveway
    erosion of, 101
    improvements, 118–19
    permits and, 21–22
    repairs, 120–22
    water/sewer lines and, 217
Drywall
    ceilings, 157
    repairs, 135–37
Dupont, 146

E
Electrical, 223–28
    lighting, 223–26. *See also*
        Lighting
    switches and outlets,
        227–28
    wiring and breakers,
        226–27
End caps, 174
Energy efficiency
    insulation, 168–70
    windows and, 108–9

Entryway, 171–72
Environmental Protection
    Agency (EPA), 156
Estimates for improvement,
    242–43
Exterior improvements,
    combining, 123–26
Exterior structures, 75–90
    decks, 75–77
    garages, 86–88
    gazebos, 78–79
    hot tubs and spas, 82–84
    patios, 77–78
    playground equipment, 56,
        57, 88–90
    pools, 80–81
    storage sheds, 84–86
External obsolescence, 237

F
Fair market value, 234
Family room, 183–84
Faucets, 218–19
Fees (required approval), 21–23
Fences, 110–13
Fertilizer, lawn, 59
Filed plat of subdivision, 115
Filtration systems, 217
Final inspection, 24
Fireplaces, 160–63
    direct-vent, 161, 162–63,
        183–84
    odors and, 167
    wood burning, 161–62
Firewood, 57
First impressions, 55, 131–32
Fish hook jets, 220
Flooring, 132–35
    bathroom, 193
    carpet, 132–34
    ceramic tile, 134–35
    in foyer/entryway, 171
    hardwood, 135
    vinyl/linoleum, 134
Florescent lighting, 182, 225
Footings, 23–24

Forced–air heating systems, 209–10
Foundation(s)
  basement, 206–7
  brick ledge, 103
  footings, 23–24
  sewer lines and, 217
  signs of damage to, 105, 120, 136
  slab, 24, 203–6
  "stress cracks," 136
Foyer, 171–72
Frost laws, 116
Functional obsolescence, 237
Furnaces, 208–10
Furniture, 152–55, 177
  in home office, 186

G

Garages, 86–88
Gazebos, 78–79
Glass, in doors and sidelights, 106
Granite countertops, 145
Grass. *See* Lawns
Gravel driveways, 118
Grout sealer, 146
Gutters, 100–102

H

Half bath, 186–88
Half-wall, 173
Hardware, doors and, 152
Hardwood flooring, 135, 172
Hazardous materials/waste, 46
Heating, ventilating, and air conditioning systems (HVAC), 208–14
  air-conditioning systems, 211–12
  central heating systems, 209
  direct and indirect processes compared, 208
  furnaces, 208–10
  space heaters, 209
  thermostats, 213–14

Home equity line of credit (HELOC), 242
Home Improvement Retailing, 5
Home office, 14, 185–86
Homeowner associations, 32–33
Home sales price, average, 4
Hot tubs, 82–84
Hot water heaters, 214–16

I

Impact value rating system, 11–12
Improvements
see also specific area of improvement
  exterior, combining, 123–26
  property and grounds, combining, 72–74
Income capitalization method, 238
Inspections, required, 23–25
Insulated doors, 106
Insulation, 24, 168–70
Insurance
  replacement cost appraisal and, 236–37
  subcontractors and, 42–43, 45
International Data Corporation (IDC), 185
Invisible fences, 110, 111
Irrigation systems, 63–67

J–K

Joint Center for Housing Studies, 5
Junk, removing, 55, 122–23
Kiosks (gazebos), 78–79
Kitchen, 14, 177–79
  appliances, 179–80
  cabinets, 142–44, 178
  countertops, 144–47, 178–79
  faucets, 218–19
  island, 178

lighting, 179, 225
pantry, 181–83
sinks, 221–22

L

Laminate countertops, 147
Landscaping, 58–60, 61–63
  driveways and, 118–19, 120
  as "fence," 111
  water/sewer lines and, 216–17
Laundry room, 14, 188–90
Lawns, 58–60, 63–67
Leaded glass, 106
Liability, swimming pools and, 81
Licensing, 42–43
Liens, mechanics', 51–52
Lighting, 223–26
  atmosphere and, 224
  bathroom, 187–88, 192–93
  closet, 194
  florescent, 182, 225
  kitchen, 179
  outdoor, 67–69
  pantry, 182
Linoleum flooring, 134
Liquidated damages, 46
Living room, 174–76
Location, 13, 16

M–N

Market value, 235
Masonry, 102–5
Master bedroom, 191
Mechanics' liens, 51–52
Media room, 14
Mildew, 207
Miniblinds, 163–64
Mirrors, 158–60
Mold, 167, 207
Molding, 148–51, 176
Muriatic acid, 104
Nail pops, 136
National Association of Home Builders, 13, 178, 181

O

Odors, 71, 165–68
Organization
    closet, 195
    laundry room, 190
Outlets, 227–28. *See also* Electrical
Output analysis, 244–46

P

Paint/painting, 176, 190–91
    ceilings and, 157
    exterior, 91–93
    finishes, 139
    interior, 137–40, 175
    types, 138
    wood siding, 94
Paintings (art), 175
Pantry, 14, 181–83
Patios, 15, 77–78
Pedestal sink, 222
Permits, 21–23
Pet(s)
    invisible fences and, 111
    odors and, 167
    property/grounds and, 69–72
Photos, 175
Physical depreciation, 237
Pier-and-beam foundation, 203, 204–5
Plants
    exterior. *See* Landscaping
    houseplants, 155, 172, 175–76
Playground equipment, 56, 57, 88–90
Plumbing
    hot water heaters, 214–16
    kitchen/bathroom faucets, 218–19
    sinks, 221–22
    water and sewer lines, 216–18
    whirlpool tubs, 219–21
Pools, 80–81
Popcorn ceiling, 156

Porch
    adding, 114–17
    improving an existing, 113–14
Post-tensioned cable system, 203, 204
Powder room, 186–88
Power washing
    brick, 105
    decks, 76
    driveways, 122
    fences, 111
Price concerns, 13
Profit margin, 246
Property analysis worksheet, 240–41
Property and grounds, 55–74
    combining improvements, 72–74
    general cleanup, 55–58
    irrigation systems, 63–67
    landscaping, 61–63
    lawns, 58–60
    outdoor lighting, 67–69
    pets and, 69–72
Property taxes, 13
Property valuation. *See* Valuation

Q–R

Quality, of workmanship/ materials, 48–49
Rain gutters, 100–102
Rain sensing device, 66
Real estate brokers, 125
Rebar system, 203–4
Recreational vehicles, removing, 122–23
Refrigerator, 179–80
Renovation industry, 5
Replacement cost approach, 236
Restrictive covenants, 115
Return on investment (ROI), 238, 246
Roof
    cleaning, 98–100
    pitch, 7

replacement, 96–98
    shingles, 97–98
Room additions, 197–99, 227
Rough inspection, 24

S

Sales comparison method, 238–39
Sales price, 4
Sandler, Merle, 185
Sconces, 225
Scott's Fertilizer, 59
Screened porches, 114
Seal coating, 122
Setback line, 115
Sewer lines, driveways and, 121
Shades, 164–65
Sheds, storage, 84–86
Shelving
    closet, 194–95
    pantry, 182
Short-wall, 173
Sidewalk
    improvements, 118–19
    repairs, 121
Siding, 94–96
Silestone, 146
Sinks, 221–22
Site superintendent, 20
Slab foundation, 24
Space heaters, 209
Spas, 82–84
Specific point jets, 220
Sprinkler systems, 63–67
Stained glass, 106
Stairway (interior), 172–74
Stamping, 77
Storage, interior, 189
Storage sheds, 84–86
Stove, 180
Structural issues
    basement foundations, 206–7
    slab foundations, 203–6
Structures, exterior. *See* Exterior structures
Study (office), 185–86

Subcontractors, 34–52
   comparing and accepting
     proposals, 48–50
   contractor agreements,
     43–46
   finding qualified, 40–42
   hiring, *vs.* do-it-yourself,
     34–37
   licensing/insurance/bond-
     ing requirements, 42–43
   mechanics' liens and, 51–52
   payments to, 50–51
   pros and cons of using,
     37–40
   warranties and, 47
Substitution premise, 239
Summerhouses (gazebos),
   78–79
Sump pump, 206
Sunroom, 14, 198–99
Swimming pools, 80–81
Swing sets, 56, 57, 89–90
Switches, 227–28
Symphony Homes, 7, 20–21, 47,
   94, 110, 140, 148, 168–69,
   192, 223

T

Tendons, 204
Thermostats, 213–14
Tile
   ceramic flooring, 134–35
   countertops, 145–46
   in foyer, 172
Toys, 58
Tree houses, 88

Trees, 61–63
Trim and molding, 138, 139,
   148–51

U

U.S. Census Bureau, 3, 185
U.S. Home Office Forecast,
   2002–2007, 185
Utility bills, 169–70
Utility lines, 121
Utility room, 188–90

V

Valuation
   primary principles of,
     231–34
   secondary principles of,
     234–35
"Value Play Rehab Analyzer,"
   240
Vanity sinks, 222
Vapor barrier, 206
Vehicles, removing junky,
   122–23
Ventilating. *See* Heating,
   ventilating, and air
   conditioning systems (HVAC)
Vertical blinds, 164
Vinyl flooring, 134, 172
Vinyl siding, 94–95
Vinyl windows, 109–10

W–Z

Wallpaper, 140–42, 175, 176,
   190

Wall sconces, 225
Warranties, 46, 47
Washtub, 189
Waste, hazardous, 46
Water
   in basement, 206–7
   filtration systems, 217–18
   water and sewer lines, 121,
     216–18
Water heaters
   fast recovery, 215
   types of, 215
   whirlpool tubs and, 220
Waterproofing, 206–7
Wax sealers, on doors, 107
Whirlpool tubs, 14, 219–21
Window(s), 107–10
   double-glazed 108–9
   in family room, 184
   in powder room, 187
   window coverings, 163–65,
     175
Wiring, 226–27. *See also*
   Electrical
Wood
   hardwood flooring, 135
   paneling, 184
   treatment of, for outside
     use, 75–76, 89
Wood-burning fireplaces,
   161–62
Wrought-iron fences, 111
Yield, of asset, 238
Zoned air, 211
Zoning ordinances, 115

Share the message!

Bulk discounts
Discounts start at only 10 copies. Save up to 55% off retail price.

Custom publishing
Private label a cover with your organization's name and logo. Or, tailor information to your needs with a custom pamphlet that highlights specific chapters.

Ancillaries
Workshop outlines, videos, and other products are available on select titles.

Dynamic speakers
Engaging authors are available to share their expertise and insight at your event.

Call Dearborn Trade Special Sales at 1-800-245-BOOK (2665) or e-mail trade@dearborn.com

Dearborn™
Trade Publishing
A **Kaplan Professional** Company